THE ROYAL HISTORICAL SOCIETY
ANNUAL BIBLIOGRAPHY OF BRITISH AND IRISH HISTORY
Publications of 1982

ROYAL HISTORICAL SOCIETY

ANNUAL BIBLIOGRAPHY OF BRITISH AND IRISH HISTORY

Publications of 1982

General Editor: G. R. Elton

A. Bennett
R. Boyce
N. Brooks
R.A. Griffiths
M.W.C. Hassall
D.A.L. Morgan
J.S. Morrill
G. Mac Niocaill
A.T.Q. Stewart
C.A. Whatley
J.A. Woods

HARVESTER PRESS LIMITED

HUMANITIES PRESS INC

For the Royal Historical Society

First published in 1983 for
The Royal Historical Society by
THE HARVESTER PRESS LIMITED
Publisher: John Spiers
16 Ship Street, Brighton, Sussex
and in the USA by
HUMANITIES PRESS INC.,
Atlantic Highlands, New Jersey 07716

British Library Cataloguing in Publication Data
Annual bibliography of British and Irish history.
– Publications of 1982
1. Great Britain – History – Bibliography –
Periodicals
016.941 Z2016
ISBN 0-7108-0681-7

Humanities Press Inc.
ISBN 0-391-02942-8

Printed and bound in Great Britain by
Biddles Ltd, Guildford and King's Lynn

CONTENTS

PREFACE

The Bibliography is meant in the first place to serve the urgent needs of scholars, which has meant subordinating absolutely total coverage and refinements of arrangement to speed of production. Nevertheless, it is comprehensive and arranged for easy use. Because the sectional headings are those approved by section editors they are not uniform. Searchers are advised to use the subdivisions in conjunction with the Subject Index which, apart from covering all place and personal names, is designed to facilitate a thematic and conceptual analysis.

Pieces contained in collective works (under Bc and sometimes in a chronological section) are individually listed in the appropriate place and there referred to by the number the volume bears in the Bibliography.

Items covering more than two sections are listed in B; any that extend over two sections appear as a rule in the first and are cross-referenced at the head of the second.

Reliance on the British National Bibliography has necessitated the use of its 'Cataloguing in Publication' (i.e. before publication) cards. These have been entered only if the fact of publication has been independently established, but in some cases the item itself could not be seen so that occasionally the pagination has had to be omitted.

The editors wish to express their gratitude for the assistance received from the Institute of Historical Research, London (especially Miss Rosemary Taylor), the International Medieval Bibliography, Leeds (especially Dr R.J. Walsh), and Miss Jill Alexander of the Cambridge University Library.

Abbreviations

Arch. – Archaeological
B. – Bulletin
HMSO – Her Majesty's Stationery Office
J. – Journal
P. – Proceedings
Q. – Quarterly
R. – Review
Soc. – Society
T. – Transactions
UP – University press

PREFACE

A. AUXILIARY

(a) *Bibliography and Archives*

1. Stein, G. *Freethought in the United Kingdom and the Commonwealth: a descriptive bibliography*. Westport/London: Greenwood Press; 1981. Pp xxiii, 193.
2. Everitt, A.; Tranter, M. *English local history at Leicester 1948–1978: a bibliography of writings by members of the Department of English Local History, University of Leicester.* Leicester; the Department; 1981. Pp 87.
3. Knight, R.J.B. (ed.). *Guide to the manuscripts in the National Maritime Museum, vol. 2: Public records, business records and artificial collections.* London; Mansell; 1980. Pp xxxiii, 216.
4. Cantwell, J., 'The Public Record Office: the legal and departmental records,' *J. of Legal History* 2 (1981), 227–37.
5. Sawyer, P.H.; Walsh, R.J. (ed.). *International Medieval Bibliography: publications of January–June 1981.* Leeds; 1982. Pp lvi, 270.
6. Field, C.D., 'Bibliography of Methodist historical literature, 1979,' *P. of the Wesley Historical Soc.* 43 (1981), 21–4.
7. Riley, D.W., 'The Methodist archives: some recent accessions,' ibid. 18–20.
8. University of Nottingham. *The papers of Henry Kirke White 1785–1806.* Nottingham; Manuscript Department of the University; 1981. Pp 31.
9. Gilbert, V.F. (ed.). *Labour and social history theses: American, British and Irish university theses and dissertations in the field of British and Irish labour history, presented between 1900 and 1978.* London; Mansell; 1982. Pp 200.
10. Maclean, V. *A short-title catalogue of household and cookery books published in the English tongue 1701–1800.* London; Prospect; 1981. Pp xxiv, 197.
11. Smith, H. *The British labour movement to 1970: a bibliography.* London; Mansell; 1981. Pp xviii, 250.
12. Rhodes, D.E. *A catalogue of incunabula in all the libraries of Oxford outside the Bodleian.* Oxford; Clarendon; 1982. Pp xli, 444.
13. Swanton, M. *Medieval art in Britain; a select bibliography.* London; Portico; 1981. Pp 64.
14. Keen, R.A. *Catalogue of the papers of the missions of the Africa (Group 3) Committee, vol. 7: New Zealand mission 1809–1914.* London; Church Missionary Soc.; 1981. Pp 92.
15. Knighton, C.S. (ed.). *Catalogue of the Pepys Library at Magdalene*

College Cambridge, vol. V, pt. ii: Modern manuscripts. Woodbridge; D.S. Brewer; 1981. Pp xxvi, 275.

16. Golden, J. *A list of the papers and correspondence of George Bellas Greenough (1778–1855), held in the Manuscripts Room, University College London Library.* London; The College; 1981. Pp 46.
17. *Catalogue of the archives of the Royal Observatory, Edinburgh, 1764–1937.* Edinburgh; The Observatory; 1982.
18. Vage, J.A. *The records of the bishop of Exeter's consistory court to 1660: a list with introduction.* Exeter; Devon Record Office; 1981. Pp 11, 17.
19. *Cheshire Record Office and Chester Diocesan Record Office* (revd.). Cheshire Record Office; 1982. 42 leaves.
20. Van der Kiste, J. *Queen Victoria's family: a select bibliography.* Biggleswade; Clover; 1982. Pp vi, 68.
21. University of Nottingham, Manuscripts Department. *Papers of Sir William Denison.* Nottingham; The Department; ?1981. Pp 15.
22. Stratford, J. *Catalogue of the Jackson Collection of manuscript fragments in the Royal Library, Windsor Castle.* London; Academic Press; 1981. Pp xiii, 106.
23. Surtees, P.K. *Bibliography on Somerset House.* London; Inland Revenue Library; 1978. Pp 7.
24. King's College, London. *Liddell Hart Centre for Military Archives: consolidated list of accessions.* London; The College; 1981. 38 leaves.
25. British Library. *'Rough Register' of acquisitions of the Department of Manuscripts, 1976–1980.* London; Swift's; 1982 (List & Index Soc. Special Series 15).
26. Public Record Office. *Prize papers (HCA 32), index 1776–86, 1793–1803.* London; Swift's; 1982 (List & Index Soc. 183–4).
27. Public Record Office. *Exchequer, Augmentation Office; index to letters patent Henry III–Charles I.* London; Swift's; 1982 (List & Index Soc. 185).
28. Public Record Office. *Lord Steward's Department; list, 1598–1870.* London; Swift's; 1982 (List & Index Soc. 186).
29. Public Record Office. *Chancery: patent rolls, 14 James I.* London; Swift's; 1982 (List & Index Soc. 187).
30. Robinson, S.; Brook, M. *An introductory bibliography of the hosiery and lace industries in Nottingham and district to 1920.* Nottingham; University Library; 1982. Pp ix, 14.
31. McCann, A. (ed.). *The Petworth House archives: a catalogue, vol. 2.* Chichester; West Sussex County Council; 1979. Pp xi, 111.
32. Bird, D.T. *A catalogue of sixteenth-century medical books in Edinburgh libraries.* Edinburgh; Royal College of Physicians; 1982. Pp xxxii, 298.
33. *A select bibliography and source guide to the Romans in Falkirk district.* Falkirk District Council; 1982. Pp 104.

34. Huntington Library, California. *Guide to British historical manuscripts in the Huntington Library*. San Marino; The Library; 1982. Pp xiv, 448.
35. Bergess, W. *Supplement to the Kent bibliography (compiled by the late George Bennett)*. London; Library Association; 1981. Pp vii, 368.
36. Farrant, S. *Medieval Sussex: a bibliography*. Brighton; Centre for Continuing Education; 1980. Pp 40.
37. Sawyer, P.H.; Walsh, R.J. (ed.). *International medieval bibliography; publications of July–December 1981*. Leeds; 1982. Pp lii, 252.
38. Elton, G.R. (ed.). *Annual bibliography of British and Irish history: publications of 1981*. Brighton; Harvester; 1982. Pp ix, 196.
39. British Library. *Catalogue of additions to the manuscripts, 1951–1955*. London; British Library; 1982. Pp 714.
40. Dolphin, P.; Grant, E.; Lewis, E. *The London region: an annotated geographical bibliography*. London; Mansell; 1981. Pp xiv, 379.
41. Tobias, R.C., 'Victorian bibliography for 1981,' *Victorian Studies* 27 (1982), 521–610.
42. Graham, T.W., 'A list of articles on Scottish history published during the year 1981,' *Scottish Historical R.* 61 (1982), 166–74.
43. Creaton, H.J. (ed.). *Writings on British history 1967–1968*. London; Institute of Historical Research; 1982. Pp xx, 231.
44. Pickles, D.J. *A select bibliography of the founding and history of the Girl Guide Movement in the United Kingdom, 1907–1930*. London; Ealing College of Higher Education; 1981. Pp 14.
45. Keen, R.A. *Catalogue of the papers of the missions of the Africa (Group 3) Committee, vol. 2: Nigeria missions 1844–1934*. 2nd ed. London; Church Missionary Soc.; 1981. 102 leaves.
46. *A bibliography of the publications of the Royal Dublin Society from its foundation in the year 1731 together with a list of bibliographical material relative to the Society* (3rd ed.). Dublin; the Society; 1982. Pp 53.
47. Neveu, B., 'A contribution to an inventory of Jacobite sources,' Bc22, 138–58.
48. Nelson, J., 'Bibliography: Anglo-Saxon England 1970–81,' *Medieval Prosopography* 3/1 (1982), 109–12.

(b) *Works of Reference*

1. McNulty, A.; Troop, H. *Directory of British oral history collections, vol. 1*. Colchester; Oral History Soc.; 1981. Pp 60.
2. Feather, J. *The English provincial book trade before 1850: a checklist of secondary sources*. Oxford Bibliographical Soc.; 1981. Pp vi, 37.

3. Royal Commission on Ancient and Historical Monuments in Wales. *An inventory of the ancient monuments in Glamorgan; vol. 4: Domestic architecture from the Reformation to the industrial revolution; Part 1: The greater houses.* Cardiff; HMSO; 1981. Pp xl, 379.
4. Storey, R.; Edwards, S. *Supplement to the Guide to the Modern Records Centre, University of Warwick Library.* Coventry; the Library; 1981. Pp 116.
5. Raimo, J.W. (ed.). *A guide to manuscripts relating to America in Great Britain and Ireland* (revd. ed.). London; Mansell; 1979. Pp xxv, 467.
6. Houfe, S. *The dictionary of British book illustrators and caricaturists, 1800–1914.* Woodbridge; Antique Collectors' Club; 1978. Pp 520.
7. Adkins, L. & R.A. *A thesaurus of British archaeology.* Newton Abbot; David & Charles; 1982. Pp 319.
8. Smith, D.M. *A supplementary guide to the archive collections in the Borthwick Institute of Historical Research.* York; The Institute; 1980. Pp i, 77.
9. Greenall, R.L. (ed.). *The Leicester newspapers 1850–74: a guide for historians.* University of Leicester; 1980. Pp viii, 61.
10. Smart, V. *Sylloge of Coins of the British Isles, 28: cumulative index of vols. 1–20.* Oxford UP for British Academy; 1981. Pp 118.
11. Hope, M. *Index to the Proceedings of the British Academy, vols. 1–63.* Ibid.; 1981. Pp 85.
12. Caplan, D. *Independent review of the work of the Royal Commission on Historical Manuscripts.* London; Civil Service Dept Library; 1980. Pp 66.
13. Bellamy, J.M.; Saville, J. (ed.). *Dictionary of Labour biography*, vol. 6. London; Macmillan; 1982. Pp xxxi, 309.
14. Coyne, L.; Doyle, D.; Pickstone, J. *A guide to the records of health services in the Manchester region (Kendal to Crewe).* Manchester; UMIST; 1981. 2 vols.
15. Ormond, R.; Rogers, M. (ed.). *Dictionary of British portraiture: vol. 3, The Victorians – historical figures born between 1800 and 1860* (ed. E. Kilmurray); *vol. 4, The twentieth century – historical figures born before 1900* (ed. A. Davies). London; Batsford; 1981. Pp 228, 176.
16. Richard, S. *British government publications. Indexes to chairmen of committees and commissions of enquiry, 1, 1800–1899; to chairmen and authors, 3, 1941–1978.* London; Library Association; 1982.
17. Cobb, H.S., 'Modern political collections in the House of Lords Record Office,' *Archives* 15 (1981), 67–78.
18. Colvin, H.; Crook, J.M.; Friedman, T. (ed.). *Architectural drawings from Lowther Castle, Westmorland.* London; Soc. of Architectural Historians; 1980. Pp 17.

19. Hooke, J.M.; Kain, R.J.P. *Historical change in the physical environment: a guide to sources and techniques.* London; Butterworth; 1982. Pp xxi, 236.
20. Gaffney, C.; Murray, P.; Gilmour, C.; Forbes, E.G. *Index of fellows of the Royal Society of Edinburgh elected from 1783 to 1882: containing their dates of birth, death and election to that Society, primary occupation or institutional affiliation.* University of Edinburgh; 1980. Pp 153.
21. *Guide to London local history resources: London Borough of Camden.* London; the Borough; 1982. Pp 34.
22. Tuson, P. (ed.). *A brief guide to sources for Middle East studies in the India Office Library Records.* London; the Library; 1982. Pp 20.
23. Haan, H.; Krieger, K.-F.; Niedhart, G. *Einführung in die englische Geschichte.* Munich; Beck; 1982. Pp 326.
24. Foster, J.; Sheppard, J. *British archives: a guide to archive resources in the United Kingdom.* London; Macmillan; 1982. Pp xv, 533.
25. Royal Commission on Historical Monuments. *An inventory of the historical monuments in the county of Northampton, vol. 4: Archaeological sites in Northamptonshire.* London; HMSO; 1982. Pp xxii, 226.
26. *Record repositories in Great Britain: a geographical directory* (7th ed.). London; HMSO; 1982. Pp 31.
27. Emmison, F.G.; Smith, W.J. *Material for theses in local record offices and libraries.* London; Historical Association; 1982. Pp iv, 48.
28. Alban, J.R. *Calendar of Swansea freemen's records from 1760.* Swansea City Council; 1982. Pp v, 86.
29. Perkin, M.R. (ed.). *The book trade in Liverpool to 1805: a directory.* Liverpool Bibliographical Soc.; 1981. Pp x, 35.

(c) *Historiography*

1. Aldsworth, F.G., 'Parish boundaries on record,' *Local Historian* 15 (1982), 34–40.
2. Hoskins, W.G. *Fieldwork in local history* (2nd ed.). London; Faber; 1982. Pp 208.
3. Eyck, F. *G.P. Gooch: a study in history and politics.* London; Macmillan; 1982. Pp 520.
4. Milsom, S.F.C., 'F.W. Maitland,' *P. of the British Academy* 66 (1982 for 1980), 265–81.
5. Ellison, L., 'Petty sessions records and social deprivation,' *Local Historian* 15 (1982), 74–9.
6. Pocock, J.G.A., 'The limits and divisions of British History; in search of the unknown subject,' *American Historical R.* 87 (1982), 311–36.

7. Pocock, J.G.A., 'Virtues, rights, and manners: a model for historians of political thought,' *Political Theory* 9 (1981), 353–68.
8. Harris, O., 'Households and their boundaries,' *History Workshop* 13 (1982), 143–52.
9. Boreham, J.M. *The census and how to use it.* Brentwood; Essex Soc. for Family History; 1982. Pp 20.
10. Schofield, J.; Palliser, D.M.; Harding, C. (ed.). *Recent archaeological research in English towns.* London; Council for British Archaeology; 1981. Pp x, 125.
11. Tribe, K. *Genealogies of capitalism.* London; Macmillan; 1981. Pp xvi, 175.
12. Ashworth, W., 'The newest and truest economic history?,' [rev. article] *Economic History R.* 2nd ser. 35 (1982), 434–42.
13. Chilton, C.W., 'The universal British directory – a warning,' *Local Historian* 15 (1982), 144–6.
14. Sutherland, G., 'A view of education records in the nineteenth and twentieth centuries,' *Archives* 15 (1981), 79–85.
15. Gosden, P., 'Twentieth-century archives of education as sources for the study of education policy and administration,' ibid. 86–95.
16. King, E., 'John Horace Round and the *Calendar of Documents preserved in France*,' Bc16, 93–103.
17. Shaw, G. *British directories as sources in historical geography.* Norwich; Geo Abstracts; 1982. Pp 60.
18. Beales, D.E.D. *History and biography: an inaugural lecture.* Cambridge UP; 1982. Pp 36.
19. Harvey, P.D.A. *The historian and the written word: an inaugural lecture.* Durham; the University; 1982. Pp 12.
20. Gorman, J.L. *The expression of historical knowledge.* Edinburgh UP; 1982. Pp viii, 123.
21. Mayhew, A., ' "The first economic revolution" as fiction,' *Economic History R.* 2nd ser. 35 (1982), 568–71. – North, D.C., 'Reply,' ibid. 572.
22. Gathercole, P., 'Gordon Childe: man or myth?,' *Antiquity* 46 (1982), 195–8.
23. Madden, A.F., 'The Commonwealth, Commonwealth history, and Oxford, 1905–1971,' Bc8, 7–29.
24. Robinson, R.E., 'Oxford in imperial historiography,' Bc8, 30–48.
25. Symonds, R., 'Oxford and India,' Bc8, 49–72.
26. Fieldhouse, D.K., 'Keith Hancock and imperial economic history: a retrospect forty years on,' Bc8, 144–63.
27. Mason, J., 'Accounting records and business history,' *Business History* 24 (1982), 293–9.
28. Houston, R.A.; Smith, R.M., 'A new approach to family history?,' *History Workshop* 14 (1982), 120–31.
29. Stephenson, D., 'The early career of J.H. Round: the shaping of a

historian,' *Essex Archaeology and History* 12 (1981 for 1980), 1–10.

30. Boyden, P.B., 'J.H. Round and the beginnings of the modern study of Domesday Book: Essex and beyond,' ibid. 11–24.
31. Powell, W.R., 'J. Horace Round, the county historian: the *Victoria County Histories* and the Essex Archaeological Society,' ibid. 25–38.
32. Lutz, A., 'Das Studium der Angelsächsischen Chronik im 16. Jahrhundert: Nowell und Joscelyn,' *Anglia* 100 (1982), 301–56.

B. GENERAL

(a) *Long Periods: National*

1. Smith, D.B. *Curling: an illustrated history.* Edinburgh; Donald; 1981. Pp vii, 232.
2. Bradley, I. *The English middle classes.* London; Collins; 1982.
3. Beard, G. *Craftsmen and interior decoration in England 1660–1820.* Edinburgh; Bartholomew; 1981. Pp xxiv, 311.
4. Blakeney, M., 'Sequestered piety and charity – comparative analysis,' *J. of Legal History* 2 (1981), 207–26.
5. Russell, R. *Lost canals and waterways of Britain.* Newton Abbot; David & Charles; 1982. Pp 304.
6. Murdoch, J. *The English miniature.* London; Yale UP; 1982.
7. Hudson, K. *Pawnbroking – an aspect of British social history.* London; Bodley Head; 1982. Pp 166.
8. Falkus, M.; Gillingham, J. *Historical atlas of Britain.* London; Granada; 1981. Pp 223.
9. Vaughan-Thomas, W.; Hales, M. *Secret landscapes: mysterious sites, deserted villages and forgotten places of Great Britain and Ireland.* Exeter; Webb & Bower; 1980. Pp 208.
10. Field, J. *Place-names of Great Britain and Ireland.* Newton Abbot; David & Charles; 1980. Pp 208.
11. Brunskill, R.W. *Houses.* London; Collins; 1982. Pp 224.
12. Townshead, C., 'Martial law: legal and administrative problems of civil emergency in Britain and the empire, 1800–1940,' *Historical J.* 25 (1982), 167–95.
13. Robbins, K., 'Papal progress,' *History Today* 32/6 (1982), 12–17.
14. Duffy, E., 'The bishop of Rome and the catholics of England,' ibid. 5–12.
15. Woolf, N., 'The sovereign remedy: touch-pieces and the King's Evil, part II,' *British Numismatic J.* 50 (1981 for 1980), 91–116.
16. Borsay, P., 'Culture, status and the English urban landscape,' *History* 67 (1982), 1–12.

17. Rodwell, W. *The archaeology of the English church: the study of historic churches and churchyards.* London; Batsford; 1981. Pp 192.
18. Gibson, R. *The family doctor: his life and history.* London; Allen & Unwin; 1981. Pp xv, 214.
19. Wilkinson, G. *A history of Britain's trees.* London; Hutchinson; 1981. Pp 176.
20. Squibb, G.D. *Precedence in England and Wales.* Oxford; Clarendon; 1981. Pp xviii, 139.
21. Johnston, W.R. *Great Britain's great empire: an evaluation of the British imperial experience.* St Lucia/London; University of Queensland Press; 1981. Pp xvii, 207.
22. Gunstone, A. *Lincolnshire collections: Sylloge of coins of the British Isles, vol. 27.* Oxford UP for British Academy; 1981. Pp 172.
23. Warhurst, M. *Merseyside County museums: ancient British issues and later coins from English, Irish and Scottish mints to 1279 and associated foreign coins (Sylloge of coins of the British Isles, vol. 29).* Oxford UP for British Academy; 1982. Pp 132.
24. Addison, W. *Local styles of the English parish church.* London; Batsford; 1982. Pp 192.
25. Nevett, T.R. *Advertising in Britain: a history.* London; Heinemann; 1982. Pp xiii, 231.
26. Weller, J.B. *History of the farmstead: the development of energy sources.* London; Faber; 1982. Pp 248.
27. Conzen, M.R.G. (ed. J.W.R. Whitehead). *The urban landscape: historical development and management.* London; Academic Press; 1981. Pp vii, 166.
28. *Home Office 1782–1982: to commemorate the bicentenary of the Home Office.* London; Home Office; 1981. Pp 48.
29. Brown, K.D. *The English labour movement 1700–1951.* Dublin; Gill & Macmillan; 1982. Pp 322.
30. Hamilton, O. *The divine country: the British in Tuscany 1372–1980.* London; Deutsch; 1982. Pp xiv, 190.
31. Ollard, R. *An English education: a perspective of Eton.* London; Collins; 1982. Pp 216.
32. Edwards, A.M. *The design of suburbia: a critical study in environmental history.* London; Pembridge; 1981. Pp viii, 281.
33. Flinn, M.W., 'The population history of England, 1541–1871 [review article],' *Economic History R.* 2nd ser. 35 (1982), 443–57.
34. Soltow, L., 'The land tax redemption records, 1798–1963,' ibid. 427–33.
35. Wyatt, G., 'Famility stability through the ages,' *Local Historian* 15 (1982), 132–5.
36. Burnett, J., 'Autobiographies of childhood: the experience of education,' *History Today* 32/9 (1982), 8–15.

37. Yelling, J.A., 'Rationality in the common fields,' *Economic History R.* 2nd ser. 35 (1982), 409–15.
38. Mason, P. *The English gentleman.* London; Deutsch; 1982.
39. Aldrich, R. *An introduction to the history of education.* London; Hodder & Stoughton; 1982. Pp 188.
40. Brunskill, R.W. *Traditional farm buildings of Britain.* London; Gollancz; 1982. Pp 160.
41. Thomas, D.A. *Royal admirals 1327–1981.* London; Deutsch; 1982. Pp 200.
42. Muir, R. *The lost villages of Britain.* London; Joseph; 1982. Pp 285.
43. Rowley, T.; Wood, J. *Deserted villages.* Princes Risborough; Shire; 1982. Pp 72.
44. Routledge, R., 'The legal status of Jews in England 1190–1790,' *J. of Legal History* 3 (1982), 91–124.
45. Cohen, J., 'The history of imprisonment for debt and its relation to the development of discharge in bankruptcy,' ibid. 153–71.
46. Sykes, C.S. *Black sheep.* London; Chatto & Windus; 1982. Pp 285.
47. Howson, G. *A history of mathematics teaching in England.* Cambridge UP; 1982. Pp x, 294.
48. Williams, M.E. *The Venerable English College, Rome: a history: 1579–1979.* London; Associated Catholic; 1979. Pp xii, 256.
49. Taylor, C.S., 'Archaeology and the origins of open-field agriculture,' Bc3, 13–21.
50. Hall, D., 'The origins of open-field agriculture — the archaeological fieldwork evidence,' Bc3, 22–38.
51. Campbell, R.H., 'Introductory essay [on Scottish industrial history],' Bc4, pp. vii–xxxix.
52. Gammon, V., ' "Babylonian performances": the rise and suppression of popular church music, 1660–1870,' Bc7, 62–88.
53. McAdoo, H.R., 'Anglican/Roman Catholic relations, 1717–1980: a detection of themes,' Bc9, 143–281.
54. Hall, A.R.; Kenward, H.K. (ed.). *Environmental archaeology in the urban context.* London; Council for British Archaeology; 1982. Pp 132.
55. Mays, J.O'D. *The 'splendid shilling': a social history of an engaging coin.* Burley; New Forest Leaves; 1982. Pp 186.
56. Rainbow, B. et al. *English psalmody prefaces: popular methods of teaching, 1562–1835.* Clifden; Boethius Press; 1982. Pp 158.
57. Jenkins, D.T.; Ponting, K.G. *The British wool textile industry, 1770–1914.* London; Heinemann Educational; 1982. Pp 388.
58. Muthesius, S. *The English terraced house.* London; Yale UP; 1982. Pp 288.
59. Aldcroft, D.H., 'Urban transport problems in historical perspective,' Bc24, 220–35.
60. Blake, R. (ed.). *The English world: history, character and people.* London; Thames & Hudson; 1982. Pp 268.

(b) *Long Periods: Local*

1. Foster-Smith, J.R. *The non ferrous mines of the South Wales area.* Sheffield; Northern Mine Research Soc.; 1981. Pp 54.
2. Winter, C.W.R. *The ancient town of Yarmouth.* Newport; Isle of Wight County Press; 1981. Pp 208.
3. Whetter, J. *The history of Falmouth.* Redruth; Dyllansow Truran; 1981. Pp 190.
4. Adlam, B. *The book of Dorchester, county town of Dorset.* Buckingham; Barracuda; 1981. Pp 136.
5. Armstrong, M.E. (ed.). *An industrial island: a history of Scunthorpe.* Scunthorpe Borough Museum; 1981. Pp xiv, 218.
6. Johnson, S., 'Borrowdale, its land tenure and the records of the Lawson manor,' *T. of the Cumberland and Westmorland Antiquarian and Arch. Soc.* 81 (1981), 63–71.
7. Morris, R.W. *Yorkshire through place names.* Newton Abbot; David & Charles; 1982. Pp 192.
8. Warrington, G., 'The copper mines of Alderley Edge and Mottram St Andrew, Cheshire,' *J. of the Chester Arch. Soc.* 64 (1981), 47–73.
9. Thornes, R.C.N. *West Yorkshire, a noble scene of industry: the development of the county 1500 to 1830.* Wakefield; West Yorks. Metropolitan County Council; 1981. Pp x, 59.
10. University of Nottingham (Extra-Mural Studies). *The navigable waterways of Nottinghamshire: a survey in industrial archaeology.* Nottingham; the Department & WEA; 1981. Pp 77.
11. Port, M.H., 'Lowther Hall and Castle,' *T. of the Cumberland & Westmorland Antiquarian and Arch. Soc.* 81 (1981), 123–36.
12. O'Leary, T.J., 'Excavations at Upper Borough Walls, Bath, 1980,' *Medieval Archaeology* 25 (1981), 1–30.
13. Robinson, F.W. & B.A. *A history of Long Sutton and district (South Lincolnshire).* Long Sutton & District Civic Trust; 1981. Pp xviii, 303.
14. Crocker, J. (ed.). *Charnwood Forest, a changing landscape.* Loughborough Naturalists' Club; 1981. Pp 184.
15. Whitfield, G. *The Royal College of Physicians: the first thirty seven registrars of the college.* Univ. of Birmingham; 1981. Pp 193.
16. Kennedy, C. *Harewood: the life and times of an English country house.* London; Hutchinson; 1982. Pp 192.
17. Woodman, F. *The architectural history of Canterbury Cathedral.* London; Routledge; 1981. Pp xviii, 282.
18. Ingram, R.W. (ed.). *Coventry.* Manchester UP; 1981. Pp l, 712.
19. Belgion, H. *Titchmarsh past and present.* Kettering; the author; 1979. Pp 128.
20. Underwood, A. *Bedford Modern School of the black and red.* Bedford; The School; 1981. Pp 288.

21. Harrison, B.J.D.; Dixon, G. (ed.). *Gisborough before 1900.* Gisborough; G. Dixon; 1981. Pp xvi, 270.
22. Williams, G.H. *The western defences of Portsmouth harbour, 1400–1800.* Portsmouth City Council; 1979. Pp 74.
23. Barker, F.; Hyde, R., 'Crossing the Thames: London bridges that might have been,' *History Today* 32/6 (1982), 22–8.
24. Keeling-Roberts, M. *In retrospect: a short history of the Royal Salop Infirmary.* Wem; the author; 1981. Pp xvii, 102.
25. Smith, J.S., 'The rise and fall of Aberdeen's granite industry,' *Aberdeen University R.* 49 (1982), 163–7.
26. Christiansen, R. *Thames and Severn.* Newton Abbot; David & Charles; 1981. Pp 205.
27. Sweeny, J.O. *A numismatic history of the Birmingham Mint.* Birmingham Mint; 1981. Pp xii, 245.
28. Poppy, I.V., 'The homes of the Vaughan, part II,' *Brycheiniog* 19 (1980–1), 96–104.
29. Roese, H.E., 'The history of a South Wales family through public records,' ibid. 69–73.
30. Hasker, L. *The place which is called Fulanham: an outline history of Fulham from Roman times until the start of the Second World War.* London; Fulham & Hammersmith Hist. Soc.; 1981. Pp ii, 220.
31. Glover, C.; Riden, P. (ed.). *William Woolley's History of Derbyshire.* Chesterfield; Derbyshire Record Soc.; 1981. Pp lviii, 276.
32. Hart, C.R. *The North Derbyshire archaeological survey to A.D. 1500.* Chesterfield; North Derbyshire Arch. Trust; 1981. Pp xiv, 179.
33. Dodgson, J.McN. *The place-names of Cheshire, part 5.* 2 vols. English Place-Name Soc.; 1981. Pp 426.
34. Hasenson, A. *The history of Dover harbour.* London; Aurum; 1980. Pp 475.
35. Bailey, S. *Canonical houses of Wells.* Gloucester; Sutton; 1982. Pp 192.
36. Riches, A.; Coutley, H.M. *Victorian church building and restoration in Suffolk.* Woodbridge; Boydell; 1982. Pp 480.
37. Yasumoto, M., 'Industrialisation and demographic change in a Yorkshire parish,' *Local Population Studies* 27 (1981), 10–25.
38. Prior, M. *Fisher Row: fishermen, bargemen and canal boatmen in Oxford, 1500–1900.* Oxford; Clarendon; 1982. Pp xxii, 406.
39. *Lower Swansea Valley: legacy and future.* Swansea City Council; 1982. Pp 84.
40. Buckley, J.A. *A history of South Crofty mine.* Redruth; Dyllansow Truran; ?1980. Pp 224.
41. Nicholson, S. (ed.). *The changing face of Liverpool 1207–1727: archaeological survey of Merseyside.* Liverpool; Merseyside Arch. Soc.; 1982. Pp 48.

42. Bush, R.; Allen, G. *The book of Wellington: the story of a market town.* Buckingham; Barracuda; 1981. Pp 140.
43. Delaforce, J. *Anglicans abroad: the history of the chaplaincy and church of St James at Oporto.* London; SPCK; 1982. Pp ix, 140.
44. Dymond, D.; Betterton, A. *Lavenham: 700 years of textile making.* Woodbridge; Boydell & Brewer; 1982. Pp vi, 121.
45. Wiliam, E. *Traditional farm buildings in north-east Wales, 1500–1900.* Cardiff; National Museum of Wales; 1982. Pp 334.
46. Dyer, C. *The Guild of Freemen of the City of London: a record of its formation and history.* London; the Guild; 1982. Pp ix, 192.
47. Jenkin, A.K.H. *Mines of Devon: north and east of Dartmoor.* Exeter; Devon Library Services; 1981. Pp xi, 226.
48. Neville, G. *Religion and society in Eastbourne 1735–1920.* Eastbourne Local History Soc.; 1982. Pp 32.
49. Baker, T.F.T. (ed.). *A history of the county of Middlesex, vol. 7: Acton, Chiswick, Ealing and Willesden parishes.* Oxford UP for Institute of Historical Research (Victoria County History); 1982. Pp xx, 280.
50. Wright, A.P.M. (ed.). *A history of the county of Cambridge and the Isle of Ely, vol. 8: Armingford and Thriplow hundreds.* Idem; 1982. Pp xvi, 301.
51. Davies, M. *Glynogwr and Gilfach Goch: a history.* Cowbridge; D. Brown; 1981. Pp 229.
52. Plumley, N.M. *The organs and music masters of Christ's Hospital.* London; Christ's Hospital; 1981. Pp 94.
53. Hobley, B., 'The archaeology of London Wall,' *London J.* 7 (1981), 3–14.
54. Scott, W.N. *Coryton: the history of a village.* London; Mobil; 1981. Pp 47.
55. Bailey, N. *Fitzrovia.* New Barnet; Historical Publications; 1981. Pp 72.
56. Shipsides, F.; Wall, R. *Bristol: maritime city.* Bristol; Redcliffe; 1981. Pp 144.
57. Jennings, S.; Karshner, M.M.; Milligan, W.R.; Williams, S.V. *Eighteen centuries of pottery from Norwich.* Norwich; Univ. of East Anglia; 1981. Pp xii, 281.
58. Winnifrith, J., 'Land ownership in Appledore, 1500–1900,' *Archaeologia Cantiana* 97 (1982 for 1981), 1–6.
59. Williams, G.A. *The Welsh in their history* [collected papers]. London; Croom Helm; 1982. Pp 224.
60. Fenlon, I. *Cambridge music manuscripts, 900–1700.* Cambridge UP; 1982. Pp 174.
61. Wright, P.P. *Hunky punks: a study of Somerset stonecarving.* Amersham; Avebury Publishing; 1982. Pp x, 159.
62. Entwistle, K. *From Bodeltone to Bolton-on-Sands: the story of a village.* London; Euromonitor; 1982. Pp xi, 241.

63. McKinley, R. *The surnames of Lancashire.* London; Leopard's Head; 1981. Pp xiii, 501.
64. Knowles, J. *A history of Whiston.* Huyton; Knowsley Libraries; 1982. Pp vii, 137.
65. Tye, D. *A village school: Boughton Monchelsea 1850–1970.* Sittingbourne; Prototype; 1982. Pp 140.
66. Gibbs, J.M. *Morels of Cardiff: the history of a family shipping firm.* Cardiff; Amgueddfa Genedlaethol Cymru; 1982. Pp 183.
67. Lewis, J.M. *The Ewenny potteries.* Idem; 1982. Pp x, 126.
68. Messenger, M.J. *North Devon clay: the history of an industry and its transport.* Truro; Twelveheads Press; 1982. Pp 104.
69. Shoesmith, R. *Hereford excavations, vol. 2: Excavations on and close to the defences.* London; Council for British Archaeology; 1982. Pp 120.
70. Batey, M. *Oxford gardens: the university's influence on garden history.* Amersham; Avebury Publishing; 1982. Pp xvi, 256.
71. Lowe, D.; Richards, J. *The city of lace* [Nottingham]. Nottingham Lace Centre; 1982. Pp iv, 90.
72. Porteous, J.D., 'Surname geography: a study of the Mell family name c. 1538–1980,' *T. Institute of British Geographers* new ser. 7 (1982), 395–418.
73. Steer, F.W., 'St. Philip Howard, Arundel and the Howard connexion in Sussex,' Bc17, 209–222.
74. Exley, V., 'The Exley family of Rawdon,' *Bradford Antiquary* new ser. 47 (1982), 87–97.
75. Lister, M., 'Old Bradford charities,' ibid. 118–28.
76. Course, E.A., 'Transport history in Hampshire and the Isle of Wight,' *Southern History* 4 (1982), 221–35.
77. Pointon, A.G. *Methodists in West Somerset: their place and influence in the life of the community: the story of the West Somerset Circuit, 1790–1980.* Minehead; the author; 1982. Pp v, 106.
78. Wade-Martins, P. (ed.). *East Anglian archaeology, report no. 14: Norfolk: Trowse, Horning, deserted medieval villages, King's Lynn.* Dereham; Norfolk Arch. Unit; 1982. Pp viii, 133.
79. Brownlow, J. *Melton Mowbray, queen of the shires.* Wymondham; Sycamore; 1980. Pp 271.
80. Kerrigan, C. *A history of Tower Hamlets.* London; the borough; 1982. Pp viii, 95.
81. Chilton, C.W. *Early Hull printers and booksellers: an account of the printing, bookselling and allied trades from their beginnings to 1840.* Hull City Council; 1982. Pp 274.
82. Anderson, D.N. *Glasgow through the looking-glass: history of a city seen through its costume.* Milngavie; Heatherbank Press; 1982. Pp 94.
83. Richards, B. *History of the Llynfi valley.* Cambridge; D. Brown; 1982. Pp 366.

84. Thompson, P.; McKenna, L.; Sackillop, J. *Ploughlands and pastures: the imprint of agrarian history in four Cheshire townships – Peckforton, Haughton, Bunbury, Huxley*. Chester Libraries and Museums; 1982. Pp 112.
85. Bartlett, C. et al.; ed. Watts, G. *Titchfield: a history*. Titchfield Historical Soc.; 1982. Pp 143.
86. Roberts, B., 'Townfield origins: the case of Cockfield, county Durham,' Bc3, 145–61.
87. Harvey, M., 'The origins of planned field systems in Holderness, Yorkshire,' Bc3, 184–201.
88. Philipps, A. *Glasgow's Herald 1783–1983*. Glasgow; Drew; 1982. Pp 192.
89. Russell, E. & R.C. *Landscape changes in South Humberside: the enclosures of thirty-seven parishes.* Hull; Humberside Leisure Services; 1982. Pp 159.
90. Hague, J.; Robinson, M. (ed.). *Crookes: the history of a Sheffield village.* Sheffield; Crookes Residents' Association; 1982. Pp 77.
91. Waugh, J. *The vale of Bonny in history and legend.* Falkirk District Council; 1981. Pp 211.
92. Bennett, E. *The worshipful Company of Carmen of London* (new ed.). Buckingham; Barracuda; 1982. Pp 244.
93. Birley, R., 'The cathedral library [at Wells],' Bc23, 204–12.
94. Dunning, R.W., 'The bishop's palace [at Wells],' Bc23, 227–47.
95. Wilson, R.D.S. *The Feildens of Witton Park: the chronicles of a Lancashire family*. Blackburn; Borough Council; 1982. Pp 92.

(c) *Collective Volumes*

1. Robbins, K. (ed.). *Religion and humanism* (Studies in Church History, 17). Oxford; Blackwell; 1981[2]. Pp xii, 365.
2. Scott, B.G. (ed.). *Studies of early Ireland: essays in honour of M.V. Duignan.* Association of Young Irish Archaeologists; 1982. Pp 143.
3. Rowley, T. (ed.). *The origins of open-field agriculture.* London; Croom Helm; 1982. Pp 258.
4. *Scottish industrial history: a miscellany*. Scottish History Soc.; 1978. Pp xxxix, 221.
5. Webster, C. (ed.). *Biology, medicine and society 1840–1940.* Cambridge UP; 1981. Pp xi, 344.
6. Custance, R. *Winchester College: sixth-centenary essays.* Oxford UP; 1982. Pp xxiii, 515.
7. Yeo, E. & S. (ed.). *Popular culture and class conflict, 1590–1914: explorations in the history of labour and leisure.* Brighton; Harvester; 1981. Pp xii, 315.
8. Madden, A.F.; Fieldhouse, D.K. (ed.). *Oxford and the idea of the Commonwealth.* London; Croom Helm; 1982. Pp vii, 167.
9. Haase, W. (ed.). *Rome and the Anglicans: historical and doctrinal*

aspects of Anglican-Roman Catholic relations. Berlin/New York; de Gruyter; 1982. Pp 301.

10. Mews, S. (ed.). *Religion and national identity* (Studies in Church History, 18). Oxford; Blackwell; 1982. Pp xvi, 618.
11. Pickering, W.S.F. (ed.). *A social history of the diocese of Newcastle, 1882–1982.* Stocksfield; Oriel Press; 1981. Pp xiv, 338.
12. Minchinton, W. (ed.). *Reactions to social and economic change, 1750–1939.* University of Exeter; 1979. Pp 117.
13. Whitelock, D.; McKitterick, R.; Dumville, D. (ed.). *Ireland in early medieval Europe: essays in memory of Kathleen Hughes.* Cambridge UP; 1982. Pp x, 406.
14. Prest, J. (ed.). *Balliol studies.* London; Leopard's Head Press; 1982. Pp xi, 224.
15. Barker, T.; Drake, M. (ed.). *Population and society in Britain 1850–1980.* London; Batsford; 1982. Pp 221.
16. Brown, R.A. (ed.). *Proceedings of the Battle Conference on Anglo-Norman studies, IV, 1981.* Woodbridge; Boydell; 1982. Pp 224.
17. Kitch, M.J. *Studies in Sussex church history.* London; Leopard's Head Press; 1981. Pp xv, 260.
18. Dickson, T. (ed.). *Capital and class in Scotland.* Edinburgh; Donald; 1982. Pp vi, 286.
19. Kettenacker, L.; Schlenke, M.; Seier, H. (ed.). *Studien zur Geschichte Englands und der deutsch-britischen Beziehungen (Festschrift für Paul Kluke).* Munich; Wilhelm Fink; 1981. Pp 397.
20. Walvin, J. (ed.). *Slavery and British society, 1776–1846.* London; Macmillan; 1982. Pp 272.
21. Shiels, W.J. (ed.). *The Church and healing* (Studies in Church History 19). Oxford; Blackwell; 1982. Pp xxiv, 440.
22. Cruickshanks, E. (ed.). *Ideology and conspiracy: aspects of Jacobitism, 1689–1759.* Edinburgh; Donald; 1982. Pp xi, 231.
23. Colchester, L.S. (ed.). *Wells Cathedral: a history.* West Compton House; Open Books; 1982. Pp xii, 263.
24. Slaven, A.; Aldcroft, D.H. (ed.). *Business, banking and urban history: essays in honour of S.G. Checkland.* Edinburgh; Donald; 1982. Pp xiv, 235.
25. Dwyer, J.; Mason, A.; Murdoch, A. (ed.). *New perspective on the politics and culture of early modern Scotland.* Edinburgh; Donald; 1982. Pp vii, 329.
26. Detsicas, A. (ed.). *Collectanea Historica: essays in memory of Stuart Rigold.* Maidstone; Kent Arch. Soc.; 1981. Pp xiv, 304.
27. Pierce, S.M. (ed.). *The early church in western Britain and Ireland: studies presented to C.A. Ralegh Radford.* British Arch. Reports: British Series 102; 1982. Pp x, 388.

(d) *Genealogy and Heraldry*

1. Graham, N.H. *The genealogist's consolidated guide to parish registers, copies and indexes in the Inner London area, 1538 to 1837* (rev. ed.). Birchington; N.H. Graham; 1981. Pp 129.
2. Koe, W.S. *The jackdaws: a history of the Scandinavian family named Kaae, anglicised to Koe, and its connections.* Buckland; R.G. Taylor; 1981. Pp xi, 144.
3. *Charlton parish register 1813–1840.* London; Charlton Soc.; n.d. 69 leaves.
4. Gladwish, V.E.R. *The rape of Hastings family of de Gladwyshe, 1225–1980.* Somersham; UPEC Publications; 1981. Pp 182.
5. Hudleston, R.; Boumphrey, R.S., 'A supplement to Cumberland families and heraldry, part I,' *T. of the Cumberland and Westmorland Antiquarian and Arch. Soc.* 81 (1981), 27–47.
6. Cornwall County and Diocesan Record Office. *Handlist of pedigrees and heraldic documents.* Truro; the Office; 1981. Pp 18.
7. *A guide to the genealogical sources in Guildhall Library* (2nd ed.). London; the Library; 1981. Pp 44.
8. Carter, B.J. *Location of documents for Wiltshire parishes, parts 4–7.* Swinton; the compiler; 1981.
9. Keast, J. & R. (ed.). *Cornish epitaphs.* Redruth; Dyllansow Truran; 1981. Pp 64.
10. Gibbs, R. *Pedigree of the family of Gibbs of Pytte in the parish of Clyst St George* (4th ed.). London; the author; 1981. Pp xxi, 170.
11. Dennys, R. *Heraldry and the heralds.* London; Cape; 1982. Pp xviii, 285.
12. *The parish registers of St Mary, Bishophill Junior, York, 1813–1837.* York Family History Soc.; 1981. Pp iii, 123.
13. Shellis, P. *Registers of St Philip's, the cathedral church of Birmingham: marriages 1715–1800.* Birmingham & Midland Soc. for Genealogy and Heraldry; ?1981. Pp 111.
14. Collins, L. *Marriage licences: abstracts and indexes in the Library of the Society of Genealogists.* London; the Society; 1981. Pp 19.
15. *Monumental inscriptions: East Leake, East Leake (Baptist), Rempstone, Sandiacre (Derbyshire), South Muskham, West Leake.* Nottinghamshire Family History Soc.; 1981. Pp 63.
16. *Registers of the church of St Giles, Sheldon, part 2: baptisms 1683–1858, marriages 1684–1858, burials 1683–1841.* Sedley; Birmingham and Midland Soc. for Genealogy and Heraldry; 1980. Pp 124.
17. *Registers of St Michael & All Angels, Adbaston, Staffs: part 2: baptisms, marriages and burials 1727–1839.* Idem; 1980. Pp i, 89.
18. *Registers of St Kenelm's, Clifton-upon-Teme, Worcestershire: 1598–1837.* Idem; 1982. Pp 149.

19. *Index to 1851 census, vol. 2: Norton & Campsall.* Doncaster Soc. for Family History; 1982. Pp 28.
20. Richards, M.E.; Martin, H.C. *Handlist of genealogical sources.* Gloucestershire Record Office; 1982. Pp iv, 139.
21. Gibson, J.S.W. *Quarter sessions records for family historians: a select list.* Plymouth; Federation of Family History Societies; 1982. Pp 32.
22. Gibson, J.S.W. *Bishops' transcripts and marriage licences: bonds and allegations: a guide to their location and indexes* (2nd ed.). Banbury; Gulliver; 1982. Pp 32.
23. Staffordshire Parish Registers Society. *Newcastle under Lyme parish register.* Birmingham & Midland Soc. for Genealogy and Heraldry; 1981. Pp 354.
24. *Registers of the chapelry of St Michael & All Angels, Little Witley, Worcestershire: baptisms 1680–1846, marriages 1680–1836, burials 1680–1744.* Idem; 1982. Pp i, 47.
25. Browning, D.J.; Pope, F.R.; Turner, A.D. *The registers of Rainford chapel.* Bishops Stortford; Browning; 1981. Pp iv, 54. – The same. *The registers of Rainford chapel in the parish of Prescot: baptisms and burials 1813–1837.* The same; 1982. Pp v, 59.
26. De Breffny, B. *Irish family names: arms, origins, and locations.* Dublin; Gill & Macmillan; 1982. Pp 192.
27. *Birth briefs.* Sleaford; Soc. for Lincolnshire History and Archaeology; 1982. Pp 100.
28. Ratcliffe, R. *Alphabetical index of surnames in the 1851 census of Lincolnshire: part 1: Gainsborough registration district.* The same; 1982. Pp 78.
29. *Registers of the church of St Mary, Swynnerton, Staffordshire: baptisms, marriages and burials 1558–1812.* Birmingham and Midland Soc. for Genealogy and Heraldry; 1982. Pp viii, 138.
30. Ailes, A. *The origins of the royal arms of England: their development to 1199.* Reading University (Reading Medieval Studies, no. 2); 1982. Pp 126.

C. ROMAN BRITAIN

(a) *Archaeology*

1. Hill, P.R., 'Stonework and the archaeologist: including a stonemason's view of Hadrian's Wall,' *Archaeologia Aeliana* 5th ser. 9 (1981), 1–22.
2. Jobey, I., 'Excavations on the Romano-British settlement at Aiddle Gunnar Peak, Barrasford, Northumberland,' ibid. 51–74.

3. Allason-Jones, L.; Shorer, P.H.T.; Coulston, J.C., 'Museum notes,' ibid. 347–51.
4. Bellhouse, R.L., 'Roman sites on the Cumberland coast: Mile fortlet 20 Low Mire,' *T. of the Cumberland and Westmorland Antiquarian and Arch. Soc.* 81 (1981), 7–13.
5. Shotter, D.C.A., 'Further Roman coins from Docker Moor,' ibid. 159–60.
6. Not used.
7. Bryant, G.F. *The early history of Barton upon Humber: prehistory to the Norman Conquest.* Barton Civic Soc.; 1981. Pp 73.
8. Burnett, A.M. (ed.). *Coin hoards from Roman Britain.* London; British Museum; 1981. Pp iv, 121.
9. Webster, G., 'The excavation of a Romano-British rural establishment at Barnsley Park: part I,' *Bristol & Gloucestershire Arch. Soc. T.* 99 (1982 for 1981), 21–77.
10. Hunter, A.G., 'Building-excavations at the Cross, Gloucester,' ibid. 79–107.
11. Rawes, B. (ed.)., 'Archaeological review No. 5,' ibid. 172–9.
12. Musson, C.R., 'Prehistoric and Romano-British settlements in northern Powys and western Shropshire: recent evidence from aerial photography and excavation,' *Arch. J.* 138 (1982 for 1981), 5–7.
13. Barker, P., 'The Montgomery area,' ibid. 7–9.
14. Frere, S.S., 'Fordean Gaer,' ibid. 17–18.
15. Frere, S.S., 'Brandon Camp,' ibid. 25.
16. Stanford, S.C., 'Roman and native around Leintwardine,' ibid. 25–6.
17. Webster, G., 'Wroxeter,' ibid. 33.
18. Taylor, H.M.; Yonge, D.D., 'The ruined church at Stone-by-Faversham: a re-assessment,' ibid. 118–45.
19. Harrison, A.C., 'Rochester 1974–75,' *Archaeologia Cantiana* 97 (1982 for 1982), 95–136.
20. Black, E.W., 'The Roman villa at Darenth,' ibid. 159–83.
21. Painter, K.S., 'Two Roman silver ingots from Kent,' ibid. 201–7.
22. Tatton-Brown, T.W.T.; Bennett, P.; Rady, J.; Blockley, K. & P., 'Interim report on excavations in 1981 by the Canterbury Archaeological Trust,' ibid. 275–93.
23. Perkins, D.R.J., 'A Roman bronze head from Margate,' ibid. 307–11.
24. Pollard, R.J., 'Two cremations of the Roman period from St Augustine's College, Canterbury,' ibid. 318–24.
25. Anon., 'Investigation and excavations during the year,' ibid. 325–6.
26. Pooter, T.W. and C.F. *A Romano-British village at Granford, March, Cambridgeshire.* London; British Museum; 1982. Pp viii, 133.
27. Cunliffe, B.W.; Fulford, M.G. *Corpus signorum imperii Romani,*

I/2: Bath and the rest of Wessex. Oxford UP for British Academy; 1982. Pp 59.

28. Bland, R. (ed.). *Coin hoards from Roman Britain, vol. 3: The Blackmoor hoard*. London; British Museum; 1982. Pp v, 115.
29. Potter, T.W.; Jackson, R.P.J., 'The Roman site of Stonea, Cambridgeshire,' *Antiquity* 56 (1982), 111–20.
30. Hodges, R.; Wildgoose, M., 'Roman or native in the White Peak: the Roystone Grange project and its regional implications,' *Derbyshire Arch. J.* 101 (1981), 42–57.
31. Ling, R.; Courtney, T., 'Excavations at Carsington, 1979–80,' ibid. 58–76.
32. Brassington, M., 'The Roman roads of Derbyshire,' ibid. 88–92.
33. Neal, D.S. *Roman mosaics in Britain: an introduction to their schemes and a catalogue of paintings*. London; Soc. for the Promotion of Roman Studies; 1981. Pp 127.
34. Wedlake, W.J. et al. *The excavation of the shrine of Apollo at Nettleton, Wiltshire, 1956–1971*. London; Soc. of Antiquaries; 1982. Pp xx, 267.
35. Liddle, P. *Leicestershire archaeology: the present state of knowledge; vol. 1: to the end of the Roman period*. Leicester; Leics. Museums Service; 1982. Pp 52.
36. King, C.E., 'A hoard of clipped siliquae in the Preston Museum,' *Numismatic Chronicle* 141 (1981), 40–64.
37. Boon, G.C.; Hassall, M. *Report on the excavations at Usk 1965–1976: the coins, inscriptions and graffiti*. Cardiff; University of Wales Press; 1982. Pp x, 72.
38. Jobey, G., 'The settlement at Doubstead and Romano-British settlement on the coastal plain between Tyne and Forth,' *Archaeologia Aeliana* 5th ser. 10 (1982), 1–23.
39. Allason-Jones, L.; Gillam, J.P., 'Roman pottery from Hadrian's Wall turret 27A,' ibid. 199–200.
40. Bennett, J., 'The Great Chesters "pilum murale",' ibid. 200–5.
41. Henig, M., 'A Roman finger ring from Durham,' ibid. 207.
42. Green, M., 'The Roman wheel-brooch from Lakenheath (Suffolk) and a note on the typology of wheel-brooches,' *B. of the Board of Celtic Studies* 30 (1982), 168–75.
43. Butcher, A., 'Two Roman zoomorphic brooches from Richborough,' Bc26, 3–13.
44. Johnson, S., 'The construction of the Saxon Shore fort at Richborough,' Bc26, 14–19.
45. Young, C., 'The late Roman mill at Ickham and the Saxon Shore,' Bc26, 32–40.
46. Green, C.S., 'The cemetery of a Romano-British community at Poundbury, Dorchester, Dorset,' Bc27, 61–76.

(b) *History*

1. Holder, P.A. *The Roman army in Britain.* London; Batsford; 1982. Pp 160.
2. Green, M., 'Wheel-god and ram-headed snake in Roman Gloucestershire,' *Bristol and Gloucestershire Arch. Soc. T.* 99 (1982 for 1981), 109–15.
3. Webster, G., 'The Welsh marches and the early Roman campaigns,' *Arch. J.* 138 (1982 for 1981), 1–5.
4. Rivet, A.F.L.; Smith, C. *The place-names of Roman Britain.* London; Batsford; 1979. Pp xviii, 526.
5. Breeze, D.J. *The northern frontier of Roman Britain.* London; Batsford; 1982. Pp 188.
6. Morris, J. *Londinium: London in the Roman empire* [revd by S. Macready]. London; Weidenfeld & Nicolson; 1982. Pp xvi, 384.
7. Wilkes, J.J., 'New standards for Roman Britain [review article],' *History* 67 (1982), 405–13.
8. Potter, T.W.; Whitehouse, D.B., 'A Roman building in the Cambridgeshire fens, and some parallels near Rome,' *World Archaeology* 14 (1982), 218–23.
9. Gratwick, A.S., 'Latinitas Britannica: was British Latin archaic?,' Da2, 1–79.
10. Philp, B., 'Richborough, Reculver and Lympne: a reconsideration of three of Kent's late-Roman shore-forts,' Bc26, 41–9.
11. Knight, J., 'In tempore Iustini consulis: contacts between the British and Gaulish churches before Augustine,' Bc26, 54–62.
12. Buckland, P.C., 'The Malton burnt grain: a cautionary tale,' *Yorkshire Arch. J.* 54 (1982), 53–61.
13. Frend, W.H.C., 'Romano-British Christianity in the west: comparison and contrast,' Bc27, 5–16.
14. McKillop, S., 'A Romano-British baptismal liturgy,' Bc27, 35–48.

D. ENGLAND 450–1066

See also Ca7

(a) *General*

1. Campbell, J. *The Anglo-Saxons.* Oxford; Phaidon; 1982. Pp 272.
2. Brooks, N.P. (ed.). *Latin and the vernacular languages in early medieval Britain.* Leicester UP; 1982. Pp 192.
3. Graham-Campbell, J., 'The Vikings in England,' *History Today* 32/7 (1982), 40–3.

4. Clemoes, P. (ed.). *Anglo-Saxon England, X.* Cambridge UP; 1982. Pp ix, 326.
5. Sawyer, P.H., 'Conquest and colonization: Scandinavians in the Danelaw and in Normandy,' *P. of the Eighth Viking Congress*, ed. H. Bekker-Nielsen et al. (Odense UP; 1981), 123–31.
6. Jensen, G.F., 'Scandinavian settlement in the Danelaw in the light of place-names in Denmark,' ibid. 133–45.
7. Cox, H.J.; Whittle, A.W.R. *Settlement patterns in the Oxford region.* London; Council for British Archaeology; 1982. Pp 160.
8. Dolley, M., 'The palimpsest of Viking settlement on Man,' *P. of the Eighth Viking Congress*, ed. H. Bekker-Nielsen et al. (Odense UP; 1981), 173–81.
9. Witney, K.P. *The kingdom of Kent.* Chichester; Phillimore; 1982.
10. Dumville, D., 'The "six" sons of Rhodri Mawr: a problem in Asser's *Life of King Alfred,*' *Cambridge Medieval Celtic Studies* 4 (1982), 5–18.

(b) *Politics and Institutions*

1. Davis, R.H.C., 'Alfred and Guthrum's frontier,' *English Historical R.* 97 (1982), 803–10.
2. Williams, H., '*Princeps Merciorum gentis*: the family, career and connections of Aelfhere, ealderman of Mercia 956–83,' Da4, 143–72.
3. Stafford, P., 'The laws of Cnut and the history of Anglo-Saxon royal premises,' Da4, 173–90.
4. Rosenthal, J.T., 'The swinging pendulum and the turning wheel: the Anglo-Saxon state before Alfred,' *The Early Middle Ages, Acta* 6 (1982 for 1979), 95–115.

(c) *Religion*

1. Meyer, M.A., 'Patronage of the West Saxon royal nunneries in late Anglo-Saxon England,' *Revue Bénédictine* 91 (1981), 332–58.
2. Hinton, D.A.; Keene, S.; Qualmann, K.E., 'The Winchester Reliquary,' *Medieval Archaeology* 25 (1981), 45–77.
3. Whitelock, D.; Brett, M.; Brooke, C.N.L. (ed.). *Councils and synods with other documents relating to the English Church, I: A.D. 871–1204* (2 parts). Oxford; Clarendon; 1981. Pp lxxi, 1151.
4. Owen, G.R. *Rites and religions of the Anglo-Saxons.* Newton Abbot; David & Charles; 1981. Pp 216.
5. Lapidge, M., 'The author of CCCC 163,' *T. of the Cambridge Bibliographical Soc.* 8 (1981), 18–28.
6. Fell, C.E., 'Anglo-Saxon saints in Old Norse sources and vice versa,' *P. of the Eighth Viking Congress*, ed. H. Bekker-Nielsen & al. (Odense UP; 1981), 95–106.

7. Thacker, A.T., 'Chester and Gloucester: early ecclesiastical organization in two Mercian burhs,' *Northern History* 18 (1982), 199–211.
8. Jackson, F.H., 'Brigomaglos and St. Brioc,' *Archaeologia Aeliana* 5th ser. 10 (1982), 61–5.
9. Thomas, C., 'East and west: Tintagel, mediterranean imports and the early insular church,' Bc27, 17–34.
10. Bodwell, W., 'From mausoleum to minster: the early development of Wells cathedral,' Bc27, 49–60.
11. Swanton, M.; Pearce, S., 'Lustleigh, South Devon: its inscribed stone, the churchyard and its parish,' Bc27, 139–44.
12. Pearce, S., 'Estates and church sites in Dorset and Gloucestershire: the emergence of a Christian society,' Bc27, 117–38.
13. Henderson, C.G.; Bidwell, P.T., 'The Saxon minster at Exeter,' Bc27, 145–76.
14. Gelling, M., 'Some meanings of *stow*,' Bc27, 187–97.
15. Cubbon, A.M., 'The early church in the Isle of Man,' Bc27, 257–82.
16. Not used.
17. Briggs, G.W.D., 'The church of St. Andrew, Bolam, Northumberland,' *Archaeologia Aeliana* 5th ser. 10 (1982), 125–42.
18. Keep, D., 'Cultural conflicts in the missions of Saint Boniface,' Bc10, 47–57.
19. Banton, N., 'Monastic reform and the unification of tenth-century England,' Bc10, 71–85.
20. Dawtry, A., 'The Benedictine revival in the north: the last bulwark of Anglo-Saxon monasticism?,' Bc10, 87–98.
21. Whitelock, D., 'Bishop Ecgred, Pehtred and Niall,' Bc13, 47–68.
22. Mayr-Harting, H., 'St. Wilfrid in Sussex,' Bc17, 1–17.
23. Rodwell, W., 'The Anglo-Saxon and Norman churches at Wells,' Bc23, 1–23.

(d) *Economic Affairs and Numismatics*

1. Metcalf, D.M., 'Continuity and change in English monetary history c. 973–1086, part I,' *British Numismatic J.* 50 (1981 for 1980), 20–49.
2. Blackburn, M.A.S.; Metcalf, D.M. (ed.). *Viking-age coinage in the northern lands.* 2 vols. British Arch. Reports (International Series 122, i & ii). Oxford UP; 1981.
3. Blackburn, M.A.S.; Jonsson, K., 'The Anglo-Saxon and Anglo-Norman element in north European coin finds,' Dd2, 147–256.
4. Kluge, B., 'Das angelsächsiche Element in den slawischen Münzfunden des 10. bis 12. Jahrhunderts: Aspekte einer Analyse,' Dd2, 257–328.
5. Metcalf, D.M., 'Some 10th century runes: statistical analysis of

the Viking-age hoards and the interpretation of wastage rates,' Dd2, 329–82.

6. Sawyer, P.H., 'Fairs and markets in early medieval England,' *Danish Medieval History: New Currents*, ed. N. Skyum-Nielsen and N. Lund (Copenhagen; Museum Tusculanum Press; 1981), 153–68.
7. Hooke, D., 'Open-field agriculture – the evidence from the pre-Conquest charters of the West Midlands,' Bc3, 39–63.
8. Oxley, J., 'Nantwich: an eleventh-century salt town and its origins,' *T. of the Historic Soc. of Lancashire and Cheshire* 131 (1982 for 1981), 1–19.

(e) *Intellectual and Cultural*

1. Jacobs, N., 'The Old English heroic tradition in the light of Welsh evidence,' *Cambridge Medieval Celtic Studies* 2 (1981), 9–20.
2. Dumville, D.N., '*Beowulf* and the Celtic world: the uses of evidence,' *Traditio* 37 (1981), 109–60.
3. Whatley, G., 'The figure of Constantine the Great in Cynewulf's *Elene*,' ibid. 161–202.
4. Lapidge, M., 'The study of Latin texts in late Anglo-Saxon England: (1) The evidence of Latin glosses,' Da2, 99–140.
5. Page, R.I., 'The study of Latin texts in late Anglo-Saxon England: (2) The evidence of English glosses,' Da2, 141–65.
6. Cowdrey, H.E.J., 'Bede and the "English People",' *J. of Religious History* 11 (1981), 501–23.
7. Bately, J. (ed.). *The Old English Orosius* [Early English Text Soc., supplementary series 6]. Oxford UP; 1980. Pp cxix, 433.
8. Ray, R., 'What do we know about Bede's Commentary?,' *Recherches de théologie ancienne et médiévale* 49 (1982), 1–20.
9. Olson, G., 'Bede as historian: the evidence from his observations on the life of the first Christian community at Jerusalem,' *J. of Ecclesiastical History* 33 (1982), 519–30.
10. Hill, J.M., 'Beowulf and the Danish succession: gift giving as an occasion for complex gesture,' *Medievalia et Humanistica* new ser. 11 (1982), 177–97.
11. Thomson, R., 'Identifiable books from the pre-Conquest library of Malmesbury Abbey,' Da4, 1–20.
12. Sims-Williams, 'Mildred of Worcester's collection of Latin epigrams and its continental counterparts,' Da4, 21–38.
13. Bately, J.M., 'Lexical evidence for the authorship of the prose psalms in the Paris Psalter,' Da4, 69–96.
14. Lapidge, M., 'Byrthferth of Ramsey and the early sections of the *Historia Regum* attributed to Symeon of Durham,' Da4, 97–123.
15. Baker, P.S., 'Byrthferth's *Enchiridion* and the computus in Oxford, St John College 17,' Da4, 123–42.

16. Herren, M.J. (ed.). *Insular Latin studies: papers on Latin texts and manuscripts of the British Isles, 550–1066 A.D.* Toronto; Pontifical Institute; 1981. Pp x, 188.
17. Lapidge, M., 'The present state of Anglo-Latin studies,' De16, 45–82.
18. Stevens, W.M., 'Scientific instruction in early insular schools,' De16, 83–111.
19. Wieland, G., '*Geminus stilus*: studies in Anglo-Latin hagiography,' De16, 113–33.
20. Dumville, D.N., 'English libraries before 1066: use and abuse of the manuscript evidence,' De16, 153–78.
21. Dodwell, C.R. *Anglo-Saxon art: a new perspective.* Manchester UP; 1982. Pp xv, 308.
22. Brooks, N.P., 'The oldest document in the College archives? The Micheldever forgery [at Winchester],' Bc6, 189–238.
23. Blagg, T., 'Some Roman architectural traditions in the early Saxon churches of Kent,' Bc26, 50–3.
24. Zettel, P.H., 'Saints' lives in Old English: Latin manuscripts and vernacular accounts: Aelfric,' *Peritia* 1 (1982), 17–37.
25. Cross, J.E., 'Saints' lives in Old English: Latin manuscripts and vernacular accounts: the Old English Martyrology,' ibid. 38–62.

(f) *Society and Archaeology*

1. Hawkes, S.C.; Pollard, M., 'The gold bracteates from sixth-century Anglo-Saxon graves in Kent in the light of the new find from Finglesham,' *Frühmittelalterliche Studien*, ed. K. Hauck, 15 (1981), 316–70.
2. Firby, M.; Lang, J., 'The pre-Conquest sculpture at Stonegrave,' *Yorkshire Arch. J.* 53 (1981), 17–29.
3. Hillam, J., 'An English tree-ring chronology, A.D. 404–1216,' *Medieval Archaeology* 25 (1981), 31–44.
4. Härke, H., 'Anglo-Saxon laminated shields at Petersfinger – a myth,' ibid. 141–4.
5. Arnold, C.J.; Wardle, P., 'Early medieval settlement patterns in England,' ibid. 145–9.
6. Huggins, P.J., 'Yeavering measurements: an alternative view,' ibid. 150–3.
7. Watkin, J.; Mann, F., 'Some late Saxon finds from Lilla House, N. Yorks, and their context,' ibid. 153–7.
8. Cook, A.M. *The Anglo-Saxon cemetery at Fonaby, Lincolnshire.* Sleaford; Soc. for Lincolnshire History and Archaeology; 1981. Pp 108.
9. Not used.
10. Cambridge, E., 'C.C. Hodges and the nave of Hexham Abbey,' *Archaeologia Aeliana* 5th ser. 7 (1979), 159–68.
11. Thomas, C. *A provisional list of imported pottery in post-Roman*

western Britain and Ireland. Redruth; Institute of Cornish Studies; 1981. Pp 32.

12. Williams, J.H. *Saxon and medieval Northampton.* Northampton Development Corporation; 1982. Pp 52.
13. Addyman, P.; Pearson, N.; Tweddle, D., 'The Coppergate helmet,' *Antiquity* 55 (1982), 189–94.
14. Morris, C.D., 'Viking and native in northern England: a case-study,' *P. of the Eighth Viking Congress*, ed. H. Bekker-Nielsen (Odense UP; 1981), 223–44.
15. O'Connor, T.; Wilkinson, M. *Animal bones from Flaxengate, Lincoln, c. 870–1500.* London; Council for British Archaeology; 1982. Pp 52.
16. Perring, D. *Early medieval occupation at Flaxengate, Lincoln.* The same; 1981. Pp 47.
17. Beresford, G., 'Goltho manor, Lincolnshire: the buildings and their surrounding defences, *c.* 850–1150,' Bc16, 13–36.
18. St Joseph, J.K.S., 'Sprouston, Roxburghshire: an Anglo-Saxon settlement discovered by air reconnaisance,' Da4, 191–200.
19. Hauck, K., 'Zum zweiten Band der Sutton Hoo-Edition,' *Frühmittelalterliche Studien* 16 (1982), 319–62.
20. Barker, K., 'The early history of Sherborne,' Bc27, 77–116.
21. McCarthy, M.R., 'Thomas Chadwick and post-Roman Carlisle,' Bc27, 241–57.
22. Skipp, V., 'The evolution of settlement and open-field topography in North Arden down to 1300,' Bc3, 162–83.
23. Rahtz, P.A., 'Celtic society in Somerset A.D. 400–700,' *B. of the Board of Celtic Studies* 30 (1982), 176–200.
24. Jenkins, F., 'The church of All Saints, Shuart in the Isle of Thanet,' Bc26, 147–54.

E. ENGLAND 1066–1500

See also Df12, 15–17, 22

(a) *General*

1. Highfield, J.R.L.; Jeffs, R. (ed.). *The crown and local communities in England and France in the fifteenth century.* Gloucester; Sutton; 1981. Pp 192.
2. Hector, L.C.; Harvey, B.F. (ed.). *The Westminster chronicle, 1381–94.* Oxford; Clarendon; 1982. Pp lxxvii, 563.
3. Morris, J. (ed.). *Domesday Book; vol. 4: Hampshire* (ed. J. Mumby); *vol. 15: Worcestershire* (ed. F. & C. Thorn); *vol. 16: Gloucestershire* (ed. J.S. Moore); *vol. 18: Cambridgeshire* (ed.

A. Rumble). Chichester; Phillimore; 1981, 1982, 1982, 1981. Unpaginated.

4. Fraser, C.M. (ed.). *Northern petitions illustrative of life in Berwick, Cumbria and Durham in the 14th century [from PRO, Ancient Petitions]*. Surtees Soc. 194 (1982 for 1981). Pp 292.
5. Hilton, R.H., 'The international background: some problems of medieval social history,' *Danish Medieval History: New Currents*, ed. N. Skyum-Nielsen and N. Lund (Copenhagen; Museum Tusculanum Press; 1981), 11–21.
6. Galbraith, V.H. *Kings and chroniclers: essays in English medieval history* [collected papers]. London; Hambledon Press; 1982. Unpaginated.
7. McFarlane, K.B. *England in the fifteenth century: collected essays* (G.L. Harriss, intr.). Ibid; 1982. Pp xxvii, 279.
8. Reeves, A.C. *Lancastrian Englishmen.* Washington, DC; University Press of America; 1982. Pp 419.
9. Carpenter, C., 'Fifteenth-century biographies [review article],' *Historical J.* 25 (1982), 729–34.
10. Barrow, G.W.S., 'Das mittealterliche englische und schottische Königtum: ein Vergleich,' *Historisches Jahrbuch* 102 (1982), 362–89.

(b) *Politics*

1. Mooers, S.L., ' "Backers and Stabbers"; problems of loyalty in Robert Curthose's entourage,' *J. of British Studies* 21 (1981–2), 1–17.
2. Barron, C.M., 'London and the crown,' Ea1, 88–109.
3. Styles, D.; Allmand, C.T., 'The coronations of Henry VI,' *History Today* 32/5 (1982), 28–33.
4. Kekewich, M., 'The attainder of the Yorkists in 1459: two contemporary accounts,' *B. of the Institute of Historical Research* 55 (1982), 25–34.
5. Horowitz, M.R., 'Richard Empson, minister of Henry VII,' ibid. 35–49.
6. Keefe, T.K., 'King Henry II and the earls,' *Albion* 13 (1981), 191–222.
7. McNiven, P., 'Legitimacy and consent: Henry IV and the Lancastrian title, 1399–1406,' *Mediaeval Studies* 44 (1982), 470–88.
8. Hallam, E.M., 'Royal burial and the cult of kingship in France and England, 1060–1330,' *J. of Medieval History* 8 (1982), 359–80.
9. Crouch, D., 'Geoffrey de Clinton and Roger, earl of Warwick: new men and magnates in the reign of Henry I,' *B. of the Institute of Historical Research* 55 (1982), 113–24.
10. Clementi, D.R., 'The documentary evidence for the crisis of

government in England in 1258,' *Parliaments, Estates and Representation* 1 (1981), 99–108.

11. Knowles, C.H., 'The resettlement of England after the Barons' War, 1264–67,' *T. of the Royal Historical Soc.* 5th ser. 32 (1982), 25–41.
12. Liddell, W.H.; Wood, R.G.E. (ed.). *Essex and the great revolt of 1381.* Essex Record Office; 1982. Pp 106.
13. Dobson, R.B., 'Remembering the peasants' revolt, 1381–1981,' Eb12, 1–20.
14. Dyer, C.C., 'The causes of the revolt in rural Essex,' Eb12, 21–36.
15. Grieve, H.E.P., 'The rebellion and the country town,' Eb12, 37–54.
16. Prescott, A.J., 'Essex rebel bands in London,' Eb12, 55–66.
17. Wood, R.G.E., 'Essex manorial records and the revolt,' Eb12, 67–84.
18. Newfield, G. *The rising of 1381: an annotated bibliography with special reference to St Albans.* Hatfield Polytechnic; 1981. Pp 19.
19. Hare, J.N., 'The Wiltshire risings of 1450: political and economic discontent in mid-fifteenth century England,' *Southern History* 4 (1982), 13–31.
20. Lewis, W.G., 'The exact date of the battle of Banbury [i.e. Edgecote], 1469,' *B. of the Institute of Historical Research* 55 (1982), 194–6.

(c) *Constitution, Administration and Law*

1. Adams, N.; Donahue, C. (ed.). *Select cases from the ecclesiastical courts of the province of Canterbury c. 1200–1301.* London; Selden Soc. vol. 95; 1981. Pp xxx, 756.
2. Harding, A. (ed.). *The roll of the Shropshire eyre of 1256.* London; Selden Soc. vol. 96; 1981 [i.e. 2]. Pp lxxiv, 403.
3. Genet, J.-P., 'Political theory and the relationship in England and France between the crown and local communities,' Ea1, 19–32.
4. Virgoe, R., 'The crown, magnates and local government in 15th-century East Anglia,' Ea1, 72–87.
5. Green, J.A., ' "Praeclarum et magnificum antiquitatis momentum": the earliest surviving pipe roll,' *B. of the Institute of Historical Research* 55 (1982), 1–17.
6. Crook, D., 'The later eyres,' *English Historical R.* 97 (1982), 241–68.
7. Sharpe, J.A., 'The history of crime in late medieval and early modern England: a review of the field,' *Social History* 7 (1982), 187–203.
8. Wood, C.T., 'Celestine V, Boniface VIII, and the authority of parliament,' *J. of Medieval History* 8 (1982), 45–62.

9. Cheney, C.R. *The papacy and England, 12th to 14th centuries: historical and legal studies* [collected papers]. London; Variorum Reprints; 1982. Pp 346.
10. Cheney, C.R. *The English church and its laws, 12th–14th centuries* [collected papers]. Ibid.; 1982. Pp 348.
11. Duggan, C. *Canon law in medieval England* [collected papers]. Ibid.; 1982. Pp 340.
12. Groot, R.D., 'The jury of presentment before 1215,' *American J. of Legal History* 26 (1982), 1–24.
13. Henderson, E.G., 'Legal rights to land – the early chancery,' ibid. 97–122.
14. Bates, D., 'The origins of the justiciarship,' Bc16, 1–12.
15. Hyams, P., 'The common law and the French connection,' Bc16, 77–92.
16. Rumble, A.R., 'The purposes of the *Codex Wintoniensis*,' Bc16, 153–66.
17. Keefe, T.K., 'The 1165 levy for the army of Wales,' *Notes & Queries* 227 (1982), 194–6.
18. Cazel, F.A., Jr. (ed.). *Roll of divers accounts for the early years of the reign of Henry III (etc).* London; Pipe Roll Soc. new ser. 44, for 1974–5; 1982. Pp 153.
19. Virgoe, R., 'The parliamentary subsidy of 1450,' *B. of the Institute of Historical Research* 55 (1982), 125–38.
20. Ault, W.O., 'The vill in medieval England,' *P. of the American Philosophical Soc.* 126 (1982), 188–211.
21. Pool, P.A.S., 'The tithings of Cornwall,' *J. of the Royal Institution of Cornwall*, 8/4 (1981), 275–337.
22. Picken, W.M.M., 'The earliest borough charter of East Looe [c. 1220],' ibid. 350–7.
23. Bellamy, B., 'The Rockingham Forest perambulation of 1299,' *Northamptonshire Past & Present* 6/6 (1982–3), 303–8.
24. Birrell, J., 'Who poached the king's deer? A study in thirteenth-century crime,' *Midland History* 7 (1982), 9–25.
25. Summerson, H., 'Crime and society in medieval Cumberland,' *T. of the Cumberland and Westmorland Antiquarian and Arch. Soc.* 82 (1982), 111–24.
26. De Windt, A.R. & E.B. (ed.). *Royal justice and the medieval English countryside: the Huntingdonshire eyre of 1286, the Ramsey Abbey banlieu court of 1287, and the assizes of 1287–88.* Toronto; Pontifical Institute; 1981. 2 vols. Pp xv, 766.
27. Greenway, D.E., 'A newly discovered fragment of the hundred rolls of 1279–80,' *J. of the Soc. of Archivists* 7 (1982), 73–7.
28. Lloyd, P., 'The coroners of Leicestershire in the early 14th century,' *T. of the Leicestershire Arch. and Historical Soc.* 56 (1980–1), 18–32.
29. May, P., 'Newmarket and its market court, 1399–1413,' *P. of the Suffolk Institute of Archaeology and History* 35 (1981), 31–9.

30. Kinney, T.L., ' "Two secuturs and an overseer make three thieves": popular attitudes toward false executors of wills and testaments,' *Fifteenth-Century Studies* 3 (1980), 93–105.
31. Horrocks, R.; Hammond, P.W. (ed.). *British Library Harleian Manuscript 433. Vol. 3: second register of Edward V and miscellaneous material.* Gloucester; Alan Sutton; 1982. Pp 260.
32. Meekings, C.A.F. *Studies in thirteenth-century justice and administration* [collected papers]. London; Hambledon Press; 1982.
33. Sayles, G.O. *Scripta diversa.* Ibid.; 1982. Pp xi, 371.
34. Richardson, H.G.; Sayles, G.O. *The English parliament in the middle ages* [collected papers]. Ibid.; 1981. Unpaginated.
35. Roskell, J.S. *Parliament and politics in late medieval England* [collected papers]. 2 vols. Ibid.; 1982. Unpaginated.
36. Harvey, M., 'Ecclesia Anglicana, cui noster Christus vos prefecit: the power of the crown in the English church during the great schism,' Bc10, 229–41.
37. Palmer, R.C. *The county courts of medieval England.* Princeton UP; 1982. Pp xvii, 360.
38. Allmand, C.T.; Armstrong, C.A.J. (ed.). *English suits before the parlement of Paris, 1420–1436.* London; Royal Hist. Soc. (Camden 4th ser., 26); 1982. Pp 328.
39. Gordon, M.D., 'Royal power and fundamental law in western Europe, 1350–1650: the crown lands,' *Diritto e Potere nella Storia Europea* (Florence; Olschki; 1982), 255–70.
40. Turner, R.V., 'Twelfth- and thirteenth-century English law and government: suggestions for prosopographical approaches,' *Medieval Prosopography* 3/2 (1982), 21–34.

(d) *External Affairs*

1. Hyams, P.R., 'Some coin export from 12th-century Yorkshire to the Holy Land,' *Coinage in the Latin East*, ed. P.W. Edbury and D.M. Metcalf (British Arch. Reports, International Series 77, 1980), 133–5.
2. Allmand, C.T., 'Local reaction to the French reconquest of Normandy [1449–50]: the case of Rouen,' Ea1, 146–61.
3. Allmand, C.T.; Armstrong, C.A.J. (ed.). *English suits before the parlement of Paris, 1420–1436.* London; Royal Historical Soc. (Camden 4th series 26); 1982. Pp vii, 328.
4. Legge, D.M., 'William the Marshal and Arthur of Brittany,' *B. of the Institute of Historical Research* 55 (1982), 18–24.
5. Petit, K., 'Le mariage de Philippa de Hainault, reine d'Angleterre (1328),' *Le Moyen Age* 87 (1981), 373–85.
6. Palmer, J.J. 'Froissart et le héraut Chandos,' ibid. 88 (1982), 271–92.
7. Capra, P., 'Les espèces, les ateliers, les frappes et les émissions monétaires en Guyenne anglo-gasconne aux XIVe et XVe

siècles,' *Numismatic Chronicle* 139–40 (1979–80), 139–54; 132–64.

8. Elias, E.R.D., 'The gros au lion of Aquitaine,' ibid. 141 (1981), 65–70.
9. Loud, G.A., 'The *Gens Normannorum* – myth or reality?,' Bc16, 104–16.
10. Spear, D.S., 'The Norman empire and the secular clergy,' *J. of British Studies* 21 (1982), 1–10.
11. Mesmin, S.C., 'Waleran, count of Meulan, and the leper hospital of S. Gilles de Pont-Audemer,' *Annals de Normandie* 32 (1982), 3–19.
12. Chibnall, M. (ed.). *Charters and custumals of the abbey of Holy Trinity, Caen.* Oxford UP for British Academy; 1982. Pp liv, 163.
13. Mayer, H.E., 'Henry II of England and the Holy Land,' *English Historical R.* 97 (1982), 721–39.
14. Gillingham, J.B., 'Roger of Howden on crusade,' *Medieval Historical Writing in the Christian and Islamic Worlds*, ed. D.O. Morgan (London; School of Oriental and African Studies; 1982), 60–75.
15. Parsons, J.C., 'Eleanor of Castile and the countess Margaret of Ulster: an essay on a possible kinship,' *Genealogists' Magazine* 20 (1982), 335–40.
16. Stones, E.L.G., 'The mission of Thomas Wale and Thomes Delisle from Edward I to pope Boniface VIII in 1301,' *Nottingham Medieval Studies* 26 (1982), 8–28.

(e) *Religion*

1. Swanson, R.N. *A calendar of the register of Richard Scrope, archbishop of York, 1398–1405, part I.* York; Borthwick Institute; 1981. Pp x, 147.
2. Dahmus, J.W., 'Henry IV of England: an example of royal control of the Church in the fifteenth century,' *J. of Church and State* 23 (1981), 35–46.
3. Brockwell, C.W., 'The historical career of Bishop Reginald Pecock, D.D.: the Poore Scoleris Myrrour or a case study in famous obscurity,' *Harvard Theological R.* 74 (1981), 177–207.
4. Martin, A., 'The Middle English versions of *The Ten Commandments*, with special reference to Rylands English MS 85,' *B. of the John Rylands University Library of Manchester* 64 (1981), 191–217.
5. Gradon, P., 'Langland and the ideology of dissent,' *P. of the British Academy* 66 (1982 for 1980), 179–205.
6. Töpfer, B., 'John Wyclif – mittelalterlicher Ketzer oder Vertreter einer frühreformatorischen Ideologie?,' *Jahrbuch für Geschichte des Feudalismus* 5 (1981), 89–124.

7. Clark, J.P.H., 'Predestination in Christ according to Julian of Norwich,' *Downside R.* 100 (1982), 79–91.
8. Howell, M., 'Abbatial vacancies and the divided *mensa* in medieval England,' *J. of Ecclesiastical History* 33 (1982), 173–92.
9. Blake, D., 'The development of the chapter of the diocese of Exeter, 1050–1161,' *J. of Medieval History* 8 (1982), 1–11.
10. Seaby, P., 'King Stephen and the interdict of 1148,' *British Numismatic J.* 50 (1981 for 1980), 50–60.
11. Davies, R.G., 'The episcopal appointments in England and Wales of 1375,' *Mediaeval Studies* 44 (1982), 306–32.
12. Smith, D.M., 'Suffragan bishops in the medieval diocese of Lincoln,' *Lincolnshire History and Archaeology* 17 (1982), 17–27.
13. Archer, M. (ed.). *The register of Bishop Philip Repingdon 1405–1419; vol. 3: Memoranda 1414–1419.* Lincoln Record Soc. (vol. 74); 1982. Pp 327.
14. Clark, J.P.H., 'Nature, grace and the trinity in Julian of Norwich,' *Downside R.* 100 (1982), 203–20.
15. Clark, J.P.H., 'Walter Hilton and the psalm commentary *qui habitat*,' *Downside R.* 341 (1982), 235–62.
16. Barker, P.S.D., 'The motherhood of God in Julian of Norwich's theology,' ibid. 290–304.
17. Hodgson, P. (ed.). *The Cloud of Unknowing and related treatises on contemplative prayer.* Analecta Carthusiana 3; 1982. Pp lxii, 234.
18. Hogg, J., 'Unpublished texts in the Carthusian Northern Middle English religious miscellany, B.L. Add. MS 37049,' *Essays in Honour of Erwin Stürzl* (Salzburg University; 1980), 241–84.
19. Hendrix, G., 'Is Mechtild of Hackeborn's Booke of Gostlye Grace translated from Middle Dutch?,' *Recherches de théologie ancienne et médiévale* 49 (1982), 242–4.
20. Ellis, R., ' "Flores ad fabricandum . . . coronam": an investigation into the use of the Revelations of St. Bridget in 15th-century England,' *Medium Aevum* 51 (1982), 163–86.
21. Baker, D.C.; Murphy, J.L.; Hall, L.B. (ed.). *The late medieval religious plays of Bodleian MSS Digby 133 and e Museo 160.* Oxford UP for EETS; 1982. Pp cix, 284.
22. Millett, B. (ed.). *Hali Meidhad.* The same; 1982. Pp lviii, 85.
23. Evans, G.R., ' "Omnibus hiis litteratior": Gilbert Crispin, noted theologian,' *Studi Medievali* 3rd ser. 22 (1981), 695–716.
24. McEvoy, J., 'Notes on the prologue of St Aelred of Rievaulx's *De spirituali amicitia*, with a translation,' *Traditio* 37 (1981), 396–411.
25. Macek, E.A., 'Fifteenth-century lay piety,' *Fifteenth-Century Studies* 1 (1978), 157–83.
26. Belfield, G., 'Cardinal Beaufort's almshouse of Noble Poverty at

St Cross, Winchester,' *P. of the Hampshire Field Club and Arch. Soc.* 38 (1982), 103–11.

27. Baldwin, A., 'A reference in *Piers Plowman* to the Westminster sanctuary,' *Notes & Queries* 227 (1982), 106–8.
28. Hirsh, J.C., 'Church and monarch in the *Carmen de Hastingae proelio*,' *J. of Medieval History* 8 (1982), 353–7.
29. Haigh, C.A.; Loades, D.M., 'The fortunes of the shrine of St. Mary of Caversham,' *Oxoniensia* 46 (1981), 62–72.
30. Burrows, T., 'Monastic benefactors in medieval Yorkshire,' *J. of Religious History* 12 (1982), 3–8.
31. Hosker, P., 'The Stanleys of Lathom and ecclesiastical patronage in the north-west of England during the fifteenth century,' *Northern History* 18 (1982), 212–29.
32. Nelson, J.L., 'The rites of the Conqueror,' Bc16, 117–32.
33. Gransden, A., 'Baldwin, abbot of Bury St Edmunds, 1065–1097,' Bc16, 65–76.
34. Blake, D.W., 'An original bull of pope Eugenius III,' *Devon and Cornwall Notes and Queries* 34 (1981), 307–11.
35. Blake, D.W., 'Osbern bishop of Exeter, 1072–1103,' *T. of the Devonshire Association* 114 (1982), 63–9.
36. Blake, D.W., 'The bishops of Exeter 1138–1160,' ibid. 71–8.
37. Orme, N., 'The medieval chantries of Exeter cathedral, parts I–III,' *Devon and Cornwall Notes and Queries* 34 (1981), 319–26; 35 (1982), 12–21, 67–71.
38. Frankforter, A.D., 'The origin of episcopal registration procedures in medieval England,' *Manuscripta* 26 (1982), 67–89.
39. Raban, S. *Mortmain legislation and the English church, 1350–1500.* Cambridge UP; 1982. Pp xiii, 216.
40. Davies, R.G., 'The Anglo-Papal Concordat of Bruges, 1375: a reconsideration,' *Archivum Historiae Pontificiae* 19 (1981), 97–146.
41. Wilson, P.A., 'The parentage of bishop Strickland [of Carlisle, 1400–19],' *T. of the Cumberland and Westmorland Antiquarian and Arch. Soc.* 82 (1982), 91–6.
42. Horn, J.M. (ed.). *The Register of Robert Hallum bishop of Salisbury 1407–17.* Canterbury & York Soc. 72; 1982. Pp xviii, 344.
43. Harper-Bill, C.; Mortimer, R. (ed.). *Stoke by Clare Cartulary: B.L. Cotton Appx. XXI, part 1.* Woodbridge; Boydell; 1982. Pp x, 150.
44. Gervers, M. *The Hospitaller cartulary in the British Library (Cotton MS Nero E vi): a study of the ms. and its composition, with a critical edition of two fragments of earlier cartularies for Essex.* Toronto; Pontifical Institute; 1981. Pp 386.
45. Holdsworth, C.J. (ed.). *Rufford charters, vols. 3 and 4.* Nottingham; Thoroton Soc. vols. 32, 34; 1980, 1981. Pp 429–675.
46. Michelmore, D.J.H. (ed.). *The Fountains Abbey lease book.*

Yorkshire Arch. Soc. Record Series, 140 (1981 for 1979–80). Pp lxxxv, 369.

47. Foreville, R. *Thomas Becket dans la tradition historique et hagiographique* [collected papers]. London; Variorum; 1981. Pp 348.
48. Jancey, M. (ed.). *St Thomas Cantilupe bishop of Hereford: essays in his honour.* Friends of Hereford Cathedral; 1982. Pp 209.
49. Burson, M.C., 'Emden's *Registers* and the prosopography of medieval English universities,' *Medieval Prosopography* 3/2 (1982), 35–51.
50. Tudor, V., 'Reginald of Durham and St. Godvie of Finchale: learning and religion on a personal level,' Bc1, 37–48.
51. Hill, R.M.T., 'A soldier's devotions [Henry duke of Lancaster],' Bc1, 77–83.
52. Goodman, A., 'Henry VII and Christian renewal,' Bc1, 115–25.
53. Mason, E., '*Pro statu et incolumnitate regni mei*: royal monastic patronage, 1066–1154,' Bc10, 99–117.
54. Hudson, A., 'Lollardy: the English heresy?,' Bc10, 261–83.
55. Lapidge, M., 'The cult of St Indract at Glastonbury,' Bc13, 179–212.
56. Kemp, E., 'The medieval bishops of Chichester,' Bc17, 19–33.
57. Lawrence, C.H., 'St. Richard of Chichester,' Bc17, 35–55.
58. Fines, J., 'Bishop Reginald Pecock and the Lollards,' Bc17, 57–75.
59. Gervers, M. (ed.). *The Cartulary of the Knights of St. John of Jerusalem: Essex.* Oxford UP for British Academy; 1982. Pp lxxxiv, 735.

(f) *Economic Affairs*

1. Saul, A., 'The herring industry at Great Yarmouth c. 1280–c. 1400,' *Norfolk Archaeology* 38 (1981), 33–43.
2. Langdon, J., 'The economics of horses and oxen in medieval England,' *Agricultural History R.* 30 (1982), 31–40.
3. Archibald, M.M., 'The Queenhithe hoard of late-fifteenth century forgeries,' *British Numismatic J.* 50 (1981 for 1980), 61–6.
4. Allin, C.E. *The medieval leather industry in Leicester.* Leicestershire County Council; 1981. Pp 30.
5. Crossley, D.W. (ed.). *Medieval industry.* London; Council for British Archaeology; 1981. Pp vii, 156.
6. Rahtz, P.A., 'Medieval milling,' Ef5, 1–15.
7. Ryder, M.L., 'British medieval sheep and their wool types,' Ef5, 16–28.
8. Crossley, D.W., 'Medieval iron smelting,' Ef5, 29–41.
9. Tylecote, R.F., 'The medieval smith and his methods,' Ef5, 42–50.

10. Goodall, I.H., 'The medieval blacksmith and his products,' Ef5, 51–62.
11. Goodall, A.R., 'The medieval bronzesmith and his products,' Ef5, 63–71.
12. Blanchard, I.S.W., 'Lead mining and smelting in medieval England and Wales,' Ef5, 72–84.
13. Greeves, T.A.P., 'The archaeological potential of the Devon tin industry,' Ef5, 85–95.
14. Moorhouse, S.A., 'The medieval pottery industry and its markets,' Ef5, 96–125.
15. Drury, P.J., 'The production of brick and tile in medieval England,' Ef5, 126–42.
16. Hunter, J.R., 'The medieval glass industry,' Ef5, 143–50.
17. Meredith, R., 'Millstone making at Yarncliff in the reign of Edward IV,' *Derbyshire Arch. J.* 101 (1981), 102–6.
18. Lloyd, T.H. *Alien merchants in England in the high middle ages.* Brighton; Harvester; 1982. Pp 253.
19. Bridbury, A.R. *Medieval English clothmaking: an economic survey.* London; Heinemann; 1982. Pp xiii, 125.
20. Hanham, A., 'Profits on English wool exports, 1472–1544,' *B. of the Institute of Historical Research* 55 (1982), 139–47.
21. Britnell, R.H., 'Essex markets before 1350,' *T. of the Essex Arch. Soc.* 13 (1981), 15–21.
22. Drury, J.L., 'Early goat-keeping in Upper Weardale, co. Durham,' *T. of the Architectural and Arch. Soc. of Durham and Northumberland* new ser. 6 (1982), 23–5.
23. Lomas, R.A., 'A northern farm at the end of the middle ages: Elvethall Manor, Durham, 1443/4–1513/14,' *Northern History* 18 (1982), 26–53.
24. Shiel, N., 'Hammered coins from Exeter in Rougemont House [*temp.* Edward I–Charles I],' *P. of the Devon Arch. Soc.* 38 (1980), 125–7.
25. Stewart, I., 'The burial date of the Eccles hoard [?1230],' *Numismatic Chronicle* 140 (1980), 194–7.
26. Munro, J.H., 'Mint policies, ratios and outputs in the Low Countries and England, 1335–1420: some reflection on new date,' ibid. 141 (1981), 71–116.
27. Nightingale, P., 'Some London moneyers, and reflections on the organization of English mints in the 11th and 12th centuries,' ibid. 142 (1982), 34–50.
28. Prestwich, M., 'The crown and the currency: the circulation of money in late 13th- and early 14th-century England,' ibid. 51–65.
29. Fox, H.S.A., 'Approaches to the adoption of the Midland system [of fields],' Bc3, 64–111.
30. Campbell, B., 'Commonfield origins – the regional dimension,' Bc3, 112–29.

(g) *Social Structure and Population*

1. Kealey, E.J. *Medieval medicus: a social history of Anglo-Norman medicine.* Baltimore/London; Johns Hopkins UP; 1981. Pp x, 211.
2. Finucane, R.C., 'Sacred corpse, profane carrion: Social ideals and death rituals in the later middle ages,' *Mirrors of Mortality: studies in the social history of death*, ed. J. Whaley (London; Europa Publications; 1981), 40–60.
3. Dodd, J.P., 'The growth of a middle class in Frodsham Manor 1300–62,' *J. of the Chester Arch. Soc.* 64 (1981), 32–40.
4. Campbell, B.M.S., 'The extent and layout of commonfields in Eastern Norfolk,' *Norfolk Archaeology* 38 (1981), 5–32.
5. Dyer, C., 'Deserted medieval villages in the West Midlands,' *Economic History R.* 2nd ser. 35 (1982), 19–34.
6. Kermode, J.I., 'Urban decline? The flight from office in late medieval York,' *Economic History R.* 2nd ser. 35 (1982), 179–98.
7. Saul, A., 'English towns in the late middle ages: the case of Great Yarmouth,' *J. of Medieval History* 8 (1982), 75–88.
8. *Medieval Coventry – a city divided?* Coventry Branch of Historical Association; 1981. Pp iii, 58.
9. Hurst, Lindsay C., 'Porphyria revisited,' *Medical History* 26 (1982), 179–82.
10. Gatrell, P., 'Historians and peasants: studies of medieval English society in a Russian context,' *Past and Present* 96 (1982), 22–50.
11. Gottfried, R.S. *Bury St Edmunds and the urban crisis: 1290–1539.* Princeton/Guildford; Princeton UP; 1982. Pp xvi, 313.
12. Barley, M.W., 'The medieval borough of Torksey: excavations 1963–8,' *Antiquaries J.* 61 (1981), 264–91.
13. Raftis, J.A. *A small town in late medieval England: Godmanchester 1278–1400.* Toronto; Pontifical Institute; 1982. Pp xiii, 479.
14. Hulton, R.H., 'The small town and urbanisation: Evesham in the middle ages,' *Midland History* 7 (1982), 1–8.
15. Hilton, R.H., 'Lords, burgesses and hucksters,' *Past and Present* 97 (1982), 3–15.
16. Hilton, R.H., 'Towns in societies – medieval England,' *Urban History Yearbook* (1982), 7–13.
17. Reynolds, S., 'Medieval urban history and the history of political thought,' ibid. 14–23.
18. Holt, J.C. *Robin Hood.* London; Thames & Hudson; 1982. Pp 208.
19. Holt, J.C., 'Feudal society and the family in early medieval England: I. The revolution of 1066,' *T. of the Royal Historical Soc.* 5th ser. 32 (1982), 193–212.

20. Walker, S.S., 'Free consent and the marriage of feudal wards in medieval England,' *J. of Medieval History* 8 (1982), 123–34.
21. De Aragon, R., 'The growth of secure inheritance in Anglo-Norman England,' ibid. 381–91.
22. Rowney, L., 'Arbitration in gentry disputes in the later middle ages,' *History* 67 (1982), 367–76.
23. Berrill, N.J., 'The Reynes monuments and their possible implications for local genealogy,' *Records of Buckinghamshire* 22 (1980), 105–24.
24. Blatchly, J., 'Two 14th-century Ufford family memorials recorded by Isaac Johnson,' *P. of the Suffolk Institute of Archaeology and History* 35 (1981), 67–8.
25. Lewis, C.P., 'Herbert the jerkin maker: a Domesday tenant identified,' *T. of the Historic Soc. of Lancashire and Cheshire* 131 (1981), 159–60.
26. Dodd, J.P., 'The population of Frodsham manor, 1349–50,' ibid. 21–33.
27. Groome, N., 'The Black Death in the hundred of Higham Ferrers,' *Northamptonshire Past and Present* 6 (1982–3), 309–11.
28. Postles, D., 'Barkby 1086–1524,' *T. of the Leicestershire Arch. and Historical Soc.* 56 (1980–1), 46–61.
29. Watts, V.E., 'Some Northumbrian fishery names, I,' *T. of the Architectural and Arch. Soc. of Durham and Northumberland* new ser. 6 (1982), 89–92.
30. Holt, J.C. *What's in a name? Family nomenclature and the Norman Conquest.* Reading; the University (Stenton lecture); 1982. Pp 23.
31. Dodgshon, R., 'The interpretation of subdivided fields: a study in private or commercial interests?,' Bc3, 130–44.
32. Lytle, G.F., 'Patronage and the election of Winchester scholars during the late middle ages and Renaissance,' Bc6, 167–88.
33. Rose, R.K., 'Cumbrian society and the Anglo-Norman church,' Bc10, 119–35.
34. Catto, J., 'The first century of Balliol men, 1260–1360,' Bc14, 1–16.
35. Niles, P., 'Baptism and the naming of children in late medieval England,' *Medieval Prosopography* 3/1 (1982), 95–107.
36. Oggins, R.S. & V.D., 'Hawkers and falconers: the prosopography of a branch of the royal household,' ibid. 63–94.

(h) *Naval and Military*

1. Rose, S. (ed.). *The navy of the Lancastrian kings: accounts and inventories of William Soper, keeper of the king's ships, 1421–1427.* London; Allen & Unwin (Navy Records Soc. 123); 1982. Pp 288.
2. Bennett, P.; Frere, S.S.; Stow, S.; Anstee, J. *Excavations at*

Canterbury Castle (The archaeology of Canterbury, vol. 1). Maidstone; Kent Arch. Soc.; 1982. Pp 236.

3. Higham, R.A.; Allan, J.P., 'Excavations at Okehampton castle, Devon; part II: the bailey, a preliminary,' *P. of the Devon Arch. Soc.* 38 (1980), 49–51.
4. Markuson, K.W., 'Excavations on the Green Lane access site, Barnstaple, 1979,' ibid. 67–90.
5. Wood, M., 'Barnstaple, North Gate, east abutment,' ibid. 123–4.
6. Drage, C., 'Nottingham Castle: the gatehouse of the outer bailey,' *T. of the Thoroton Soc.* 85 (1981), 48–55.
7. Gibb, J.H.P., 'The medieval castle at Dunster,' *Somerset Archaeology and National History* 125 (1981), 1–15.
8. Sharp, M. (ed.). *Accounts of the constables of Bristol castle in the 13th and early 14th centuries.* Bristol Record Soc. 34 (1982). Pp lxiii, 128.
9. Prestwich, M., 'English castles in the reign of Edward II,' *J. of Medieval History* 8 (1982), 159–78.
10. Thorne, P.F., 'Clubs and maces in the Bayeux tapestry,' *History Today* 32/10 (1982), 48–50.
11. Gillingham, J., 'The introduction of knight service into England,' Bc16, 53–64.

(i) *Intellectual and Cultural*

1. Lee, B.S., ' "This is no fable": historical residues in two medieval *exempla,*' *Speculum* 56 (1981), 728–60.
2. McCulloch, F., 'Saints Albans and Amphibalus in the works of Matthew Paris: Dublin, Trinity College MS 117,' ibid. 761–85.
3. Harris, M.A., 'Influences on the thought of Alan of Tewkesbury,' *J. of Ecclesiastical History* 33 (1982), 1–14.
4. Langston, D.C., 'Scotus and Ockham on the univocal concept of Being,' *Franciscan Studies* 39/17 (1982 for 1979), 105–29.
5. Adams, M.M., 'Was Ockham a Humean about efficient causality?,' ibid. 5–48.
6. Mantello, F.A.C., 'Letter CXXXI ascribed to Robert Grosseteste: a new edition of the text,' ibid. 165–79.
7. D'Angelo, B., 'Poesia francescana inglese prima di Geoffrey Chaucer (d. 1400),' *Archivum Franciscanum Historicum* 75 (1982), 320–61.
8. Scott, J. (ed.). *The early history of Glastonbury: an edition, translation and study of William of Malmesbury's 'De antiquitate Glastonie ecclesie'.* Woodbridge; Boydell & Brewer; 1981. Pp viii, 224.
9. Wickham, G. *Early English stages, 1300–1660, vol. 3: plays and their makers to 1576.* London; Routledge; 1981. Pp xxxvii, 357. 357.
10. Benskin, M., 'The letters ‹p› and ‹y› in later middle English and

some related matters,' *J. of the Soc. of Archivists* 7 (1982), 13–30.

11. Clough, C.H. (ed.). *Profession, vocation and culture in later medieval England: essays dedicated to the memory of A.R. Myers.* Liverpool UP; 1982. Pp xi, 262.
12. Kermode, J.I., 'The merchants of three northern English towns [York, Beverley, Hull],' Ei11, 7–50.
13. Davies, R.G., 'The episcopate,' Ei11, 51–89.
14. Storey, R.L., 'Gentleman-bureaucrats,' Ei11, 90–129.
15. Jewell, H.M., 'The cultural interests and achievements of the secular personnel of the local administration,' Ei11, 130–54.
16. Allmand, C.T., 'The civil lawyers,' Ei11, 155–80.
17. Ives, E.W., 'The common lawyers,' Ei11, 181–217.
18. Orme, N., 'Schoolmasters, 1307–1509,' Ei11, 218–41.
19. Lucas, P.J., 'The growth and development of English literary patronage in the later middle ages and the early Renaissance,' *The Library* 6th ser. 4 (1982), 219–48.
20. Rosenthal, J.T., 'Aristocratic cultural patronage and book bequests, 1350–1500,' *B. of the John Rylands University Library of Manchester* 64 (1982), 522–48.
21. Field, P.J.C., 'The last years of Sir Thomas Malory,' ibid. 433–56.
22. Goering, J., 'The *De dotibus* of Robert Grosseteste,' *Mediaeval Studies* 44 (1982), 83–109.
23. Lewry, P.O., 'Four graduation speeches from Oxford manuscripts (*c.* 1270–1310),' ibid. 138–80.
24. Tachan, K.H., 'The problem of the *species in medio* at Oxford in the generation after Ockham,' ibid. 394–443.
25. Murdoch, J.E., 'William of Ockham and the logic of infinity and continuity,' *Infinity and Continuity in Ancient and Medieval Thought*, ed. N. Kretzmann (Ithaca; Cornell UP; 1982), 165–206.
26. Stump, E., 'Theology and physics in *De sacramento altaris*: Ockham's theory of indivisibles,' ibid. 207–30.
27. Sylla, E.D., 'Infinite indivisibles and continuity in 14th-century theories of alteration,' ibid. 258–69.
28. Kretzmann, N., 'Continuity, contrariety, contradiction, and change,' ibid. 270–96.
29. Spade, P.V., 'Quasi-Aristotelianism [Richard Kilrington],' ibid. 297–307.
30. Smalley, B. *Studies in medieval thought and learning* [collected papers]. London; Hambledon Press; 1982. Pp 430.
31. Duclow, D.F., 'Anselm's *Proslogion* and Nicholas of Cusa's Wall of Paradise,' *Downside R.* 338 (1982), 22–30.
32. Lerer, S., 'John of Salisbury's Virgil,' *Virarium* 20 (1982), 24–39.
33. Flori, J., 'La chevalerie selon Jean de Salisbury: nature, fonction, idéologie,' *Revue d'histoire ecclésiastique* 77 (1982), 35–77.

34. McEvoy, J. *The philosophy of Robert Grosseteste.* Oxford; Clarendon; 1982. Pp 506.
35. McEvoy, J., 'Questions of authenticity and chronology concerning works attributable to Robert Grosseteste and edited 1940–80, I,' *B. de philosophie médièvale* 23 (1981), 64–90.
36. Hughes, B.B., '*De regulis generalibus*: a 13th-century English mathematical tract on problem-solving,' *Viator* 11 (1980), 209–24.
37. Harvey, M.M., 'Harley MS 3049 and two *questiones* of Walter Hunt, O. Carm.,' *T. of the Architectural and Arch. Soc. of Durham and Northumberland* new ser. 6 (1982), 45–7.
38. Getz, F.M., 'Gilbertus Anglicus anglicized [Wellcome MS 537],' *Medical History* 26 (1982), 436–42.
39. Cobban, A.B., 'Theology and law in the medieval colleges of Oxford and Cambridge,' *B. of the John Rylands University Library of Manchester* 65 (1982), 57–77.
40. Sammut, A. *Unfredo duca di Gloucester e gli umanisti italiani.* Padua; Antenore; 1980. Pp xxiv, 247.
41. Bérard, R.N., 'Grapes of the cask: a triptych of medieval English monastic historiography [Bede, Jocelin de Brakelond, Matthew Paris],' *Studia Monastica* 24 (1982), 75–104.
42. Bouet, P., 'La *Felicitas* de Guillaume le Conquérant dans les *Gesta Guillelmi* de Guillaume de Poitiers,' Bc16, 37–52.
43. Warren, W.L., 'Biography and the medieval historian,' *Medieval Historical Writing in the Christian and Islamic Worlds*, ed. D.O. Morgan (London; School of Oriental and African Studies; 1982), 5–18.
44. Gransden, A., 'Politics and historiography during the Wars of the Roses,' ibid. 125–48.
45. Gransden, A. *Historical writing in England, II: c. 1307 to the early 16th century.* London; Routledge; 1982. Pp xxiv, 644.
46. Genet, J.-Ph., 'Essoi de bibliométrie médièvale: l'histoire dans les bibliothèques anglaises,' *Revue française d'histoire du livre* 16 (1977), 17–22.
47. Stow, G.B., 'Bodleian Library MS Bodley 316 and the dating of Thomas Walsingham's literary career,' *Manuscripta* 25 (1981), 67–76.
48. Ashbee, P., 'William Worcestre and the Isles of Scilly,' *Cornish Archaeology* 19 (1980), 109–11.
49. Owen, D.D.R., 'The epic and history: *Chanson de Roland* and the *Carmen de Hastingae proelio*,' *Medium Aevum* 51 (1982), 18–34.
50. Gardiner, E., 'A solution to the problem of the dating in the *Vision of Tundale*,' ibid. 85–91.
51. Crawford, T.D., 'On the linguistic competence of Geoffrey of Monmouth,' ibid. 152–62.
52. Murdoch, B., 'Pascon Agan Arluth: the literary position of the

Cornish poem of the Passion,' *Studi Medievali* 3rd ser. 22 (1981), 821–36.

53. Haske, A., 'The manuscript of the Cornish Passion poem,' *Cornish Studies* 9 (1981), 23–8.
54. Pickering, O.S.; Görlach, M., 'A newly discovered manuscript of *South English Legendary*,' *Anglia* 100 (1982), 109–23.
55. Doyle, A.I., 'Two medieval service-books from the parish of Lanchester,' *T. of the Architectural and Arch. Soc. of Durham and Northumberland* new ser. 6 (1982), 19–22.
56. Nicholls, J., 'A courtesy poem from Magdalene College, Cambridge, Pepys MS 1236,' *Notes and Queries* 227 (1982), 3–10.
57. Powell, S., 'Connections between the *Fasciculus Morum* and Bodleian MS Barlow 24,' ibid. 10–14.
58. Jacobs, N., 'Sir Degarré, Lay le Freine, Beves of Hamtoun, and the "Auchinleck Bookshop" [in London, c. 1330–40],' ibid. 294–301.
59. O'Carroll, M., 'Notes on some vernacular phrases found in [Bodleian] MS Laud Misc. 511 [sermons],' ibid. 301–3.
60. Fox, D., 'Stephen Scrope, Jacques Legrand and the word "mankyndely",' ibid. 400.
61. Powell, S., 'A new dating of John Mirk's *Festial*,' ibid. 487–9.
62. Schmidt, A.V.C., 'Langland's "Book of Conscience" and Alanus de Insulis,' ibid. 482–4.
63. Orme, N., 'Langland and education,' *History of Education* 11 (1982), 251–66.
64. Jewell, H.M., ' "The bringing up of children in good learning and manners": a survey of secular educational provision in the north of England, *c.* 1350–1550,' *Northern History* 18 (1982), 1–25.
65. Curley, M.J., 'A new edition of John of Cornwall's *Prophetia Merlini*,' *Speculum* 57 (1982), 217–49.
66. Turville, Petre, T., 'The lament for Sir John Berkeley [d. 1375],' ibid. 332–9.
67. Greenberg, C., 'John Shirley and the English book trade,' *Library* 6th ser. 4 (1982), 369–80.
68. Bornstein, D., 'Sir Anthony Woodville as the translator of Christian de Pisan's *Livre du corps de policie*,' *Fifteenth-Century Studies* 2 (1979), 9–20.
69. Krieg, M.F., 'Latinate color terminology in Middle English medical and herbal treatises,' ibid. 135–42.
70. Baird, L.T., 'The physician's "urynals and jurdones": urine and uroscopy in medieval medicine and literature,' ibid. 1–8.
71. Miller, E., 'Christ, Ypocras, and a felt hat: pragmatic approaches to 15th-century medicine,' ibid. 151–7.
72. Reeves, A.C., 'The world of Thomas Hoccleve,' ibid. 187–202.
73. Scattergood, V.J., '*Sir Gawain and the Green Knight* and the sins of the flesh,' *Traditio* 37 (1981), 347–71.

74. Vantuono, W., 'John de Mascy of Sale and the *Pearl* poems,' *Manuscripta* 25 (1981), 77–88.
75. Hanna, R., 'Leeds University Library MS Brotherton 501: a redescription [*The Price of Conscience* etc],' ibid. 26 (1982), 38–42.
76. Fletcher, A.J., 'Marginal glosses in the N-Town manuscript, B.L. MS Cotton Vespasian D. viii,' ibid. 25 (1981), 113–17.
77. Jaech, S.L.J., 'English political prophecy and the dating of MS Rawlinson C. 813,' ibid. 141–50.
78. Corbett, M., 'An East Midland revision of the *Northern Homily Cycle* [Bute MS],' ibid. 26 (1982), 100–7.
79. Heffernan, T.J., 'The rediscovery of the Bute Manuscript of the *Northern Homily Cycle*,' *Scriptorium* 36 (1982), 118–29.
80. Hanna, R., 'The archaeology of a manuscript: Huntington Library HM 266 [Walter Hilton, *Scala Perfectionis*],' ibid. 99–102.
81. Goffart, W., 'The subdivisions of Trevet's *Chronicles* in Bodleian Library MS Fairfax 10,' ibid. 96–8.
82. Wynn, P., 'The conversion story of Nicholas Trevet's "Tale of Constance",' *Viator* 13 (1982), 259–74.
83. Scott, K.L., 'Lydgate's Lives of Saints Edmund and Fremund: a newly located manuscript in Arundel Castle,' ibid. 335–66.
84. Malvern, M.M., 'An earnest "monyscyon" and "thinge delectabyll" realized verbally and visually in *A Disputacion betwyx the body and wormes*, a Middle English poem inspired by tomb art and northern spirituality,' ibid. 415–43.
85. Klene, J., 'Chaucer's contribution to a popular topos: the world upside-down,' ibid. 11 (1980), 321–34.
86. Wurtele, D., 'The penitence of Geoffrey Chaucer,' ibid. 335–59.
87. Coleman, W.E., 'Chaucer, the *Teseida* and the Visconti library at Pavia: a hypothesis,' *Medium Aevum* 51 (1982), 91–101.
88. Goodall, P., 'Chaucer's "burgesses" and the aldermen of London,' ibid. 284–92.
89. Minnis, A.J., 'John Gower, *sapiens* in ethics and politics,' ibid. 49 (1980), 207–29.
90. Olsson, K., 'Natural law and John Gower's *Confessio Amantis*,' *Medievalia et Humanistica* new ser. 11 (1982), 229–61.
91. Clogan, P.M., 'Literary genres in a medieval textbook,' ibid. 199–209.
92. Sheingorn, P., 'The moment of resurrection in the Corpus Christi plays,' ibid. 111–29.
93. Morgan, W., ' "Who was then the gentleman?": social, historical, and linguistic codes in the *Mystère d'Adam*,' *Studies in Philology* 79 (1982), 101–21.
94. Revard, C., '*Gilote et Johane*: an interlude in B.L. MS Harley 2253,' ibid. 122–46.
95. Hellinga, L. *Caxton in focus: the beginning of printing in England.* London; British Library; 1982. Pp 109.

96. Partner, P., 'William of Wykeham and the historians,' Bc6, 1–36.
97. Lytle, G.F., ' "Wykehamist culture" in pre-Reformation England,' Bc6, 129–66.
98. Ransford, R., 'A kind of Noah's ark: Ailred of Rievaulx and national identity,' Bc10, 137–46.
99. McHardy, A.K., 'Liturgy and propaganda in the diocese of Lincoln during the Hundred Years' War,' Bc10, 215–27.
100. Dawtry, A., 'The *modus medendi* and the Benedictine Order in Anglo-Norman England,' Bc21, 25–38.
101. Mason, E., ' "Rocamadour in Quercy above all other churches": the healing of Henry II,' Bc21, 39–54.
102. Rosenthal, J.T., 'Bede's *Life of Cuthbert*: preparatory to *The Ecclesiastical History*,' *Catholic Historical R.* 68 (1982), 599–611.

(j) *Visual Arts*

1. Cherry, J., 'A 12th-century mortar from Ryston Hall, Norfolk,' *Norfolk Archaeology* 38 (1981), 67–73.
2. Mellor, J.E.; Pearce, T. (ed.). *The Austin Friars, Leicester.* Leicestershire County Council; 1981. Pp viii, 175.
3. Jones, R.H. *Medieval houses at Flaxengate, Lincoln* (The Archaeology of Lincoln, vol. IX/1). London; Council for British Archaeology; 1980. Pp 56.
4. Schwartzbaum, E., 'Three Tournai tombstones in England,' *Gesta* 20/1 (1981), 89–97.
5. Parker, E.C., 'Master Hugo as sculptor: a source for the style of the Bury Bible,' ibid. 99–109.
6. Haney, K.E., 'The immaculate imagery in the Winchester Psalter,' ibid. 111–18.
7. Caviness, M.H. *The windows of Christ Church cathedral, Canterbury* (Corpus Vitrearum Medii Aevi, Great Britain II). Oxford UP for British Academy; 1981. Pp 372.
8. Coe, B. *Stained glass in England: 1150–1550.* London; Allen; 1981. Pp 143.
9. Gage, J., 'Gothic glass: two aspects of a dionysian aesthetic,' *Art History* 5 (1982), 36–58.
10. Heslop, T.A., 'A walrus ivory pyx and the *Visitatio Sepulchris*,' *J. of the Warburg and Courtauld Institutes* 44 (1981), 157–60.
11. Wilmott, T., 'The arms of Fitzwalter on leather scabbards from London,' *T. of the London and Middlesex Arch. Soc.* 32 (1981), 132–9.
12. Rhodes, M., 'A pair of 15th-century spectacle frames from the city of London,' *Antiquaries J.* 62 (1982), 57–73.
13. Lewis, J.M., 'A medieval ring-brooch from Oxwich castle, West Glamorgan,' ibid. 126–9. [Made in London].

14. Fawcett, R., 'St Mary at Wireton in Norfolk and a group of churches attributed to its mason,' ibid. 35–56.
15. Drage, C., 'Two medieval cross-slabs from Edwalton church, Notts.,' *T. of the Thoroton Soc.* 85 (1981), 113–14.
16. Drage, C.; Garton, D., 'A 14th-century effigy from Headon church, Notts.,' ibid. 115–16.
17. Behrens, G.A., 'Conservation work on the Cartmel Fell figure of Christ [c. 1500],' *T. of the Cumberland and Westmorland Antiquarian and Arch. Soc.* 82 (1982), 125–34.
18. Sherman, H., 'Diverging tendencies in Gothic art: two sculptures of Abraham and Isaac at Norwich cathedral,' *Fifteenth-Century Studies* 1 (1978), 275–86.
19. Norton, E.C., 'The medieval floor-tiles of Christchurch priory,' *P. of the Dorset Natural History and Arch. Soc.* 102 (1982 for 1980), 49–64.
20. Mayes, P.; Hayfield, C., 'A late medieval pottery kiln at Holme-upon-Spalding moor, North Humberside,' *East Riding Archaeologist* 6 (1980), 99–113.
21. Hadfield, J.I., 'The excavation of a medieval kiln at Barnett's Mead, Ringmer, East Sussex,' *Sussex Arch. Collections* 119 (1981), 89–106.
22. Orton, C., 'The excavation of a late medieval/transitional kiln at Cheam, Surrey,' *Surrey Arch. Collections* 73 (1982), 49–92.
23. Cole, G.H.; Limby, J.R., 'Excavations at Park Row, Farnham, Surrey: a medieval pottery kiln,' ibid. 101–14.
24. Stratton, H.J.M.; Pardoe, B.F.J., 'The history of Chertsey Bridge,' ibid. 115–26.
25. Brown, S.W., 'The medieval Larkbeare Bridge, Exeter,' *P. of the Devon Arch. Soc.* 39 (1981), 155–8.
26. Allan, J.P.; Jupp, B., 'Recent observations in the south tower of Exeter cathedral,' ibid. 141–54.
27. Allan, J.P.; Silvester, R.J., 'Newenham Abbery, Axminster,' ibid. 159–71.
28. Crook, J., 'The Pilgrims' Hall, Winchester,' *P. of the Hampshire Field Club and Arch. Soc.* 38 (1982), 85–101.
29. Baker, N.J., 'The west range of Ulverscroft priory and its roof: a survey,' *T. of the Leicestershire Arch. and Historical Soc.* 56 (1980–1), 10–17.
30. Thurlby, M., 'A note of the 12th-century sculpture from Old Sarum cathedral,' *Wiltshire Arch. and Natural History Magazine* 76 (1981), 93–8.
31. Reeves, J.A.; Bonney, H.M., 'No. 15 Minster Street, Salisbury: a 14th-century timber-framed house,' ibid. 99–104.
32. Birch, J.; Ryder, P.F., 'New Hall, Darfield,' *Yorkshire Arch. J.* 54 (1982), 81–98.
33. Godfrey, W.E., 'Crosby Hall and its re-erection,' *T. of the Ancient Monuments Soc.* new ser. 26 (1982), 227–43.

34. Harvey, J.H., 'The church towers of Somerset,' ibid. 157–83.
35. Williams, E.H.D.; Gilson, R.G., 'Base crucks in Somerset (III) and allied roof forms,' *Somerset Archaeology and History* 125 (1981), 45–66.
36. Bridge, M.; Dunning, R.W., 'The abbey barn, Glastonbury,' ibid. 120.
37. Harding, J.M., 'Medieval vernacular roof-trusses in Surrey,' *Vernacular Architecture* 11 (1980), 39–42.
38. Sharp, H.B., 'Some mid 15th-century small-scale building repairs [on the manors of Ralph, lord Cromwell],' ibid. 20–9.
39. Woodfield, C.T.P., 'The larger medieval houses of Northamptonshire,' *Northamptonshire Archaeology* 16 (1981), 153–96.
40. Edwards, J., 'The morality of the three living and the three dead medieval wall paintings at St Mary's church, Raunds,' ibid. 148–52.
41. Edwards, J., 'A medieval wall-painting at Hailes,' *T. of the Bristol and Gloucestershire Arch. Soc.* 99 (1981), 167–9.
42. Wissolik, R.D., 'Duke William's messengers: an "insoluble reverse-order" scene of the Bayeux Tapestry,' *Medium Aevum* 51 (1982), 101–7.
43. Haney, K.E., 'A Norman antecedent for English floral ornament of the mid-twelfth century,' *Scriptorium* 36 (1982), 84–6.
44. Morgan, N.J. *Early Gothic manuscripts: I, 1190–1250.* London; Harvey Miller; 1982. Pp 276.
45. Michael, M.A., 'Some early 14th-century English drawings at Christ's College, Cambridge,' *Burlington Magazine* 124 (1982), 230–2.
46. Seymour, M., 'Manuscript portraits of Chaucer and Hoccleve,' ibid. 618–23.
47. Scott, K.L. *The Mirroure of the Worlde, MS Bodley 283 (England, c. 1470–80): the physical composition, decoration and illustration.* Oxford, Roxburgh Club; 1980. Pp xiii, 68.
48. Hogg, J. (ed.). *An illuminated Yorkshire Carthusian religious miscellany, B.L. Add. MS 37049, vol. 3: the illustrations.* Analecta Carthusiana 95; 1981. Pp 142.
49. Saith, W., 'The 15th-century manuscript *Horae* in the parochial library of Steeple Ashton [Wilts],' *Manuscripta* 25 (1981), 151–63.
50. Sutton, A.F., 'Christian Colborne, painter of Germany and London, died 1486,' *J. of the British Arch. Association* 135 (1982), 55–61.
51. Heywood, S., 'The ruined church at North Elmham,' ibid. 1–10.
52. Jansen, V., 'Dying mouldings, unarticulated springer blocks, and hollow chamfers in 13th-century architecture,' ibid. 35–54.
53. Andrew, M., 'Chichester cathedral: the problem of the Romanesque choir vault,' ibid. 11–22.
54. Johnson, G.A.L.; Dunham, K., 'The stones of Durham cathedral:

a preliminary note,' *T. of the Architectural and Arch. Soc. of Durham and Northumberland* new ser. 6 (1982), 53–6.

55. Gardner, S., 'The nave galleries of Durham cathedral,' *Art B.* 64 (1982), 564–79.
56. McAleer, J.P., 'The Romanesque transept and choir elevations of Tewkesbury and Pershore,' ibid. 549–63.
57. Dudley, C.J., 'Canterbury Cathedral: the small portrait carvings of the pulpitum, *c.* 1400,' *Archaeologia Aeliana* 97 (1982 for 1981), 185–94.
58. *Medieval art and architecture at Canterbury before 1220.* Leeds; British Arch. Association; 1982. Pp 128.
59. Gem, R.D., 'The significance of the 11th-century rebuilding of Christ Church and St Augustine's, Canterbury, in the development of Romanesque architecture,' Ej58, 1–19.
60. Strik, H.J.A., 'Remains of the Lanfranc building in the great central tower and the north-west choir/transept area,' Ej58, 20–6.
61. Fernie, E., 'St Anselms's crypt,' Ej58, 27–38.
62. Parsons, D., 'The Romanesque vices at Canterbury,' Ej58, 39–45.
63. Caviness, M., 'Canterbury cathedral clerestory: the glazing programme in relation to the campaigns of construction,' Ej58, 46–55.
64. Mair, R., 'The choir capitals of Canterbury cathedral,' Ej58, 56–66.
65. Eames, E., 'Notes on the decorated stone roundels in the Corona and Trinity chapel in Canterbury cathedral,' Ej58, 67–70.
66. Stratford, N.; Tudor-Craig, P.; Muthesius, A.M., 'Archbishop Hubert Walter's tomb and its furnishings,' Ej58, 71–93.
67. Heslop, T.A., 'The conventual seals of Canterbury cathedral, 1066–1232,' Ej58, 94–100.
68. Lawrence, A., 'Manuscripts of early Anglo-Norman Canterbury,' Ej58, 101–11.
69. Tatton-Brown, T., 'The great hall of the archbishop's palace,' Ej58, 112–19.
70. Woods, H., 'The completion of the abbey church of SS Peter, Paul and Augustine, Canterbury, by abbots Wido and Hugh of Fleury,' Ej58, 120–4.
71. Renn, D., 'The decoration of Canterbury castle keep,' Ej58, 125–8.
72. Miscampbell, C., 'A twelfth-century re-building of St Augustine's abbey, Canterbury,' Bc26, 63–5.
73. Geddes, J., 'Some tomb railings at Canterbury cathedral,' Bc26, 66–73.
74. Thorn, J.C., 'The burial of John Dygon, abbot of St Augustine's, Canterbury [1496–1510],' Bc26, 74–84.
75. West, J., 'Acton Burnell castle, Shropshire: a re-interpretation,' Bc26, 85–92.

76. Renn, D., 'Tonbridge and some other gatehouses,' Bc26, 93–103.
77. Morley, B., 'Aspects of fourteenth-century castle design,' Bc26, 104–13.
78. Taylor, A., 'Stephen de Pencestre's account as constable of Dover castle for the years Michaelmas 1272–Michaelmas 1274,' Bc26, 114–22.
79. Gilyard-Beer, R., 'Boxley abbey and the pulpitum collationis,' Bc26, 123–31.
80. Slade, H.G., 'Meopham: the parish church of St John the Baptist,' Bc26, 132–46.
81. Thompson, M., 'The significance of the buildings of Ralph, lord Cromwell (1394–1456),' Bc26, 155–62.
82. Tester, P., 'The court lodge at Horton Kirby,' Bc26, 163–72.
83. Tatton-Brown, T.; Bennett, P.; Sparks, M., 'The poor priests' hospital at Canterbury,' Bc26, 173–86.
84. Gravett, K., 'The rectory house at Cliffe-at-Hoo,' Bc26, 187–91.
85. Beresford, G., 'The timber-laced wall in England,' Bc26, 213–18.
86. Grove, A., 'Newark, Maidstone,' Bc26, 219–24.
87. Parkin, J., 'A unique aisled cottage at Petham,' Bc26, 225–30.
88. Gee, E., 'Stone from the medieval limestone quarries of south Yorkshire,' Bc26, 247–55.
89. Blair, J., 'English monumental brasses before the Black Death,' Bc26, 256–72.
90. Harvey, J.H., 'The buildings of Winchester College,' Bc6, 77–127.
91. Betley, J.H.; Taylor, C.W.G. *Sacred and satiric: medieval stone carving in the west country*. Bristol; Redcliffe; 1982. Pp 64.
92. Gransden, A., 'The history of Wells cathedral, c. 1090–1547,' Bc23, 24–51.
93. Harvey, J.H., 'The building of Wells cathedral: I, 1175–1307; II, 1307–1508,' Bc23, 52–101.
94. Tudor-Craig, P., 'Wells sculpture,' Bc23, 102–31.
95. Marks, R., 'The medieval stained glass at Wells cathedral,' Bc23, 132–47.
96. Rodwell, W., 'The building of Vicars' Close [at Wells],' Bc23, 213–27.
97. Rynne, E., 'An unnoticed constructional detail in insular church and castle building,' Bc27, 333–50.

(k) *Topography*

1. Youngs, S.M.; Clark, J., 'Medieval Britain in 1980, II: post-Conquest,' *Medieval Archaeology* 25 (1981), 187–228.
2. Alldridge, N.J., 'Aspects of the topography of early medieval Chester,' *J. of the Chester Arch. Soc.* 64 (1981), 5–31.
3. Cowell, R., 'Kirk Langley, Mackworth and Horsley: aspects of medieval settlement,' *Derbyshire Arch J.* 101 (1981), 93–101.

4. Tweedy, J.M. *Popish Elvet, part 1: The history of St Cuthbert's, Durham.* Durham; the author; 1981. Pp ii, 167.
5. May, P.; Moore, I.E. *Newmarket: medieval and Tudor.* Newmarket; the author; 1982. Pp x, 74.
6. Blair, J., 'The early history of Horne: an addendum,' *Surrey Arch. Collections* 73 (1982), 179–80.
7. MacKay, W., 'The development of medieval Ripon,' *Yorkshire Arch. J.* 54 (1982), 73–80.
8. Harvey, M., 'Irregular villages in Holderness, Yorkshire: some thoughts on their origins,' ibid. 63–71.
9. Hummler, M.R., 'An excavation in medieval Lichfield new town,' *T. of the South Staffordshire Arch. and Historical Soc.* 22 (1980–1), 85–92.
10. Bassett, S.R., 'Medieval Lichfield: a topographical review,' ibid. 93–121.
11. Mastoris, S.N., 'The boundary between the English and French boroughs of medieval Nottingham: a documentary survey,' *T. of the Thoroton Soc.* 85 (1981), 68–74.
12. Weir, C., 'The site of the Cromwell's medieval manor house at Lambley, Notts.,' ibid. 75–7.
13. Crook, D., 'Lindhurst, No Man's Wood, and the manor of Mansfield,' ibid. 78–89.
14. Cameron, A.; O'Brien, C., 'The deserted mediaeval village of Thorpe-in-the-Glebe, Notts.,' ibid. 56–67.
15. Halpin, C., 'The deserted medieval village of Thorpe, Earls Barton,' *Northamptonshire Archaeology* 16 (1981), 197.
16. Tebbutt, C.F., 'A deserted medieval farm settlement at Faulkner's Farm, Hartfield,' *Sussex Arch. Collections* 119 (1981), 107–16.
17. Hadfield, J., 'An excavation at 1–3 Tower Street, Rye, East Sussex,' ibid. 222–5.
18. Britnell, R.H., 'Abingdon: a lost Buckinghamshire hamlet,' *Records of Buckinghamshire* 22 (1980), 48–52.
19. Baines, A.H.J., 'Hasley: a Domesday manor restored,' ibid. 53–72.
20. Whitfield, M., 'The medieval fields of south-east Somerset,' *Somerset Archaeology and Natural History* 125 (1981), 17–29.
21. Reid, R.D.; Scrase, A.J., 'The great house and two lanes in Wells,' ibid. 31–43.
22. Dunning, R.W., 'The origins of Nether Stowey,' ibid. 124–6.
23. Silvester, R.J., 'An excavation at Dunkeswell,' *P. of the Devon Arch. Soc.* 38 (1980), 53–66.
24. Weddell, P.J., 'Excavations at 3–5 Lower Fore Street, Exmouth,' ibid. 91–115.
25. Draper, J., 'St. Rowald's chapel, South Street, Dorchester,' *P. of the Dorset Natural History and Arch. Soc.* 102 (1980), 112–14.
26. Jarvis, K., 'A medieval cemetery in Brownsea Island,' ibid. 134–6.

27. Harman, M.; Wilson, B., 'A medieval graveyard beside the Faringdon Road, Abingdon,' *Oxoniensia* 46 (1981), 56–61.
28. Perry, J.G., 'Interim report on the excavation at Sydenham's, Solihull, 1972–78: a moated site in the Warwickshire Arden,' *T. of the Birmingham and Warwickshire Arch. Soc.* 90 (1982 for 1980), 49–64.
29. Smith, L.D.W., 'A survey of building timber and other trees in the hedgerows of a Warwickshire estate, c. 1500,' ibid. 65–73.
30. Courtney, P., 'The monastic granges of Leicestershire,' *T. of the Leicestershire Arch. and Historical Soc.* 56 (1980–1), 33–45.
31. Tarver, A., 'Long Whatton medieval moated site: interim report,' ibid. 108–11.
32. Harding, M., 'Excavations at the moated site of Newbold Verdon,' ibid. 111–12.
33. Adams, A.W., 'A medieval building complex at Whitwell, Rutland,' ibid. 112–13.
34. Clack, P.A.G., 'The Browney valley,' *T. of the Architectural and Arch. Soc. of Durham and Newcastle* new ser. 6 (1982), 13–17.
35. Cantor, L. (ed.). *The English medieval landscape.* London; Croom Helm; 1982. Pp 225.
36. Rowley, T., 'Medieval field systems,' Ek35, 25–55.
37. Cantor, L., 'Forests, chases, parks and warrens,' Ek35, 56–85.
38. Williams, W., 'Marshland and waste,' Ek35, 86–125.
39. Cantor, L., 'Castles, fortified houses, moated homesteads and monastic settlements,' Ek35, 126–53.
40. Bigmore, P., 'Villages and towns,' Ek55, 154–92.
41. Hindle, B.P., 'Roads, and tracks,' Ek35, 193–217.
42. Keene, D., 'Town into gown: the site of the College and other lands in Winchester before the Reformation,' Bc6, 37–75.

F. ENGLAND AND WALES 1500–1714

(a) *General*

1. Hutton, R., 'Clarendon's "History of the Rebellion",' *English Historical R.* 97 (1982), 70–88.
2. Pritchard, A., 'A defence of the private life by the second duke of Buckingham,' *Huntington Library Q.* 44 (1981), 157–71.
3. Fritz, P.S., 'From "public" to "private": the royal funerals in England, 1500–1830,' *Mirrors of Mortality: Studies in the Social History of Death*, ed. J. Whaley (London; Europa Publications; 1981), 61–79.
4. Puckrein, G., 'Did Sir William Courteen really own Barbados?,' *Huntington Library Q.* 44 (1981), 135–49.

5. Morrah, P. *A royal family: Charles I and his family.* London; Constable; 1982. Pp 292.
6. Jones, F., 'The Failies of Blaiddbwll,' *National Library of Wales J.* 22 (1981), 27–37.
7. Dray, W.H., 'Presentism, inevitability and the English civil war,' *Canadian J. of History* 17 (1982), 257–74.
8. Cheetham, J.K. *Mary queen of Scots, 'the captive years': the story of Mary queen of Scots with particular reference to the buildings and monuments connected with her captivity in England.* Sheffield; Northend; 1982. Pp ix, 66.
9. Fox, A. *Thomas More: history and providence.* Oxford, Blackwell; 1982. Pp xi, 271.
10. Smith, W. *A particular description of England in 1588.* Gloucester; Sutton; 1982. Pp 124.
11. Guth, D.J.; McKenna, J.W. (ed.). *Tudor rule and revolution; essays for G.R. Elton from his American friends.* Cambridge UP; 1982. Pp xiv, 418.
12. Bridbury, A.C., 'The Lisle letters [review article],' *Economic History R.* 2nd ser. 35 (1982), 573–80.
13. Harris, F., 'The authorship of the manuscript Blenheim journal,' *B. of the Institute of Historical Research* 55 (1982), 203–6.
14. Not used.
15. Walsh, K., 'England unter Tudors und Stuarts: neue Perspektive der Forschung [review article],' *Innsbrucker Historische Studien* 4 (1981), 169–204.
16. Pennington, D.H., 'The war and the people,' Fb45, 115–36.
17. Loades, D.M., 'The origins of English protestant nationalism,' Bc10, 297–307.
18. Fletcher, A.J., 'The first century of English protestantism and the growth of national identity,' Bc10, 309–17.
19. Aylmer, G.E., 'Seventeenth-century Wykehamists,' Bc6, 281–311.

(b) *Politics*

1. Hasler, P.W. (ed.). *The House of Commons 1558–1603* (3 vols.). London; HMSO (History of Parliament); 1981 (i.e. 1982). Pp xxi, 695; ix, 509; ix, 688.
2. Zwicker, S.; Hirst, D., 'Rhetoric and disguise: political language and political arguments in *Absalom and Achitophel*,' *J. of British Studies* 21 (1981), 39–55.
3. Katz, D.S. *Philo-semitism and the readmission of the Jews to England, 1603–1655.* Oxford; Clarendon; 1982. Pp 300.
4. Bartlett, K.R., 'The English exile community in Italy and the political opposition to Queen Mary I,' *Albion* 13 (1981), 223–41.
5. Harrison, S.M. *The Pilgrimage of Grace in the Lake counties,*

1536–7. London; Royal Historical Soc. (Studies in History 27); 1981.

6. Knowles, W.E. (ed.). *Lorenzo Magalotti at the court of Charles II: his Relazione d'Inghilterra of 1668.* Waterloo; Wilfrid Laurier UP; 1980. Pp ix, 161.
7. Cole, S. *Princess over the water: a memoir of Louise Marie Stuart (1692–1713).* London; Royal Stuart Soc.; 1981. Pp 20.
8. Greaves, R.L.; Zaller, R. (ed.). *Biographical dictionary of British radicals in the seventeenth century, 1: A–F.* Brighton; Harvester; 1982. Pp xxiv, 308.
9. Russell, C.S., 'Monarchies, wars and estates in England, France, and Spain, c. 1580–1640,' *Legislative Studies Q.* 7 (1982), 205–20.
10. Cope, E.S., 'Public images of parliament during its absence,' ibid. 221–34.
11. Woolrych, A. *Commonwealth to Protectorate.* Oxford; Clarendon; 1982. Pp xii, 446.
12. Cope, E.S. *The life of a public man: Edward, first baron Montagu of Boughton, 1562–1644.* Philadelphia; American Philosophical Soc.; 1981. Pp xv, 224.
13. Loomie, A.J., 'Alonso de Cárdenas and the Long Parliament, 1640–1648,' *English Historical R.* 97 (1982), 289–307.
14. Peck, L.L., 'Court patronage and government policy: the Jacobean dilemma,' Fk36, 27–46.
15. Fritze, R.H., 'The role of family and religion in the local politics of early Elizabethan England: the case of Hampshire in the 1560s,' *Historical J.* 25 (1982), 267–87.
16. McIntosh, A.W., 'The numbers of the English regicides,' *History* 67 (1982), 195–216.
17. Challinor, P.J., 'Restoration and exclusion in the county of Cheshire,' *B. of the John Rylands University Library of Manchester* 64 (1982), 360–85.
18. Not used.
19. Not used.
20. Briscoe, A.D. *A Marian lord mayor: Sir Thomas White.* Ipswich; East Anglian Magazine; 1982. Pp 112.
21. Coates, W.H.; Young, A.S.; Snow, V.F. (ed.). *The private journals of the Long Parliament, 3 January to 5 March 1642.* New Haven/London; Yale UP; 1982. Pp xxxix, 581.
22. Bingham, C. *Relations between Mary queen of Scots and her son King James VI of Scotland.* London; Royal Stuart Soc.; 1982. Pp 14.
23. Ridley, J. *The statesman and the fanatic: Thomas Wolsey and Thomas More.* London; Constable; 1982. Pp xiii, 338.
24. Levine, M., 'The place of women in Tudor government,' Fa11, 109–23.

25. MacCaffrey, W.T., 'Parliament: the Elizabethan experience,' Fa11, 127–47.
26. Cressy, D., 'Binding the nation: the Bonds of Association, 1584 and 1696,' Fa11, 217–34.
27. Heinze, R.W., 'Proclamations and parliamentary protest, 1539–1610,' Fa11, 237–59.
28. Carter, C.H., 'Diplomatic intervention in English law enforcement: Sarmiento and James I,' Fa11, 261–84.
29. Hexter, J.H., 'Quoting the Commons, 1604–1642,' Fa11, 369–91.
30. Peck, L.L. *Northampton: patronage and politics at the court of James I.* London; Allen & Unwin; 1982. Pp x, 277.
31. Bennett, G.V., 'English Jacobitism, 1710–1715: myth and reality,' *T. of the Royal Historical Soc.* 5th ser. 32 (1982), 137–51.
32. Miller, J., 'Charles II and his parliaments,' ibid. 1–23.
33. Adams, S., 'Faction, clientage & party: English politics, 1550–1603,' *History Today* 32/12 (1982), 33–9.
34. Sharpe, K., 'Court and commonwealth [review article],' *Historical J.* 25 (1982), 735–49.
35. Casada, J.A., 'Dorset politics in the puritan revolution,' *Southern History* 4 (1982), 107–22.
36. Beer, B.L. *Rebellion and riot: popular disorder in England during the reign of Edward VI.* Kent State UP; 1982. Pp x, 259.
37. Barnard, T.C. *The English republic 1649–1660.* Harlow; Longman; 1982. Pp vii, 111.
38. *Scandal on the Corporation: royalists and puritans in mid-17th century Kingston, from the Kingston Borough Archives.* Kingston-upon-Thames; Heritage Unit Recreation Department; 1982. Pp xviii, 51.
39. Palmer, W.G., 'Oliver St John and the middle group in the Long Parliament, 1643–1645: a reappraisal,' *Albion* 14 (1982), 20–6.
40. Jones, G.H., 'The Irish fright of 1688: real violence and imagined massacre,' *B. of the Institute of Historical Research* 55 (1982), 148–53.
41. Perceval-Maxwell, M., 'Protestant faction in the impeachment of Strafford and the origins of the Irish civil war,' *Canadian J. of History* 17 (1982), 235–55.
42. McInnes, A., 'When was the English revolution?,' *History* 67 (1982), 377–92.
43. Hughes, A.L., 'Warwickshire on the eve of the civil war: a county community?,' *Midland History* 7 (1982), 42–72.
44. Weingierl, M.P., 'Parliament and the army in England 1659: constitutional thought and the struggle for control,' *Parliaments, Estates & Representation* 2 (1982), 47–55.
45. Morrill, J.S. (ed.). *Reactions to the English civil war 1642–1649.* London; Macmillan; 1982. Pp 257.

46. Morrill, J.S., 'Introduction,' Fb45, 1–28.
47. Fletcher, A.J., 'The coming of war,' Fb45, 29–50.
48. Howell, R., 'Neutralism, conservatism and political alignment in the English revolution: the case of the towns 1642–9,' Fb45, 67–88.
49. Kishlansky, M.A., 'Ideology and politics in the parliamentary armies 1645–9,' Fb45, 163–84.
50. Ashton, R., 'From cavalier to roundhead tyranny, 1642–9,' Fb45, 185–208.
51. Morrill, J.S., 'King Oliver?,' *Cromwelliana* (1981).
52. Kishlansky, M.A., 'What happened at Ware?,' *Historical J.* 25 (1982), 827–39.
53. Lake, P.G., 'Constitutional consensus and puritan opposition in the 1620s: Thomas Scott and the Spanish match,' ibid. 805–25.
54. Wende, P., 'Das Parlament und die Anfänge der englischen Revolution,' Bc19, 13–26.
55. Patterson, W.B., 'King James I and the protestant cause in the crisis of 1618–22,' Bc10, 319–34.
56. Hopkins, P., 'Sham plots and real plots in the 1690s,' Bc22, 89–110.

(c) *Constitution, Administration and Law*

1. Martin, J., 'Enclosure and the Inquisitions of 1607: an examination of Dr Kerridge's article "The returns of the Inquisitions of Depopulation",' *Agricultural History R.* 30 (1982), 41–8.
2. McIntosh, A.W. *The death warrant of King Charles I.* London; House of Lords Record Office (Mem. no. 66); 1981. Pp 20.
3. Rogers, A. (ed.). *Coming into line: local government in Clayworth 1674–1714.* University of Nottingham; 1979. Pp xxiii, 170.
4. Bindoff, S.T. (ed.). *The history of parliament: the House of Commons 1509–1558* (3 vols.). London; Secker & Warburg; 1982. Pp xv, 745; x, 656; x, 687.
5. Mather, J., 'The Civil War sheriff: his person and his office,' *Albion* 13 (1981), 242–61.
6. Foster, E.R., 'Procedure and the House of Lords in the seventeenth century,' *P. of the American Philosophical Soc.* 126 (1981), 183–7.
7. Quintrell, B.W. (ed.). *Proceedings of the Lancashire justices of the peace at the sheriff's table during assizes week, 1578–1694.* Chester; Record Soc. of Lancashire and Cheshire; 1981. Pp viii, 215.
8. Sharpe, J.A. *Defamation and sexual slander in early modern England: the church courts at York.* York; Borthwick Institute; 1980. Pp 36.
9. Hayton, D.; Jones, C. (ed.). *A register of parliamentary lists, 1660–1761.* University of Leicester History Dept.; 1979. Pp

xxvi, 168 [i.e. 170]. – The same. *A Supplement.* The same; 1982. Pp xii, 20.

10. Horstman, A., 'A new curia regis: the judicature of the House of Lords in the 1620s,' *Historical J.* 25 (1982), 411–22.
11. Guy, J.A., 'The origins of the Petition of Right reconsidered,' ibid. 289–312.
12. Elton, G.R. (ed.). *The Tudor Constitution* (2nd revd. ed.). Cambridge UP; 1982. Pp xvii, 511.
13. Guth, D.J., 'The age of debt, the Reformation and English law,' Fa11, 69–86.
14. Hoak, D.E., 'The king's privy chamber, 1547–1553,' Fa11, 87–108.
15. Bryson, W.H., 'The court of exchequer comes of age,' Fa11, 149–58.
16. Barnes, T.G., 'Mr Hudson's star chamber,' Fa11, 285–308.
17. Cockburn, J.S., 'The spoils of law: the trial of Sir John Hele, 1604,' Fa11, 309–43.
18. Gray, C.M., 'Prohibitions and the privilege against self-incrimination,' Fa11, 345–67.
19. Youngs, F.A., 'Towards petty sessions: Tudor JPs and divisions of counties,' Fa11, 201–16.
20. Rushton, P., 'Women, witchcraft and slander in early modern England: cases from the church courts of Durham, 1560–1675,' *Northern History* 18 (1982), 116–32.
21. Harriss, G.L., 'Theory and practice in royal taxation: some observations,' *English Historical R.* 97 (1982), 811–19.
22. Clifford, C.A., 'Ship money in Hampshire: collection and collapse,' *Southern History* 4 (1982), 91–106.
23. Cockburn, J.S. (ed.). *Calendar of assize records: Essex indictments, James I.* London; HMSO; 1981. Pp vii, 370.
24. Newton, K.C.; McIntosh, M.K., 'Leet jurisdiction in Essex manor courts during the Elizabethan period,' *T. of the Essex Arch. Soc.* 13 (1981), 3–14.
25. Kitching, C.J., 'The cursitors' office (1573–1813) and the Corporation of the Cursitors of Chancery,' *J. of the Soc. of Archivists* 7 (1982), 78–84.
26. Hołdys, S., 'Sejm polski i parlament angielski w XVI–XVII wieku: porównanie procedury [The Polish Sejm and the English Parliament in the 16th–17th centuries: a comparison of procedure],' *Przeglad Historyczny* 71 (1980), 497–514.
27. Dewar, M. (ed.). *The De Republica Anglorum by Sir Thomas Smith.* Cambridge UP; 1982. Pp vii, 162.
28. Cockburn, J.S. (ed.). *Calendar of assize records: Surrey indictments, James I.* London; HMSO; 1982. Pp vii, 407.
29. Davis, R.W., 'Committee and other procedures in the House of Lords, 1660–1685,' *Huntington Library Q.* 45 (1982), 20–35.
30. Quintrell, B.W., 'Government in perspective: Lancashire and the

privy council, 1570–1640,' *T. of the Historic Soc. of Lancashire and Cheshire* 131 (1982 for 1981), 35–62.

(d) *External Affairs*

1. Keeler, M.F. (ed.). *Sir Francis Drake's West Indian voyage 1585–86.* London; Hakluyt Soc.; 1981. Pp xiv, 358.
2. Jespersen, K.J.V., 'Henry VIII of England, Lübeck and the Count's War, 1533–1535,' *Scandinavian J. of History* 6 (1981), 243–75.
3. Johnson, R.R. *Adjustment to empire: the New England colonies 1675–1715.* Leicester UP; 1981. Pp xx, 470.
4. Thrower, N.J.W. (ed.). *The three voyages of Edmond Halley in the Paramore, 1698–1701.* London; Hakluyt Soc.; 1981. 2 vols. Pp 392.
5. Potter, D.L., 'The treaty of Boulogne and European diplomacy, 1549–50,' *B. of the Institute of Historical Research* 55 (1982), 50–65.
6. Quinn, D.B., 'Why they came [to colonize Maryland],' *Early Maryland in a Wider World*, ed. D.B. Quinn (Detroit; Wayne State UP; 1982), 119–48.
7. Cell, G.T. (ed.). *Newfoundland discovered: English attempts at colonisation, 1610–1630.* London; Hakluyt Soc.; 1982. Pp xviii, 310.
8. Kouri, E.I., 'Elizabethan England and Europe: forty unprinted letters from Elizabeth I to protestant powers,' *B. of the Institute of Historical Research* (Special Supplement no. 12, 1982). Pp 81.
9. Burger, P., 'Spymaster to Louis XIV: a study of the papers of the abbé Eusèbe Renaudot [support to James II],' Bc22, 111–37.

(e) *Religion*

1. Sheppard, E.M., 'The Reformation and the citizens of Norwich,' *Norfolk Archaeology* 38 (1981), 44–58.
2. Hawes, T.L.M., 'Genealogy of the Reverend Francis Blomefield,' ibid. 59–66.
3. Nuttall, G.F., 'Henry Danvers, his wife and the heavenly life,' *Baptist Q.* 29 (1982), 217–19.
4. Caraman, P., 'An English Baronius [Michael Alford],' *The Month* 263 (1982), 22–4.
5. O'Malley, T., ' "Defying the powers and tempering the spirit": a review of Quaker control over their publications, 1672–1689,' *J. of Ecclesiastical History* 33 (1982), 72–88.
6. Shriver, F., 'Hampton Court revisited: James I and the Puritans,' ibid. 48–71.

7. Whiting, R., 'Abominable idols: images and image-breaking under Henry VIII,' ibid. 30–47.
8. Gibbs, L.W., 'Richard Hooker's *via media* doctrine of justification,' *Harvard Theological R.* 74 (1981), 211–20.
9. Cheyne, E.; Barratt, D.M. *Probate records of the courts of the bishop and archdeacon of Oxford, 1516–1732, vol. 1: A–K.* Cambridge; British Record Soc.; 1981. Pp xv, 337.
10. Maclean, T., 'The recusant legend: Chideock Tichborne,' *History Today* 32/5 (1982), 11–14.
11. Foster, M., 'Thomas Allen, Gloucester Hall and the Bodleian Library,' *Downside R.* 100 (1982), 116–37.
12. Herbrüggen, H.S. *Das Haupt des Thomas Morus in der St. Dunstan-Kirche zu Canterbury.* Forschungsberichte des Landes Nordrhein-Westfalen no. 3083. Westdeutscher Verlag; 1982. Pp viii, 132.
13. Carley, J., 'Four poems in praise of Erasmus by John Leland,' *Erasmus in English* 11 (1981–2), 26–7.
14. Herbert, J.C., 'William Perkins's "A Reformed Catholic": a psycho-cultural analysis,' *Church History* 51 (1982), 7–23.
15. Condren, C., '*Sacra* before *Civile*: understanding the ecclesiastical politics of George Lawson,' *J. of Religious History* 11 (1981), 524–35.
16. Sprunger, K.L., 'English and Dutch sabbatarianism and the development of puritan social theology, 1600–1660,' *Church History* 51 (1982), 24–38.
17. Lake, P. *Moderate puritans and the Elizabethan church.* Cambridge UP; 1982. Pp viii, 357.
18. Holmes, P.J. *Resistance and Compromise: the political thought of the Elizabethan catholics.* Cambridge UP; 1982. Pp viii, 279.
19. Wunderli, R., 'Pre-Reformation London summoners and the murder of Richard Hunne,' *J. of Ecclesiastical History* 33 (1982), 209–24.
20. Davis, J.F., 'Joan of Kent, Lollardy and the English Reformation,' ibid. 225–33.
21. Hargrave, O.T., 'Bloody Mary's victims: the iconography of John Foxe's Book of Martyrs,' *Historical Magazine of the Protestant Episcopal Church* 51 (1982), 7–21.
22. Martin, J.W., 'The Elizabethan Familists: a separatist group as perceived by their contemporaries,' *Baptist Q.* 29 (1982), 267–81.
23. Lupton, L. *Courage* (A History of the Geneva Bible, vol. 10). London; Olive Tree; 1978. Pp 192.
24. Lupton, L. *Endurance* (History of the Geneva Bible, vol. 11). Ibid.; 1979. Pp 192.
25. Keeble, N.H. *Richard Baxter, puritan man of letters.* Oxford; Clarendon; 1982. Pp 216.
26. Porter, H.B. *Jeremy Taylor: liturgist (1613–1667).* London; Alcuin Club; 1979. Pp vii, 185.

27. Northeast, P. (ed.). *Boxford churchwardens' accounts 1530–1562.* Woodbridge; Boydell; 1982. Pp xv, 108.
28. Skwarczynski, P., 'Elsinore 1580: John Rogers and John Bosgrave,' *Recusant History* 16 (1982), 1–16.
29. Allison, A.F., 'Who was John Brereley? The identity of a seventeenth-century controversialist,' ibid. 17–41.
30. Hibbard, C., 'The Contribution of 1639: court and country catholicism,' ibid. 42–60.
31. Reid, D.S., 'P.R. Newman and the Durham protestations,' ibid. 15 (1981), 370–1.
32. Shakespeare, J.; Dowling, M., 'Religion and politics in mid-Tudor England through the eyes of an English protestant woman: the recollections of Rose Hickman,' *B. of the Institute of Historical Research* 55 (1982), 94–102.
33. Brigden, S., 'Youth and the English Reformation,' *Past and Present* 95 (1982), 37–67.
34. Lytle, G.F., 'Religion and the lay patron in Reformation England,' Fk36, 65–114.
35. Marotti, A.F., 'John Donne and the rewards of patronage,' Fk36, 207–34.
36. Bossy, J., 'Reluctant colonists: the English catholics confront the Atlantic,' *Early Maryland in a Wider World*, ed. D.B. Quinn (Detroit; Wayne State UP; 1982), 149–64.
37. Menard, R.R.; Carr, L.G., 'The Lords Baltimore and the colonization of Maryland,' ibid. 167–215.
38. McFarlane, I.D. *Buchanan.* London; Duckworth; 1981. Pp xvii, 574.
39. Moody, M.E., 'Trials and travels of a nonconformist layman: the spiritual odyssey of Stephan Offwood, 1564–ca. 1635,' *Church History* 51 (1982), 157–71.
40. Hajzyk, H., 'Household divinity and covenant theology in Lincolnshire c. 1595–c. 1640,' *Lincolnshire History and Archaeology* 17 (1982), 45–9.
41. Morgan, N.J., 'Lancashire Quakers and the oath, 1660–1722,' *J. of the Friends' Historical Soc.* 54 (1980), 235–54.
42. Mortimer, J. & R. (ed.). *Leeds Friends' minute book: 1692–1712.* Leeds; Yorkshire Arch. Soc.; 1980. Pp li, 269.
43. Gentles, I.J.; Sheils, W.J. *Confiscation and restoration: the archbishopric estates and the civil war.* York; Borthwick Institute; 1981. Pp 53.
44. Not used.
45. Hall, C.S., 'The general baptist church, Netherton, Dudley,' *Baptist Q.* 29 (1982), 308–18.
46. Bennett, J.S., 'Who was Fr Thomas Whitbread?,' *Recusant History* 16 (1982), 91–8.
47. Bamber, J.E., 'The skull at Wardley Hall,' ibid. 61–77.

48. Sullivan, R.E. *John Toland and the Deist controversy.* Cambridge, Mass.; Harvard UP; 1982. Pp x, 355.
49. Schüler, S. *Die Klöstersekularisation in Kent 1535–1558.* Paderborn; Schöningh; 1980. Pp 164.
50. Slavin, A.J., 'The Tudor revolution and the devil's art: Bishop Bonner's printed forms,' Fa11, 3–23.
51. McKenna, J.W., 'How God became an Englishman,' Fa11, 25–43.
52. Lehmberg, S.E., 'The reformation of choirs: cathedral musical establishments in Tudor England,' Fa11, 45–67.
53. Cross, C., 'The development of protestantism in Leeds and Hull, 1520–1640: the evidence from wills,' *Northern History* 18 (1982), 230–8.
54. Jones, N.L. *Faith by statute: parliament and the settlement of religion 1559.* London; Royal Historical Soc. (Studies in History, 32); 1982. Pp viii, 245.
55. Vage, J.A., 'Ecclesiastical discipline in the early seventeenth century: some findings and some problems from the archdeaconry of Cornwall,' *J. of the Soc. of Archivists* 7 (1982), 85–105.
56. Croft, R.D., 'Archbishop Thomas Cranmer and the education of the English clergy, 1533–1553,' *History of Education* 11 (1982), 155–64.
57. Schwartz, M.L., 'Lay anglicanism and the crisis of the English Church in the early seventeenth century,' *Albion* 14 (1982), 1–19.
58. Condick, F.M., 'The self-revelation of a puritan: Dr Alexander Leighton in the sixteen-twenties,' *B. of the Institute of Historical Research* 55 (1982), 196–203.
59. Jones, N.L., 'A bill confirming Bishop Bonner's deprivation and reinstating Bishop Ridley as the legal bishop of London, from the parliament of 1559,' *J. of Ecclesiastical History* 33 (1982), 580–5.
60. Heal, F.M., 'The archbishops of Canterbury and the practice of hospitality,' ibid. 544–63.
61. Clauss, S., 'John Wilkins' Essay Toward a Real Character: its place in seventeenth-century episteme,' *J. of the History of Ideas* 43 (1982), 531–54.
62. Bradley, R.D., 'The failure of accommodation: religious conflict between presbyterians and independents in the Westminster Assembly 1643–1646,' *J. of Religious History* 12 (1982), 23–47.
63. Morrill, J.S., 'The Church in England 1643–9,' Fb45, 89–114.
64. Kitch, M.J., 'The Reformation in Sussex,' Bc17, 77–98.
65. McCann, T.J., 'The clergy and the Elizabethan Settlement in the diocese of Chichester,' Bc17, 99–123.
66. Abercrombie, N.J., 'From Counter-Reformation to bourgeois Catholicism: recusancy in seventeenth and eighteenth century Sussex,' Bc17, 125–40.

67. Fletcher, A.J., 'Puritanism in seventeenth century Sussex,' Bc17, 141–55.
68. Kenny, A., 'Reform and reaction in Elizabethan Balliol,' Bc14, 17–51.
69. Bossy, J., 'Catholicity and nationality in the northern Counter-Reformation,' Bc10, 285–96.
70. Guy, J.R., 'The significance of indigenous clergy in the Welsh Church at the Restoration,' Bc10, 335–43.
71. Loades, D.M., 'Relations between the Anglican and Roman Catholic Churches in the 16th and 17th centuries,' Bc9, 1–53.
72. Aveling, J.C.H., 'The English clergy, catholic and protestant, in the 16th and 17th centuries,' Bc9, 33–142.
73. McGrath, P., 'Winchester College and the old religion in the sixteenth century,' Bc6, 229–80.
74. Patterson, W.B., 'Educating the Greeks: Anglican scholarships for Greek Orthodox students in the early seventeenth century,' Bc1, 227–37.
75. Walsh, M.J., 'The publishing policy of the English press at St. Omer, 1608–1759,' Bc1, 239–50.
76. Goldie, M., 'The nonjurors, episcopacy, and the origins of the Convocation controversy,' Bc22, 15–35.
77. LaRocca, J.L., 'Time, death, and the next generation: the early Elizabethan recusancy policy, 1558–1574,' *Albion* 14 (1982), 103–17.
78. Opfell, O.S. *The King James Bible translators.* Jefferson/London; McFarland; 1982. Pp v, 173.
79. Guy, J.R., 'From the Reformation to 1800 [Wells Cathedral],' Bc23, 148–78.

(f) *Economic Affairs*

1. Alsop, J.D., 'The theory and practice of Tudor taxation,' *English Historical R.* 97 (1982), 31–53.
2. Jones, J.G., 'The Wynn estate of Gwydir: aspects of its growth and development c. 1500–1580,' *National Library of Wales J.* 22 (1981), 141–69.
3. Backscheider, P.R., 'Defoe's Lady Credit,' *Huntington Library Q.* 44 (1981), 89–100.
4. Nef, J.U., 'The rise of the coal industry and its place in integral history,' *J. of Historical Geography* 8 (1982), 68–73.
5. Awty, B.J., 'French immigrants and the iron industry in Sheffield,' *Yorkshire Arch. J.* 53 (1981), 57–62.
6. Butlin, R.A. *The transformation of rural England c. 1580–1800: a study in historical geography.* Oxford UP; 1982. Pp 64.
7. Harrison, C.J., 'Elizabethan field books,' *Local Historian* 15 (1982), 67–9.

8. Alcock, N.A. (ed.), *Warwickshire grazier and London skinner, 1532–1555.* Oxford UP for British Academy; 1982. Pp xix, 281.
9. Parry, E.G., 'Brecon: occupations and society, 1500–1800,' *Brycheiniog* 19 (1980–1), 60–8.
10. Ramsay, G.D., 'A saint in the city: Thomas More at Mercers' Hall, London,' *English Historical R.* 97 (1982), 269–88.
11. Yates, E.M., 'The dispute of the salt fen,' *Norfolk Archaeology* 38 (1981), 73–8.
12. Postler, D. (ed.). *Sheffield in 1581.* Sheffield City Libraries; 1981. Pp 42.
13. Porter, S., 'Farm transport in Huntingdonshire, 1610–1749,' *J. of Transport History* 3rd ser. 3 (1982), 35–45.
14. Challis, C.E., 'The conversion of testoons: a restatement,' *British Numismatic J.* 50 (1981 for 1980), 67–80.
15. Alsop, J.D., 'Protector Somerset and warrants for payment,' *B. of the Institute of Historical Research* 55 (1982), 102–8.
16. Åström, S.-E., 'Swedish iron and the English iron industry about 1700: some neglected aspects,' *Scandinavian Economic History R.* 30 (1982), 129–41.
17. Alsop, J.D., 'Dating Edward VI's exchequer terms,' *J. of the Soc. of Archivists* 7 (1982), 31–2.
18. Phillips, J., 'The English patent as a reward for invention: the importation of an idea,' *J. of Legal History* 3 (1982), 71–9.
19. Paget, M., 'A study of manorial custom before 1625,' *Local Historian* 15 (1982), 166–83.
20. Zell, M.L., 'The mid-Tudor market in crown land in Kent,' *Archaeologia Cantiana* 97 (1982 for 1981), 53–70.
21. Nash, R.C., 'The English and Scottish tobacco trades in the seventeenth and eighteenth centuries: legal and illegal trade,' *Economic History R.* 2nd ser. 35 (1982), 354–72.
22. Not used.
23. Pounds, N.J.G. (ed.). *The parliamentary survey of the duchy of Cornwall, pt. 1.* Exeter; Devon and Cornwall Record Soc., new ser. 25; 1982. Pp xxiv, 130.
24. Gethyn-Jones, E. *George Thorpe and the Berkeley Company: a Gloucestershire enterprise in Virginia.* Gloucester; Sutton; 1982. Pp 296.
25. Denington, R.F., 'The records of Rothwell horse fair 1684–1744,' *Northamptonshire Past and Present* 6 (1982–3), 319–24.
26. Harrison, M.C., 'The probate inventory of an early seventeenth-century Northampton mercer and linen draper,' ibid. 313–17.
27. Horsefield, J.K., 'The "stop of the exchequer" revisited,' *Economic History R.* 2nd ser. 35 (1982), 511–28.
28. Bettey, J.H., 'Land tenure and manorial custom in Dorset 1570–1670,' *Southern History* 4 (1982), 33–54.
29. Martin, J.M., 'A Warwickshire market town in adversity:

Stratford-upon-Avon in the sixteenth and seventeenth centuries,' *Midland History* 7 (1982), 26–41.
30. Fieldhouse, R., 'Some evidence of surviving open fields in the seventeenth-century Pennine dales and the gradual elimination of communal agriculture,' *Yorkshire Arch. J.* 54 (1982), 111–18.
31. Ramsay, G.D. *The English woollen industry, 1500–1750.* London; Macmillan; 1982. Pp 91.
32. Grammp, W.D., 'The controversy over usury in the seventeenth century,' *J. of European Economic History* 10 (1981), 671–95.
33. Kent, J., 'A new type of George noble of Henry VIII,' Bc26, 231–4.

(g) *Social History (General)*

1. Blewett, D., 'Changing attitudes toward marriage in the time of Defoe: the case of Moll Flanders,' *Huntington Library Q.* 44 (1981), 77–88.
2. Clay, C., 'Property, settlements, financial provision for the family, and sale of land by the greater landowners,' *J. of British Studies* 21 (1981), 18–38.
3. Moore, J.S. (ed.). *Clifton and Westbury probate inventories 1609–1761.* Bristol; Avon Local History Association; 1981. Pp xlix, 247.
4. Kussmaul, A. *Servants in husbandry in early modern England.* Cambridge UP; 1981. Pp xii, 233.
5. Lindley, K. *Fenland riots and the English Revolution.* London; Heinemann Educational; 1982. Pp 276.
6. Stoate, T.L. (ed.). *Dorset Tudor subsidies: granted in 1523, 1543, 1593.* Bristol; the editor; 1982. Pp xxiv, 256.
7. Davey, C.R. (ed.). *The Hampshire lay subsidy rolls, 1586; with the city of Winchester assessment of a fifteenth and tenth, 1585.* Winchester; Hampshire County Council; 1981. Pp xi, 180.
8. Houston, R.A., 'The development of literacy: northern England, 1640–1750,' *Economic History R.* 2nd ser. 35 (1982), 199–216.
9. Elton, G.R., 'Contentment and discontent on the eve of colonization,' *Early Maryland in a Wider World*, ed. D.B. Quinn (Detroit; Wayne State UP; 1982), 105–18.
10. Coleman, D.C., 'The local and the global in early modern society, [review article],' *Historical J.* 25 (1982), 447–55.
11. Palliser, D.M., 'Tawney's century: brave new world or Malthusian trap?,' *Economic History R.* 2nd ser. 35 (1982), 339–53.
12. Cioni, M.L., 'The Elizabethan chancery and women's rights,' Fa11, 159–82.
13. Houston, R.A., 'Illiteracy in the diocese of Durham, 1663–89 and 1750–62: the evidence of the marriage bonds,' *Northern History* 18 (1982), 239–51.

14. Coward, B., 'A "crisis in the aristocracy" in the sixteenth and seventeenth centuries? The case of the Stanleys, earls of Derby, 1504–1642,' ibid. 54–77.
15. Edwards, D.G. (ed.). *Derbyshire hearth tax assessments, 1662–70.* Chesterfield; Derbyshire Record Soc.; 1982. Pp lxxxv, 225.
16. Bernard, G.W., 'The fortunes of the Greys, earls of Kent, in the early sixteenth century,' *Historical J.* 25 (1982), 671–85.
17. Hume, R., 'Educational provision for the Kentish poor, 1660–1811: fluctuations and trends,' *Southern History* 4 (1982), 123–44.
18. Hawkins, M.J., 'Wardship, royalist delinquency and too many children: the Portmans in the seventeenth century,' ibid. 55–89.
19. Houston, R.A., 'Illiteracy among Newcastle shoemakers, 1618–1740,' *Archaeologia Aeliana* 5th ser. 10 (1982), 143–7.
20. Rook, K., 'The protection of the commons, 1641,' *Bradford Antiquary* new ser. 47 (1982), 135–45.
21. Knafla, L.A., ' "Insolent and formidable felons": historical crime in early modern England [review article],' *Canadian J. of History* 17 (1982), 307–14.
22. Nadelhaft, J., 'The Englishwoman's sexual civil war: feminist attitudes toward men, women, and marriage, 1650–1740,' *J. of the History of Ideas* 43 (1982), 555–79.
23. Attreed, L.C., 'Preparation for death in sixteenth-century northern England,' *Sixteenth Century J.* 13 (1982), 37–66.
24. Hill, C., 'Dr. Tobias Crisp,' Bc14, 53–76.
25. Custance, R., 'Warden Nicholas and the mutiny at Winchester College,' Bc6, 313–50.
26. Horne, W.C., ' "Between th' petticoat and the breeches": sexual warfare and the marriage debate in *Hudibras*,' *Eighteenth-Century Studies* (1982), 132–46.

(h) *Social Structure and Population*

1. Pickles, M.F., 'Agrarian society and wealth in mid-Wharfedale, 1664–1743,' *Yorkshire Arch. J.* 53 (1981), 63–78.
2. Phillips, C., 'The population of the borough of Kendal in 1576,' *T. of the Cumberland & Westmorland Antiquarian and Arch. Soc.* 81 (1981), 57–62.
3. Dobbie, B.M.W., 'An attempt to estimate the true rate of maternal mortality, sixteenth to eighteenth centuries,' *Medical History* 26 (1982), 79–90.
4. Harris, B.J., 'Marriage sixteenth-century style: Elizabeth Stafford and the third duke of Norfolk,' *J. of Social History* 15 (1981–2), 371–82.
5. Leites, E., 'The duty to desire: love, friendship and sexuality in some puritan theories of marriage,' ibid. 383–408.
6. Munby, L.M. (ed.). *Life and death in King's Langley: wills and*

inventories 1498–1659. King's Langley Local History Soc.; 1981. Pp xxxiv, 166.

7. Dyer, A., 'Seasonality of baptisms: an urban approach,' *Local Population Studies* 27 (1981), 26–34.
8. Wyatt, G., 'Migration in south west Lancashire,' ibid. 62–4.
9. Griffiths, M., 'The Vale of Glamorgan in the 1543 lay subsidy returns,' *B. of the Board of Celtic Studies* 29 (1982), 709–48.
10. Kent, J.R., 'Population mobility and alms: poor migrants in the Midlands during the early seventeenth century,' *Local Population Studies* 27 (1981), 35–51.
11. Siraut, M., 'Physical mobility in Elizabethan Cambridge,' ibid. 65–70.
12. Palliser, D.M.; Jones, L.J., 'A neglected source for English population history: the bishops' returns of 1563 and 1603,' ibid. 155–6.
13. Barker, R., 'The local study of plague,' *Local Historian* 14 (1981), 332–40.
14. Wrightson, K., 'Alehouses, order and reformation in rural England, 1590–1660,' Bc7, 1–27.

(i) *Naval and Military*

1. Trevor-Roper, H.R., 'Prince Rupert, 1619–82,' *History Today* 33/3 (1982), 4–11.
2. Tomlinson, H., 'Ordnance building at the Tower of London, 1660–1714,' ibid. 33/4 (1982), 43–7.
3. Kenyon, J.R., 'Early artillery fortifications in England and Wales: a preliminary survey and reappraisal,' *Arch. J.* 138 (1982 for 1981), 205–40.
4. Howell, R., 'The Army and the English Revolution: the case of Robert Lilburne,' *Archaeologia Aeliana* 5th ser. 9 (1981), 299–315.
5. Junge, H.-C., ' "The fittest subject for a King's quarrel": Politik, Militär und Gesellschaft in England, 1640–1660 [review article with commentary],' *Militärgeschichtliche Mitteilungen* 29/1 (1981), 143–63.
6. Gratton, J.M., 'Thomas Dalton of Thurnham: a Lancashire royalist colonel,' *Recusant History* 16 (1982), 89–90.
7. Le Fevre, P., 'Sir George Ayscue, Commonwealth and Restoration admiral,' *Mariner's Mirror* 68 (1982), 189–202.
8. McGrath, P. *Bristol and the civil war.* Bristol; Historical Association Branch; 1981. Pp 50.
9. Hilton Jones, G., 'The recall of the British from the Dutch service,' *Historical J.* 25 (1982), 423–35.
10. Rule, M., 'The sinking of the Mary Rose,' *History Today* 32 (1982), 27–36.

11. Andrews, K.R., 'The Elizabethan seaman,' *Mariner's Mirror* 68 (1982), 245–62.
12. Hogg, A.H.A., 'The causeway earthwork and the Elizabethan redoubt on West Wickham Common,' *Archaeologia Cantiana* 97 (1982 for 1981), 71–8.
13. Colvin, H.M.; Summerson, J.; Biddle, M.; Hale, J.R.; Merriman, M. *The history of the King's Works, IV (1485–1660, part II).* London; HMSO; 1982. Pp xxviii, 826.
14. Temple, R.K.G., 'Discovery of manuscript eye-witness account of the battle of Maidstone,' *Archaeologia Cantiana* 97 (1982 for 1981), 209–20.
15. Hutton, R., 'The royalist war effort,' Fb45, 51–6.

(j) *Political Thought and History of Ideas*

1. Kinney, D., 'More's *Letter to Dorp*: remapping the trivium,' *Renaissance Q.* 34 (1981), 179–210.
2. Green, L.D., 'Modes of perception in the *Mirror for Magistrates*,' *Huntington Library Q.* 44 (1981), 117–33.
3. Winfrey, J.C., 'Charity versus justice in Locke's theory of property,' *J. of the History of Ideas* 42 (1981), 423–38.
4. Cotton, J., 'James Harrington and Thomas Hobbes,' ibid. 407–21.
5. Tennant, R.C., 'The Anglican response to Locke's theory of personal identity,' ibid. 43 (1982), 73–90.
6. Goldsmith, M.M., 'Picturing Hobbes's politics? The illustrations to *Philosophical Rudiments*,' *J. of the Warburg and Courtauld Institutes* 44 (1981), 232–7.
7. Cook, E., 'Thomas Hobbes and the "Far-Fetched",' ibid. 222–32.
8. Koontz, T.J., 'Religion and political cohesion: John Locke and Jean Jacques Rousseau,' *J. of Church and State* 23 (1981), 95–115.
9. Forsyth, M., 'The place of Richard Cumberland in the history of natural law doctrine,' *J. of the History of Philosophy* 20 (1982), 23–42.
10. Menake, G.T., 'A research note and query on the dating of Locke's *Two Treatises*,' *Political Theory* 9 (1981), 547–50.
11. Okin, S.M., ' "The Soveraign and his Counsellours",' ibid. 10 (1982), 49–75.
12. De Beer, E.S. (ed.). *The correspondence of John Locke, vol. 7: Letters nos. 2665–3286.* Oxford; Clarendon; 1981.
13. Mather, J., 'The moral code of the English civil war and interregnum,' *The Historian* 44 (1982), 207–28.
14. Green, I., 'The Publication of Clarendon's autobiography and the acquisition of his papers by the Bodleian Library,' *Bodleian Library Record* 10 (1982), 349–67.

15. Miller, J., 'The Glorious Revolution: "contract" and "abdication" reconsidered,' *Historical J.* 25 (1982), 541–55.
16. Sommerville, J.P., 'From Suarez to Filmer: a reappraisal,' ibid. 525–40.
17. Box, I., 'Bacon's *Essays*: from political science to political prudence,' *History of Political Thought* 3 (1982), 31–49.
18. Verdon, M., 'Of the laws of physical and human nature: Hobbes' physical and social cosmologies,' *J. of the History of Ideas* 43 (1982), 653–64.
19. Tuck, R., ' "The ancient law of freedom": John Selden and the civil war,' Fb45, 137–62.
20. Mulligan, L.; Richards, J.; Graham, J.K., 'A concern for understanding: a case of Locke's precepts and practice,' *Historical J.* 25 (1982), 841–57.
21. Parry, G., 'Locke on representation in politics,' *History of European Ideas* 3 (1982), 403–14.
22. Stanwood, P.G. (ed.). *Richard Hooker: Of the Laws of Ecclesiastical Polity, Books VI, VII, VIII.* Cambridge, Mass.; Belknap Press; 1981. Pp lxxvii, 644.
23. Salmon, J.H.M., 'An alternative theory of popular resistance: Buchanan, Rossaeus and Locke,' *Diritto e Potere nella Storia Europea* (Florence; Olschki; 1981), 823–49.
24. Stallmach, J., 'De Thomae Mori re publica optima et perfecta quae est nusquam ideoque "Vtopia" appelatur,' *Vox Latina* 16 (1980), 22–131.

(k) *Cultural and History of Science*

1. Martin, J.W., 'Miles Hogarde: artisan and aspiring author in sixteenth-century England,' *Renaissance Q.* 34 (1981), 359–83.
2. Fychan, C., 'Tri Chymydog Llengar,' *National Library of Wales J.* 22 (1981), 187–213.
3. Gresham, S., 'William Baldwin: literary voice of the reign of Edward VI,' *Huntington Library Q.* 44 (1981), 101–16.
4. Reed, M., 'Seventeenth-century Stowe,' ibid. 189–203.
5. Williams, A.S., 'Panegyric decorum in the reigns of William III and Anne,' *J. of British Studies* 21 (1981), 56–67.
6. Lawrence, H.; Hoyle, R., 'New maps and surveys by Christopher Saxton,' *Yorkshire Arch. J.* 53 (1981), 51–6.
7. Clough, C.H., 'A presentation volume for Henry VIII: the Charlecote Park copy of Erasmus's *Institutio principis*,' *J. of the Warburg and Courtauld Institutes* 44 (1981), 199–202.
8. Eisenach, E.J. *Two worlds of liberalism: religion and politics in Hobbes, Locke, and Mill.* Chicago/London; University of Chicago Press; 1981. Pp x, 262.
9. Cook, A.J. *The privileged playgoers of Shakespeare's London, 1576–1642.* Princeton/Guildford; Princeton UP; 1981. Pp x, 316.

10. Ravenhill, W., 'Projections for the large general maps of Britain, 1583–1700,' *Imago Mundi* 33 (1981), 21–32.
11. Schroeder, H., 'The mural paintings of the nine worthies at Amersham,' *Archaeological J.* 138 (1982 for 1981), 241–7.
12. Barkley, H. *Likenesses in line: an anthology of Tudor and Stuart engraved portraits.* London; HMSO; 1982. Pp 87.
13. Grieve, H. *A transatlantic gardening friendship.* Chelmsford; Historical Association Branch; 1981. Pp 27.
14. Not used.
15. Underwood, M.G., 'The Lady Margaret and her Cambridge connections,' *Sixteenth Century J.* 13 (1982), 67–81.
16. Croft, P.J.; Matar, N., 'The Peter Sterry MSS at Emmanuel College, Cambridge,' *T. of the Cambridge Bibliographical Soc.* 8 (1981), 42–56.
17. Hammond, P., 'Dryden's employment by Cromwell's government,' ibid. 130–6.
18. Rook, A.; Martin, L., 'John Addenbrooke M.D. (1680–1719),' *Medical History* 26 (1982), 169–78.
19. Blaim, A., 'More's *Utopia*: persuasion or polyphony?,' *Moreana* 73 (1982), 5–20.
20. Ahrens, R., 'Literaturtheorie und Aristokratie in der Tudorzeit. Ein Beitrag zur Funktion des Mäzens im England des 16. Jahrhunderts,' *Anglia* 99 (1981), 279–311.
21. Höltgen, K.J., 'Why are there no wolves in England? Philip Camerarius and a German version of Sidney's Table Talk,' ibid. 60–82.
22. Alsop, J.D., 'The invention of a selfpropelled vehicle in the 16th century,' *Technology and Culture* 22 (1981), 753–6.
23. Quinn, D.B. *Drake's circumnavigation of the globe: a review.* Exeter; The University; 1981. Pp 21.
24. Fisher, J. *A collection of early maps of London 1553–1667.* London; Guildhall Library; 1981. 21 leaves.
25. Richmond, H.M. *Puritans and libertines: Anglo-French literary relations in the Reformation.* Berkeley/London; University of California Press; 1981. Pp xii, 401.
26. Eccles, A. *Obstetrics and gynaecology in Tudor and Stuart England.* London; Croom Helm; 1982. Pp 144.
27. Tyacke, S. *Christopher Saxton and Tudor map making.* London; British Library; 1980. Pp 64.
28. Cressy, D., 'Francis Bacon and the advancement of schooling,' *History of European Ideas* 2 (1981), 65–74.
29. Treadwell, M., 'London trade publishers 1675–1750,' *The Library* 6th ser. 4 (1982), 99–134.
30. Gleason, J.B., 'The earliest evidence for ecclesiastical censorship of printed books in England,' ibid. 135–41.
31. Nash, N.F., 'English licences to print and grants of copyright in the 1640s,' ibid. 174–84.

32. Page, R.I., 'The Parker Register and Matthew Parker's Anglo-Saxon manuscripts,' *T. of the Cambridge Bibliographical Soc.* 8 (1981), 1–17.
33. Leedham-Green, E., 'A catalogue of Caius College Library 1569,' ibid. 29–41.
34. Bondos-Greene, S.A., 'The end of an era: Cambridge puritanism and the Christ's College election of 1609,' *Historical J.* 25 (1982), 197–208.
35. Parry, G. *The golden age restored: the culture of the Stuart court, 1603–42.* Manchester UP; 1981. Pp xi, 276.
36. Lytle, G.F.; Orgel, S. (ed.). *Patronage in the Renaissance.* Princeton UP; 1982. Pp xiv, 489.
37. Kipling, G., 'Henry VII and the origins of Tudor patronage,' Fk36, 117–64.
38. Smuts, M., 'The political failure of Stuart cultural patronage,' Fk36, 165–87.
39. Van Dorsten, J., 'Literary patronage in Elizabethan England: the early phase,' Fk36, 191–206.
40. Tennenhouse, L., 'Sir Walter Ralegh and the literature of clientage,' Fk36, 235–58.
41. Orgel, S., 'The royal theatre and the role of king,' Fk36, 261–73.
42. Bergeron, D.M., 'Women as patrons of English renaissance drama,' Fk36, 274–90.
43. Martin, J.W., 'The Marian regime's failure to understand the importance of printing,' *Huntington Library Q.* 44 (1981), 231–47.
44. Peacock, J., 'Inigo Jones's catafalque for James I,' *Architectural History* 25 (1982), 1–5.
45. Illsley, J., 'Admiral Lord Edward Russell and the building of St. Paul's Cathedral,' *Mariner's Mirror* 68 (1982), 305–15.
46. Hanna, R., 'Two new texts of More's *Dialogue of Comfort*,' *Moreana* 74 (1982), 5–11.
47. Yee, N.C., 'Thomas More: in defense of tribulation,' ibid. 13–26.
48. Warnicke, R., 'The Lady Margaret, countess of Richmond (d. 1509), as seen by Bishop Fisher and Lord Morley,' ibid. 47–55.
49. Searle, A., ' "A pleasing example of skill in old age": Sir Christopher Wren and Marlborough House,' *British Library J.* 8 (1982), 37–45.
50. Ashbee, A. (ed.). *Lists of payments to the King's musick in the reign of Charles II (1660–1685).* Snodland; the editor; 1981. Pp xiv, 129.
51. Dewhurst, K. (ed.). *Willis's Oxford casebook.* Oxford; Sandford; 1981. Pp xi, 199.
52. Downes, K. *The architecture of Wren.* London; Granada; 1982. Pp 96.
53. Gair, R. *The Children of Paul's: the story of a theatre company, 1553–1608.* Cambridge UP; 1982. Pp ix, 213.

54. Guerlac, H. *Newton on the continent.* Ithaca/London; Cornell UP; 1981. Pp 169.
55. Avis, F.C. *The 16th century Long Shop printing office in the Poultry.* London; Glenview; 1982. Pp 72.
56. Barker, F. *London as it might have been.* London; Murray; 1982. Pp 224.
57. Rose, E., 'Too good to be true: Thomas Lupton's Golden Rule,' Fa11, 183–200.
58. White, R., 'The architects of Bromley College, Kent,' *Architectural History* 24 (1981), 32–3.
59. Stewart, L., 'Newtonians, revolutionaries and republicans [review article],' *Canadian J. of History* 17 (1982), 314–21.
60. Cressy, D., 'Spectacle and power: Apollo & Solomon at the court of Henry VIII,' *History Today* 32/10, 16–22.
61. Duffy, M., ' "The noisie, empty, fluttring French": English images of the French 1689–1815,' *History Today* 32/9, 21–6.
62. Palliser, D.M., 'Civic mentality and the environment in Tudor York,' *Northern History* 18 (1982), 78–115.
63. Vickers, M., 'The medal of Robert Dudley, earl of Leicester in the Bibliothèque Nationale,' *Numismatic Chronicle* 141 (1981), 117–19.
64. MacDonald, M., 'Religion, social change, and psychological healing in England, 1600–1800,' Bc21, 101–25.
65. Trapp, J.B., 'John Colet and the *Hierarchies* of the Pseudo-Dionysius,' Bc1, 127–48.
66. Duffy, E., 'Valentine Greatrakes, the Irish Stroker: miracle, science and orthodoxy in Restoration England,' Bc1, 251–73.
67. Henry, J., 'Atomism and eschatalogy: catholicism and natural philosophy in the Interregnum,' *British J. for the History of Science* 15 (1982), 211–39.
68. Duchemin, P., ' "Barbarous ignorance and base detraction": the struggles of Michael Drayton,' *Albion* 14 (1982), 118–38.
69. Fores, M., 'Francis Bacon and the myth of industrial science,' *History of Technology* (1982), 57–75.
70. Horton, M., 'A group of sixteenth-century Flemish titles in England,' Bc26, 235–46.

G. BRITAIN 1714–1815

See also Ff29, 31, g17, 19, 22, k61

(a) *General*

1. Askwith, B. *Piety and wit: a biography of Harriet, countess Granville, 1785–1862.* London; Collins; 1982. Pp x, 207.

2. Bagot, O.R., 'Some eighteenth-century documents at Levens Hall,' *T. of the Cumberland & Westmorland Antiquarian and Arch. Soc.* 81 (1981), 73–82.
3. Low, D.A. *Thieves' kitchen: Regency underworld.* London; Dent; 1982.
4. Spater, George. *William Cobbett, the poor man's friend* (2 vols.). Cambridge UP; 1982. Pp xvii, 318.
5. Christie, I.R. *Wars and revolutions: Britain 1760–1815.* London; Arnold; 1982. Pp vii, 359.
6. Christie, P., 'The Gentleman's Magazine and the local historian,' *Local Historian* 15 (1982), 80–4.
7. Harris, F., 'Accounts of the conduct of Sarah, duchess of Marlborough, 1704–42,' *British Library J.* 8 (1982), 7–35.
8. Hudson, J.P., 'The Blenheim papers,' ibid. 1–6.
9. Bouce, P.G. *Sexuality in eighteenth-century Britain.* Manchester UP; 1982. Pp xii, 262.
10. Morgan, P. *The eighteenth-century renaissance.* Llandybie; Christopher Davies; 1981. Pp 174.
11. Porter, R. *English society in the eighteenth century.* London; Allen Lane; 1982. Pp 424.
12. Smout, T.C. (ed.), 'Journal of Henry Kalmeter's travels in Scotland, 1719–1720,' Bc4, 1–52.
13. Holmes, G.S. *Augustan England: professions, status and society, 1680–1730.* London; Allen & Unwin; 1982. Pp xiv, 332.
14. Pelzer, J. & L., 'The coffee-houses of Augustan London,' *History Today* 32/10 (1982), 40–7.

(b) *Politics*

1. Alsop, J.D., 'Contemporary remarks on the 1768 election in Norfolk and Suffolk,' *Norfolk Archaeology* 38 (1981), 79–82.
2. Colley, L. *In defiance of oligarchy.* Cambridge UP; 1982. Pp viii, 375.
3. Hone, J.A. *For the cause of truth: radicalism in London, 1796–1821.* Oxford; Clarendon; 1982. Pp x, 412.
4. Smith, M.J., 'The mushroom elections in Carlisle, 1784–1803,' *T. of the Cumberland & Westmorland Antiquarian and Arch. Soc.* 81 (1981), 113–21.
5. Clark, J.C.D. *The dynamics of change: the crisis of the 1750s and English party systems.* Cambridge UP; 1982. Pp xiii, 615.
6. Jones, C., 'The impeachment of the earl of Oxford and the Whig schism of 1717: four new lists,' *B. of the Institute of Historical Research* 55 (1982), 66–87.
7. Jubb, M.J., 'The cabinet in the reign of George I,' ibid. 108–10.
8. O'Gorman, F. *The emergence of the two-party system in Britain.* London; Arnold; 1982. Pp 144.
9. Olson, A.G., 'The London mercantile lobby and the coming of

the American revolution,' *J. of American History* 69 (1982), 21–41.
10. Doolittle, I.G., 'Government interference in City politics in the early eighteenth century: the work of two agents,' *London J.* 8 (1982), 170–6.
11. Drescher, S., 'Public opinion and the destruction of British colonial slavery,' Bc20, 22–48.
12. Not used.
13. Walvin, J., 'The propaganda of anti-slavery,' Bc20, 49–68.
14. Rogers, N., 'Riot and popular Jacobitism in early Hanoverian England,' Bc22, 70–88.
15. Gregg, E., 'The Jacobite career of John, earl of Mar,' Bc22, 179–200.
16. Dwyer, J.; Murdoch, A., 'Paradigms and politics: manners, morals and the rise of Henry Dundas, 1770–1784,' Bc25, 210–48.
17. Phillips, J.P. *Electoral behaviour in unreformed England: plumpers, splitters and straights.* Princeton UP; 1982. Pp xix, 353.

(c) *Constitution, Administration and Law*

1. Cooper, R.A., 'Jeremy Bentham, Elizabeth Fry, and English prison reform,' *J. of the History of Ideas* 42 (1981), 675–90.
2. Macdonagh, O. *The Inspector General: Sir Jeremy Fitzpatrick and the politics of social reform, 1783–1802.* London; Croom Helm; 1981. Pp 344.
3. Milsom, S.F.C. *The nature of Blackstone's achievement.* London; Selden Soc.; 1981 [i.e. 1982]. Pp 12.
4. Hay, D., 'War, dearth and theft in the eighteenth century: the record of the English courts,' *Past and Present* 95 (1982), 117–60.
5. Duman, D. *The judicial bench in England 1727–1875: the reshaping of a professional elite.* London; Royal Historical Soc. (Studies in History 29); 1982. Pp x, 208.
6. Polden, P., 'John Reeves as superintendent of aliens, 1803–4,' *J. of Legal History* 3 (1982), 31–51.
7. Fox, K.O. *Making life impossible: a study of military aid to the civil power in Regency England.* No publisher; 1982. Pp viii, 259.

(d) *External Affairs*

1. Brock, W.R. *Scotus Americanus: a survey of the sources for links between Scotland and America in the eighteenth century.* Edinburgh UP; 1982. Pp viii, 293.
2. Bromley, J.S., 'Britain and Europe in the eighteenth century,' *History* 66 (1981), 394–412.

3. Barber, P., 'Marlborough as imperial prince, 1704–1717,' *British Library J.* 8 (1982), 46–79.
4. Schweizer, K.W., 'William Pitt, Lord Bute, and the peace negotiations with France, May–September 1761,' *Albion* 13 (1981), 262–75.
5. Bumstead, J.M. *The people's clearance: Highland emigration to British North America, 1770–1815.* Edinburgh UP; 1982. Pp xvii, 306.
6. Jameson, H.B., 'Bonded servants on the North American continent in the eighteenth century: some new evidence from Bristol,' *Bristol & Gloucestershire Arch. Soc. T.* 99 (1982 for 1981), 127–40.
7. Jones, G.H., 'La Gran Bretagna e la destinazione di Don Carlos al trono di Toscana (1721–1732),' *Archivio Storico Italiano* 140 (1982), 47–82.
8. Philip, P. *British residents at the Cape 1795–1819: biographical records of 4800 pioneers.* Cape Town; David Philip; 1981. Pp xxiii, 484.
9. Geggus, D., 'British opinion and the emergence of Haiti 1791–1805,' Bc20, 123–49.
10. Nordmann, C., 'Choiseul and the last Jacobite attempt of 1759,' Bc22, 201–17.
11. Smith, L.B., 'Spain and the Jacobites, 1715–16,' Bc22, 159–78.
12. Berlatsky, J., 'British imperial attitudes in the early modern era: the case of Charles Ware Malet in India,' *Albion* 14 (1982), 139–52.
13. Dunthorne, H., 'British travellers in eighteenth-century Holland: tourism and the appreciation of Dutch culture,' *British J. for Eighteenth-Century Studies* 5 (1982), 77–84.
14. Tażbierski, Z., 'Europejska polityka Williama Pitta w okresie rozbiorów [William Pitt's European policy in the age of the partitions],' *Kwartalnik Historyczny* 88 (1981), 647–56.

(e) *Religion*

1. Barrie, V., 'Récherche sur la vie religieuse en Angleterre au dix-huitième siècle,' *Revue Historique* 540 (1981), 339–79.
2. Bates, E.R., 'Eighteenth-century chalices in Bath Methodism,' *P. of the Wesley Historical Soc.* 43 (1981), 29–30.
3. Boulton, D.J., 'Women and early Methodism,' ibid. 13–17.
4. Vickers, A.V., 'The John Wesley's Conversion Place Memorial,' ibid. 27–8.
5. Baker, F. (ed.). *The works of John Wesley, vol. 26: Letters, vol. 2, 1740–1755.* Oxford; Clarendon; 1982. Pp xx, 684.
6. Bellenger, D., 'The king's house, Winchester, 1792–96,' *Downside R.* 100 (1982), 101–9.
7. Duffy, E. (ed.). *Challoner and his church: a catholic bishop in*

Georgian England. London; Darton, Longman & Todd; 1981. Pp x, 203.

8. Guy, J.R., 'Eighteenth-century Gwent catholics,' *Recusant History* 16 (1982), 78–88.
9. Noulton, H.K., 'A Methodist family: ministerial succession and intermarriage,' *P. of the Wesley Historical Soc.* 43 (1981), 49–58.
10. Vickers, J.A., 'John Wesley's third London chapel,' ibid. 59–61.
11. Alsop, J.D., 'Manuscript evidence on the Quakers' Bill of 1722,' *J. of the Friends' Historical Soc.* 54 (1980), 255–7.
12. Doe, V.S. (ed.). *The diary of James Clegg of Chapel en le Frith 1708–1755, part 3: 1748–1755.* Derbyshire Record Soc. vol. 5; 1981. Pp 672–1026.
13. Elliott, B., 'The return of the Cistercians to the Midlands,' *Recusant History* 16 (1982), 99–104.
14. Hodgett, G.A.J., 'The Shacketons of Ballitore,' *J. of the Friends' Historical Soc.* 54 (1980), 217–34.
15. Sager, E.W., 'Religious sources of English pacifism from the Enlightenment to the Industrial Revolution,' *Canadian J. of History* 17 (1982), 1–26.
16. Tranter, M., 'Landlords, labourers, local preachers: rural nonconformity in Derbyshire, 1772–1851,' *Derbyshire Arch. J.* 101 (1981), 110–38.
17. Bell, A., 'Warden Huntingford and the old conservatism,' Bc6, 351–74.
18. Rattenbury, A., 'Methodism and the tatterdemalions,' Bc7, 28–61.
19. Duffy, E., ' "Englishmen in vaine": Roman Catholic allegiance to George I,' Bc10, 345–65.
20. Stafford, W., 'Religion and the doctrine of nationalism in England at the time of the French Revolution and Napoleonic wars,' Bc10, 381–95.
21. Bellenger, D.J., 'The French exiled clergy in England and national identity, 1790–1815,' Bc10, 397–407.
22. Gilley, S., 'Nationality and liberty, protestant and catholic: Robert Southey's book of the church,' Bc10, 409–32.
23. Sher, R.B., 'Moderates, managers and popular politics in mid-eighteenth-century Edinburgh: the Drysdale "bustle" of the 1760s,' Bc25, 179–209.
24. Dwyer, J., 'The heavenly city of the eighteenth-century moderate divines,' Bc25, 291–318.

(f) *Economic Affairs*

1. Barnes, T., 'Derry Ormond: some new evidence,' *National Library of Wales J.* 22 (1981), 214–25.
2. Beckett, J.V., 'Regional variation and the agricultural depression, 1730–50,' *Economic History R.* 2nd ser. 35 (1982), 35–51.

3. Carlos, A., 'The causes and origins of the North American fur trade rivalry: 1804–1810,' *J. of Economic History* 41 (1981), 777–94.
4. Duffy, I.P.H., 'The discount policy of the Bank of England during the suspension of cash payments, 1797–1821,' *Economic History R.* 2nd ser. 35 (1982), 67–82.
5. Hopkins, E., 'Working hours and the conditions during the Industrial Revolution: a re-appraisal,' ibid. 52–66.
6. Richards, E. *A history of the Highland clearances, vol. 1: Agrarian transformations and the evictions, 1746–1886.* London; Croom Helm; 1982. Pp xxii, 532.
7. Haldane, A.R.B. *The Great Fishmonger of the Tay: John Richardson of Perth & Pitfour (1760–1821).* Dundee; Abertay Historical Soc.; 1981. Pp 64.
8. Curtis, G.R., 'Roads and bridges in the Scottish Highlands: the route between Dunkeld and Inverness, 1725–1925,' *P. of the Soc. of Antiquaries of Scotland* 110 (1981 for 1978–80), 475–96.
9. Tyson, B., 'Skirwith Hall and Wilton Tenement (Kirkland Hall): the rebuilding of two Cumbrian farmsteads in the eighteenth century,' *T. of the Cumberland & Westmorland Antiquarian and Arch. Soc.* 81 (1981), 93–112.
10. Watts, M.J. & C.T., 'The Burton family of clockmakers,' ibid. 83–91.
11. Horn, P., 'An eighteenth-century land agent: the career of Nathaniel Kent (1737–1810),' *Agricultural History R.* 30 (1982), 1–16.
12. Hudson, P., 'The role of banks in the finance of the West Yorkshire wool textile industry, c. 1780–1850,' *Business History R.* 55 (1981), 379–402.
13. Inikori, J.E., 'Market structure and the profits of the British African trade in the late eighteenth century,' *J. of Economic History* 41 (1981), 745–76.
14. Schofield, R.B., 'The promotion of the Cromford Canal Act of 1789: a study in canal engineering,' *B. of the John Rylands University Library of Manchester* 64 (1981), 246–78.
15. Dyer, G.P.; Gaspar, P.P., 'The striking of proof and pattern coins in the eighteenth century,' *British Numismatic J.* 50 (1981 for 1980), 117–27.
16. Falkus, M.E., 'Early development of the British gas industry, 1790–1815,' *Economic History R.* 2nd ser. 35 (1982), 217–34.
17. Fisher, C. *Custom, work and market capitalism: the Forest of Dean colliers, 1788–1888.* London; Croom Helm; 1981. Pp xvi, 203.
18. Giggins, B.L. *Index to the fire insurance policies held at the Guildhall Library, London, covering the Milton Keynes area for the period 1710 to 1731 and the year 1793.* Milton Keynes Development Corporation; 1981. Pp 36.

19. Kennerley, E. *The Brockbanks of Lancaster: the story of an 18th century shipbuilding firm.* Lancaster Museum; 1981. Pp 27.
20. Noble, M., 'Land-tax returns and urban development,' *Local Historian* 15 (1982), 86–92.
21. Palmer, C.A. *Human cargoes: the British slave trade to Spanish America, 1700–1739.* Urbana/London; University of Illinois Press; 1981. Pp xv, 183.
22. Turnbull, G., 'Scotch linen, storms, wars and privateers: John Wilson & Son, Leeds linen merchants, 1754–1800,' *J. of Transport History* 3rd ser. 3 (1982), 47–69.
23. Turner, M., 'Arable in England and Wales: estimates from the 1801 crop return,' *J. of Historical Geography* 7 (1981), 291–302.
24. Turner, W.H.K., 'The development of flax-spinning mills in Scotland 1787–1840,' *Scottish Geographical Magazine* 98 (1982), 4–15.
25. Beresford, M.W., 'Prometheus Insured: the Sun Fire Agency in Leeds during urbanization, 1716–1826,' *Economic History R.* 2nd ser. 35 (1982), 373–89.
26. Tann, J. (ed.). *The selected papers of Boulton & Watt, vol. 1: the engine partnership.* London; Diploma; 1981. Pp xv, 425.
27. Corfield, P.J. *The impact of English towns 1700–1800.* Oxford UP; 1982. Pp vi, 206.
28. Ginter, D.E., 'A wealth of problems with the land tax,' *Economic History R.* 2nd ser. 35 (1982), 416–21. [See 32.]
29. Horn, P., 'The contribution of the propagandist to eighteenth-century agricultural improvement,' *Historical J.* 25 (1982), 313–29.
30. Musson, A.E., 'The British Industrial Revolution,' *History* 67 (1982), 252–8.
31. Smith, A.M. *Jacobite estates of the Forty-five.* Edinburgh; Donald; 1982. Pp vii, 288.
32. Wilson, G.J., 'The land tax problem,' *Economic History R.* 2nd ser. 35 (1982), 422–6.
33. Young, R., 'Following the stagecoaches,' *Local Historian* 14 (1981), 341–6.
34. Richards, E. *A history of the Highland clearances: agrarian transformation and the evictions 1746–1886.* London; Croom Helm; 1982. Pp 532.
35. Beachcroft, G., 'Balliol College accounts in the eighteenth century,' Bc14, 77–80 (+ 19 pp. of tables).
36. Greenberg, D., 'Reassessing the power patterns of the industrial revolution: an Anglo-American comparison,' *Americal Historical R.* 87 (1982), 1237–61.
37. Weatherill, L., 'Capital and credit in the pottery industry before 1770,' *Business History* 24 (1982), 243–58.
38. Payne, P.L., 'The Halbeath colliery and saltworks, 1785–1791,' Bc24, 2–34.

39. Coleman, N.E. *People, poverty and protest in Hoxne hundred 1780–1880.* Sreffing (Suffolk); 1982. Pp 83.
40. Firth, G., 'The Bradford Lime Kiln Company, 1774–1800: a pioneer of large scale industrial enterprise in Bradford,' *Bradford Antiquary* new ser. 47 (1982), 129–34.
41. Freeman, M.J. *A perspective on the geography of English internal trade during the industrial revolution: the trading economy of the textile district of Yorkshire circa 1800.* Oxford; School of Geography; 1982. Pp 36.
42. Long, W.H., 'Some notes on the size of fields after enclosure,' *Yorkshire Arch. J.* 54 (1982), 141–7.
43. McKendrick, N.; Brewer, J.; Plumb, J.H. *The birth of a consumer society: the commercialization of eighteenth-century England.* Bloomington; Indiana UP; 1982. Pp x, 345.
44. Patrick, J. *The coming of turnpikes to Aberdeenshire.* Aberdeen; King's College; 1982. Pp 55.
45. Turner, M., 'Agricultural productivity in England in the eighteenth century: evidence from crop yields,' *Economic History R.* 2nd ser. 35 (1982), 489–510.
46. Wordie, J.A. *Estate management in eighteenth-century England: the building of the Leveson-Gower fortune.* London; Royal Historical Soc. (Studies in History 30); 1982. Pp 303.

(g) *Social Structure and Population*

1. Schwarz, L.D., 'Social class and social geography: the middle classes in London at the end of the eighteenth century,' *Social History* 7 (1982), 167–85.
2. Owen, W.S.; Walton, M. (ed.). *The parish register of Sheffield, vol. 6: 1720–1736.* Yorkshire Arch. Soc.; 1981. Pp viii, 384.
3. Lindert, P.H.; Williamson, J.G., 'Revising England's social tables 1688–1812,' *Explorations in Economic History* 19 (1982), 385–408.
4. Bushaway, R.W., 'Ceremony, custom and ritual: some observations on social conflict in the rural community, 1750–1850,' Bc12, 9–29.
5. Clarke, T.; Dickson, T., 'Class and class consciousness in early industrial capitalism: Paisley 1770–1850,' Bc18, 8–60.
6. Floud, R.; Wachter, K.W., 'Poverty and physical stature: evidence on the standard of living of London boys 1770–1870,' *Social Science History* 6 (1982), 422–52.
7. Higman, B.W., 'Slavery and the development of demographic theory in the age of the industrial revolution,' Bc20, 164–94.
8. Lewis, L., 'A shoemaker's notes on a Georgian town,' Bc26, 292–303.
9. Marmoy, C.F.A. (ed.). *The case book of 'La maison de charité de Spittlefields' 1739–41.* London; Huguenot Soc.; 1981. Pp viii, 83.

10. Saito, O., 'Labour supply behaviour of the poor in the English industrial revolution,' *J. of European Economic History* 10 (1981), 633–52.
11. Beveridge, C., 'Childhood and society in eighteenth-century Scotland,' Bc25, 265–90.

(h) *Naval and Military*

1. Hickey, D.R., 'American trade restrictions during the War of 1812,' *J. of American History* 68 (1981), 517–38.
2. Houlding, J.A. *Fit for service: the training of the British Army, 1715–1795.* Oxford; Clarendon; 1981. Pp xxi, 459.
3. Howard-Vyse, V., 'Vice-Admiral Lord Collingwood,' *Mariner's Mirror* 68 (1982), 43–8.
4. McClary, B.H., 'Samuel Rogers' historic war story: a letter for Lady Bessborough,' *Huntington Library Q.* 44 (1981), 223–5.
5. Mayne, R. *The battle of Jersey.* London; Phillimore; 1981. Pp xii, 116.
6. Scott, B.W., 'The true identity of John Adams [of the *Bounty*],' *Mariner's Mirror* 68 (1982), 31–9.
7. Swanson, C.E., 'The profitability of privateering: reflections on British colonial privateers during the war of 1776–1783,' *American Neptune* 42 (1982), 36–59.
8. Thomas, E.G., 'Captain Buckle and the capture of the Glorioso,' *Mariner's Mirror* 68 (1982), 49–56.
9. Burley, P., 'Fighting for the Falklands in 1770,' *History Today* 32/6 (1982), 49–51.
10. Keppel, S. *Three brothers at Havana, 1762.* Salisbury; Michael Russell; 1981. Pp 120.
11. Cobbe, H. *Cook's voyages and peoples of the Pacific.* London; British Museum Publications; 1979. Pp 143.
12. Geggus, D., 'The British Army and the slave revolt: St Dominique in the 1790s,' *History Today* 32 (1982), 35–9.
13. Annand, A.M., 'Lord Pitsligo's horse in the army of Prince Charles Edward, 1745–6,' *J. of the Soc. for Army Historical Research* 60 (1982), 226–35.
14. Arnold, J.R., 'A reappraisal of column versus line in the Napoleonic wars,' ibid. 196–208.
15. Coad, J., 'Medway House, Chatham Dockyard,' Bc26, 273–87.
16. Spinney, J.D., 'Rodney and the Saints: a reassessment,' *Mariner's Mirror* 68 (1982), 377–89.
17. Steppler, G.A., 'British military artificers in Canada, 1760–1815,' *J. of the Soc. for Army Historical Research* 60 (1982), 150–63.

(i) *Intellectual and Cultural*

1. Binfield, C. (ed.). *Sir Francis Chantrey: sculptor to an age, 1781–1841.* University of Sheffield; 1981. Pp 103.

2. Cole, R.C., 'Samuel Johnson and the eighteenth-century Irish book trade,' *Papers of the Bibliographical Soc. of America* 75 (1981), 235–55.
3. Cookson, J.E. *The Friends of Peace: anti-war liberalism in England, 1793–1815.* Cambridge UP; 1982. Pp vi, 330.
4. Cunningham, H. *Leisure in the industrial revolution.* London; Croom Helm; 1980. Pp 222.
5. Hapgood, K., 'Library practice in the Bristol Library Society 1772–1830,' *Library History* 5 (1981), 145–53.
6. Miller, D. *Philosophy and ideology in Hume's political thought.* Oxford; Clarendon; 1982. Pp xii, 218.
7. Morrish, P.S., 'Foreign-language books in some Yorkshire subscription libraries, 1785–1805,' *Yorkshire Arch. J.* 53 (1981), 79–92.
8. Coad, J., 'Historic architecture of Chatham dockyard, 1700–1850,' *Mariner's Mirror* 68 (1982), 133–88.
9. Daiches, D. *Literature and gentility in Scotland.* Edinburgh UP; 1982. Pp 120.
10. David, R.G., 'The ice-houses of Cumbria,' *T. of the Cumberland and Westmorland Antiquarian and Arch. Soc.* 81 (1981), 137–55.
11. Feather, J., 'Country book trade apprentices 1710–1760,' *Publishing History* 6 (1982 for 1979), 85–99.
12. Hamilton-Phillips, M., 'Benjamin West and William Beckford: some projects for Fonthill,' *Metropolitan Museums J.* 15 (1981 for 1980), 157–74.
13. Harris, M., 'London printers and newspaper production during the first half of the eighteenth century,' *J. of the Printing Historical Soc.* 12 (for 1977–8), 33–51.
14. Horne, T.A., 'Envy and commercial society: Mandeville and Smith on "private vices, public benefits",' *Political Theory* 9 (1981), 551–69.
15. James, M., 'Public interest and majority rule in Bentham's democratic theory,' ibid. 49–64.
16. Standen, E.A., 'English tapestries "after the Indian manner",' *Metropolitan Museums J.* 15 (1981 for 1980), 119–42.
17. Searle, A., ' "A pleasing example of skill in old age": Sir Christopher Wren and Marlborough House,' *British Library J.* 8 (1982), 36–45.
18. Steen, P., 'Spas: pleasure or penance,' *History Today* 31/9 (1981), 21–6.
19. Stoker, D., 'The Norwich book trades before 1800,' *T. of the Cambridge Bibliographical Soc.* 8 (1981), 79–125.
20. Wright, C.J., 'Some unpublished correspondence of Sir Richard Steele,' *British Library J.* 8 (1982), 80–93.
21. Campbell, R.H.; Skinner, A.S. *Adam Smith.* London; Croom Helm; 1982. Pp 231.

22. Lowndes, W. *The Royal Crescent in Bath: a fragment of English life.* Bristol; Redcliffe; 1981. Pp 96.
23. Mackerness, E.D., 'The harvest of failure: Ebenezer Rhodes (1762–1839),' *Derbyshire Arch. J.* 101 (1981), 107–18.
24. Pottle, F.A. *Pride and negligence: the history of the Boswell papers.* New York/London; McGraw-Hill; 1982. Pp xiv, 290.
25. Rajnai, M. (ed.). *John Sell Cotman 1782–1842.* London; Herbert Press; 1982. Pp 160.
26. Rivers, I. *Books and their readers in eighteenth-century England.* Leicester UP; 1982. Pp xi, 267.
27. Smith, H.R. *David Garrick, 1717–1779.* London; British Library; 1979. Pp 80.
28. Withers, C.J., 'Gaelic-speaking in a Highland parish: Port of Menteith 1724–1725,' *Scottish Geographical Magazine* 98 (1982), 16–22.
29. Adams, B., 'A Regency pastime: the extra-illustration of Thomas Penant's "London",' *London J.* 8 (1982), 123–39.
30. Jones, J., 'Sound religion and useful learning: the rise of Balliol under John Parsons and Richard Jenkyns,' Bc14, 89–124.
31. Gembruch, W., 'Zum England-Bild des Freiherrn vom Stein,' Bc19, 27–47.
32. Seier, H., 'Heeren und England,' Bc19, 48–78.
33. Erskine-Hill, H., 'Literature and the Jacobite cause: was there a rhetoric of Jacobitism?,' Bc22, 49–69.
34. Clarke, M.; Penny, N. (ed.). *The arrogant connoisseur: Richard Payne Knight 1751–1824.* Manchester UP; 1982. Pp x, 189.
35. Jones, P., 'The Polite Academy and the presbyterians 1720–1770,' Bc25, 156–78.
36. Councer, C., 'A child of his time: canon Arthur St. Leger,' Bc26 (pages lost).
37. Teichgraeber, R., 'Rethinking *Das Adam Smith Problem*,' Bc25, 249–64 [reprint of (1982) Gi49].
38. Little, B., 'James Gibbs: architect,' *History Today* 32/12 (1982), 40–4.
39. Norton, D.F. *David Hume: common-sense moralist, sceptical metaphysician.* Princeton UP; 1982. Pp xii, 329.
40. Not used.
41. Thompson, N.W. *Malthus and the problems of economic development.* Swansea; University College; 1981. Pp 10.
42. Watkin, D. *Athenian Stuart: pioneer of the Greek revival.* London; Allen & Unwin; 1982. Pp 70, + 46 of plates.
43. Wenz, P.S., 'Berkeley's two concepts of impossibility: a reply to McKim,' *J. of the History of Ideas* 43 (1982), 673–80.
44. Ihde, H., 'Thomas Paine und sein Einfluss auf die revolutionäre Bewegung,' *Zeitschrift für Geschichtswissenschaft* 29 (1981), 144–8.
45. Campbell, R.H.; Skinner, A.S. (ed.). *The origins and nature of the*

Scottish Enlightenment: essays. Edinburgh; Donald; 1982. Pp vii, 231.

46. Campbell, R.H., 'The Enlightenment and the economy,' Gi45, 8–25.
47. Devine, T.M., 'The Scottish merchant community, 1680–1740,' Gi45, 26–41.
48. Cant, R.G., 'Origins of the Enlightenment in Scotland: the universities,' Gi45, 42–63.
49. Shepherd, C.M., 'Newtonianism in Scottish universities in the seventeenth century,' Gi45, 65–85.
50. Chitnis, R.C., 'Provost Drummond and the origins of Edinburgh medicine,' Gi45, 86–97.
51. Donovan, A.L., 'William Cullen and the research tradition of eighteenth-century Scottish chemistry,' Gi45, 98–114.
52. Cameron, J.K., 'Theological controversy: a factor in the origins of the Scottish Enlightenment,' Gi45, 116–30.
53. Sutherland, S.R., 'The presbyterian inheritance of Hume and Reid,' Gi45, 131–49.
54. MacCormick, N., 'Law and Enlightenment,' Gi45, 150–66.
55. Campbell, T.D., 'Francis Hutcheson, "father" of the Scottish Enlightenment,' Gi45, 167–85.
56. Forbes, D., 'Natural law and the Scottish Enlightenment,' Gi45, 186–204.
57. Haakonssen, K., 'What might properly be called natural jurisprudence,' Gi45, 205–25.
58. Payne, H.C. *Studies in eighteenth-century culture, vol. 11.* Madison; University of Wisconsin Press; 1982. Pp 399.
59. Atherton, H.M., 'The British defend their constitution in political cartoons and literature,' Gi58, 3–31.
60. Campbell, T.D.; Ross, I., 'The theory and practice of the wise and virtuous man: reflections on Adam Smith's response to Hume's deathbed wish,' Gi58, 65–74.
61. Myers, M., 'Reform or ruin: "A revolution in female manners" [Mary Wollstonecraft],' Gi58, 199–216.
62. Sloan, K., 'Drawing – a "polite recreation" in eighteenth-century England,' Gi58, 217–40.
63. Staves, S., 'Money for honour: damages for criminal conversation [the law and adultery],' Gi58, 279–97.
64. Svilpin, J.E., 'Johnson, humanism and "the last great revolution of the intellectual world",' Gi58, 299–310.
65. Turner, J.G., 'The sexual politics of landscape: images of Venus in eighteenth-century English poetry and landscape gardening,' Gi58, 343–66.
66. Stone, G.W. (ed.). *The stage and the page: London's 'whole show' in the eighteenth-century theatre.* Berkeley/London; University of California Press; 1981. Pp x, 251.
67. Hume, R.D., 'The multifarious forms of eighteenth-century comedy,' Gi66, 3–32.

68. Loftis, J., 'Thomson's *Tancred* and *Sigismunda*, and the demise of the drama of political opposition,' Gi66, 33–54.
69. Hughes, L., 'Afterpieces: or, That's entertainment,' Gi66, 55–70.
70. Mullen, D.C., 'Theatre structure and its effect on production,' Gi66, 73–89.
71. Allen, R.G., 'Irrational entertainment in the age of reason,' Gi66, 90–112.
72. Stone, G.W., 'The prevalence of theatrical music in Garrick's time,' Gi66, 116–22.
73. Knapp, J.M., 'English theatrical music in Garrick's time: *The Enchanter* (1760) and *May Day* (1775),' Gi66, 123–35.
74. Dircks, P.T., 'Garrick's fail-safe musical venture, *A Peep Behind the Curtain*, an English burletta,' Gi66, 136–47.
75. Lincoln, S., 'Barthelmon's setting of Garrick's *Orpheus*,' Gi66, 148–59.
76. Shattuck, C.H., 'Drama as promptbook,' Gi66, 163–91.
77. Wynne, S., 'Reviving the gesture sign: bringing the dance back alive,' Gi66, 192–208.
78. Beckerman, B., 'Schemes and shows: a search for critical norms,' Gi66, 209–28.
79. Hume, R.D. (ed.). *The London theatre world, 1660–1800.* Carbondale; Southern Illinois UP; 1980. Pp xix, 394.
80. Milhous, J., 'Company management,' Gi79, 1–34.
81. Langhans, E.A., 'The theatres,' Gi79, 35–65.
82. Visser, C., 'Scenery and technical design,' Gi79, 66–118.
83. Hughes, L., 'The evidence of the promptbooks,' Gi79, 119–42.
84. Highfill, P.H., 'Performers and performing,' Gi79, 143–80.
85. Stone, G.W., 'The making of the repertory,' Gi79, 181–209.
86. Price, C.A., 'Music as drama,' Gi79, 210–35.
87. Dedicord, H.W., 'The changing audience,' Gi79, 236–52.
88. Loftis, J., 'Political and social thought in the drama,' Gi79, 253–85.
89. Winton, C., 'Dramatic censorship,' Gi79, 286–308.
90. Kenny, S.S., 'The publication of plays,' Gi79, 309–36.
91. Donohue, J., 'The London theatre at the end of the eighteenth century,' Gi79, 337–72.

(j) *Science*

1. Coley, N.G., 'Physicians and the chemical analysis of mineral waters in eighteenth-century England,' *Medical History* 26 (1982), 123–44.
2. Harley, J.B.; Dunning, R.W. *Somerset maps: Day & Masters 1782, Greenwood 1822.* Taunton; Somerset Record Soc.; 1981.
3. Sigsworth, E.M.; Swan, P., 'An eighteenth-century surgeon and apothecary: William Elmhirst (1721–1773),' *Medical History* 26 (1982), 191–8.

4. Waites, B., 'Thomas Barker of Lyndon: eighteenth-century weatherman,' *Local Historian* 15 (1982), 70–2.
5. Beckett, J.V., 'An eighteenth-century case history: Carlisle Spedding 1738,' *Medical History* 26 (1982), 303–6.
6. Debus, A.G., 'Scientific truth and occult tradition: the medical world of Ebenezer Sibly (1751–1799),' ibid. 259–78.
7. Quist, G. *John Hunter 1728–1793.* London; Heinemann Medical; 1981. Pp xvi, 216.
8. Guy, J.R., 'Archbishop Secker as a physician,' Bc21, 127–35.
9. Rack, H.D., 'Doctors, demons and early Methodist healing,' Bc21, 137–52.
10. Champ, J.F., 'Bishop Milner, Holywell, and the cure tradition,' Bc21, 153–64.
11. Lineham, P.J., 'Restoring man's creative power: the theosophy of the Bible Christians of Salford,' Bc21, 207–23.
12. Cave, K. (ed.). *The diary of Joseph Faringdon, vols. 7/8 & 9/10.* New Haven/London; Yale UP; 1982. Pp 720, 664.
13. Fores, M., 'Technical change and the "technology" myth,' *Scandinavian Economic History R.* 30 (1982), 167–88.

H. BRITAIN 1815–1914

See also Gc5, e9, f4, 6, 8, 12, 17, 20, 34, g6, i1; Ia3, b28, e3, 4, f26, 29, 37, 40, h37, 38, j5, 7, 10, 14, 18

(a) *General*

1. Denes, G. *Story of the 'Imperial': the life and times of Torquay's great hotel.* Newton Abbot; David & Charles; 1982. Pp 158.
2. Stuart, D. *Dear Duchess: Millicent, duchess of Sutherland, 1867–1955.* London; Gollancz; 1982. Pp 215.
3. Cannadine, D., 'War and death, grief and mourning in modern Britain,' *Mirrors of mortality: studies in the social history of death*, ed. J. Whaley (London; Europa Publications; 1981), 187–242.
4. Silto, J. *A Swindon history 1840–1901.* Swindon; the author; 1981. Pp 109.
5. McCord, N., 'The making of modern Newcastle,' *Archaeologia Aeliana* 5th ser. 9 (1981), 333–46.
6. Brown, J.H. *The valley of the shadow: an account of Britain's worst mining disaster, the Senghenydd explosion.* Port Talbot; Alun Books; 1981. Pp 171.
7. Burnett, Mr. *A passenger's diary of a voyage from London to New Zealand, 1850–1851.* Workington & District Local History Soc.; 1981. Pp 30.

8. Padfield, P. *Beneath the house flag of the P. & O.* London; Hutchinson; 1981. Pp 148.
9. Black, E.C. *Feminists, liberalism and morality: the unresolvable triangle.* London; LLRS; 1981. Pp 41.
10. Sinclair, A. *The other Victoria: the Princess Royal and the great game of Europe.* London; Weidenfeld; 1981. Pp 282.
11. Mudd, D. *The Cornish Edwardians.* Bodmin; Bossiney; 1981. Pp 120.
12. Johnson, I. *Turning point: the story of Kirby le Soken, Essex, 1823 to 1862.* London; Regency Press; 1981. Pp 115.
13. Jones, I.G. *The valleys in the mid-nineteenth century: a lecture.* Standing Conference on the History of the South Wales Valleys; 1981. Pp 30.
14. Taylor, A. *Laurence Oliphant, 1829–1888.* Oxford UP; 1981. Pp xi, 306.
15. Braydon, S.; Songhurst, R. (ed.). *The diary of Joseph Sams: an emigrant in the 'Northumberland' 1874.* London; HSSO; 1982. Pp viii, 102.
16. Wood, A. *Nineteenth century Britain: 1815–1914* (2nd ed.). Harlow; Longman; 1982. Pp viii, 470.
17. Authers, W.P. (ed.). *Diary of a Devonshire squire, 1844: the journal of John Were Clarke, esquire, of Bridwell, Uffculme.* Tiverton; the editor; 1982. Pp 48.
18. Matthew, H.C.G. (ed.). *The Gladstone diaries with cabinet minutes and prime-ministerial correspondence, vols 7 (1869–June 1871) and 8 (July 1871–Dec. 1874).* Oxford: Clarendon; 1982. Pp 642, 618.
19. Gunn, J.A.W. (ed.). *Benjamin Disraeli – letters, 1815–1834.* University of Toronto Press; 1982. Pp lxviii, 482.
20. Doyle, P., 'Bishop Goss of Liverpool (1856–1872) and the importance of being English,' Bc10, 433–47.
21. Bebbington, D.W., 'Religion and national feeling in nineteenth-century Wales and Scotland,' Bc10, 489–503.
22. Aspinwall, B., 'The Scottish religious identity in the Atlantic world 1880–1914,' Bc10, 505–18.
23. Binfield, C., 'English free churchmen and a national style,' Bc10, 519–33.
24. Blatchly, J. (ed.). *A journal of excursions through the county of Suffolk 1823–1844, by David Elisha Davy.* Woodbridge; Boydell; 1982 (Suffolk Records Soc. vol. 24). Pp ix, 245.
25. Neal, F., 'The Birkenhead Garibaldi riots of 1862,' *T. of the Historic Soc. of Lancashire and Cheshire* 131 (1982 for 1981), 87–111.

(b) *Politics*

1. Bebbington, D. *The nonconformist conscience.* London; Allen & Unwin; 1982. Pp 192.
2. Scotland, N., 'Rural war in late Victorian Norfolk,' *Norfolk Archaeology* 38 (1981), 82–7.
3. Davis, R.W., 'The tories, the whigs, and Catholic Emancipation, 1827–1829,' *English Historical R.* 97 (1982), 89–98.
4. Fisher, J.R., 'The limits of deference: agricultural communities in a mid-nineteenth century campaign,' *J. of British Studies* 21 (1981), 90–105.
5. Kinzer, B.L., 'J.S. Mill and the problem of party,' ibid. 106–22.
6. Hill, J., 'Manchester and Salford politics and the early development of the Independent Labour Party,' *International R. of Social History* 26 (1981), 171–201.
7. Gash, N., 'The tortoise and the hare: Liverpool and Canning,' *History Today* 32/3 (1982), 12–19.
8. Walthew, K., 'Captain Manby and the conflagration of the palace of Westminster,' *History Today* 32/4 (1982), 21–5.
9. Not used.
10. Jones, I.G. *Explorations and explanations: essays in the social history of Victorian Wales.* Gwasg Gomer; 1981. Pp 338.
11. Hempton, D.N., 'Thomas Allan and the Methodist politics, 1800–1840,' *History* 67 (1982), 13–31.
12. Broeze, F.J.A., 'Private enterprise and the peopling of Australasia, 1831–50,' *Economic History R.* 2nd ser. 35 (1982), 235–53.
13. Parry, J.P., 'Religion and the collapse of Gladstone's first government, 1870–1874,' *Historical J.* 25 (1982), 71–101.
14. McGill, B., 'Glittering prizes and party funds in perspective, 1882–1931,' *B. of the Institute of Historical Research* 55 (1982), 88–93.
15. Gordon, P. (ed.). *The Red Earl: the papers of the fifth earl Spencer, 1835–1910; vol. I: 1835–1885.* Northamptonshire Record Soc. vol. 31; 1981. Pp xi, 328.
16. Rossi, J., 'Catholic opinion on the Eastern Question, 1876–1878,' *Church History* 51 (1982), 54–70.
17. Ball, A.R. *British political parties: the emergence of the modern party system.* London; Macmillan; 1981. Pp xiv, 292.
18. Denholm, A.F., 'Lord Ripon and Liberal party policy in Southern Africa 1892–1902,' *Australian J. of Politics and History* 27 (1982), 232–40.
19. Thomis, M.I. *Women in protest 1800–1850.* London; Croom Helm; 1982. Pp 166.
20. Claeys, G., 'Benjamin Scott Jones, alias "Philadelphus": an early Owenite socialist,' *B. of the Soc. for the Study of Labour History* 43 (1981), 14–15.
21. Fair, J.D. *British interparty conferences: a study of the procedure*

of conciliation in British politics, 1867–1921. Oxford; Clarendon; 1980. Pp xi, 354.

22. Goodway, D. *London Chartism, 1838–1848.* Cambridge UP; 1982. Pp xviii, 333.
23. Hogarth, C.E., 'Derby and Derbyshire elections, 1852–1865,' *Derbyshire Arch. J.* 101 (1981), 151–72.
24. Shannon, R. *Gladstone and Swansea 1887* [inaugural lecture]. Swansea; University College; 1982. Pp 15.
25. Kennedy, P.M.; Nicholls, A. (ed.). *Nationalist and racialist movements in Britain and Germany before 1814.* London; Macmillan; 1981. Pp xi, 210.
26. Kennedy, P.M., 'The pre-war Right in Britain and Germany,' Hb25, 1–20.
27. Searle, G., 'The revolt from the right in Edwardian Britain,' Hb25, 21–39.
28. Summers, A., 'The character of Edwardian nationalism,' Hb25, 68–87.
29. Lebzelter, G.C., 'Anti-semitism: a focal point for the British radical right,' Hb25, 88–105.
30. Rohe, K., 'The British imperialist intelligentsia and the *Kaiserreich*,' Hb25, 130–42.
31. Woodroffe, M., 'Racial theories of history and politics: the example of Houston Stewart Chamberlain,' Hb25, 143–53.
32. Fest, W., 'Jingoism and xenophobia in the electioneering strategies of British ruling elites before 1914,' Hb25, 171–89.
33. Mock, W., 'The function of race in imperialist ideologies: the example of Joseph Chamberlain,' Hb25, 190–203.
34. Young, K.; Garside, P.L. *Metropolitan London: politics and urban change, 1837–1981.* London; Arnold; 1982. Pp xiv, 401.
35. Beales, D.E.D., 'Gladstone and his diary: "Myself, the worst of all interlocutors" [review article],' *Historical J.* 25 (1982), 463–9.
36. Denholm, A.F. *Lord Ripon, 1827–1909: a political biography.* London; Croom Helm; 1982. Pp 287.
37. D'Arcy, F.A., 'Charles Bradlaugh and the English republican movement, 1868–1878,' *Historical J.* 25 (1982), 367–83.
38. Paris, M., 'Contestation ou consolidation du pouvoir? Aspects de la manipulation de thèmes traditionels dans la satire politique (Londres 1819–20),' *History of European Ideas* 3 (1982), 273–80.
39. De Rosa, P.L., 'The "Curragh Mutiny" and the House of Lords,' *Eire-Ireland* 17/2 (1982), 104–20.
40. Wilson, G.M. *Alexander McDonald: leader of the miners.* Aberdeen UP; 1982. Pp
41. Cromwell, V., 'Mapping the political world of 1861: a multidimensional analysis of House of Commons division lists,' *Legislative Studies Q.* 7 (1982), 281–97.

42. Wigley, J., 'Derby and Derbyshire during the Great Reform Bill crisis, 1830–1832,' *Derbyshire Arch. J.* 101 (1981), 139–50.
43. Morgan, T. *Churchill.* London; Cape; 1982. Pp 576.
44. *The diary of Beatrice Webb, 1: 1873–1892.* London; Virago; 1982. Pp 416.
45. Creigh, S.W., 'The origins of British strike statistics,' *Business History* 24 (1982), 95–106.
46. Kesner, R.M. *Economic control and colonial development: crown colony financial management in the age of Joseph Chamberlain.* Oxford; Clio; 1981. Pp xvii, 305.
47. Epstein, J. *The lion of freedom: Feargus O'Connor and the Chartist movement, 1832–1842.* London; Croom Helm; 1982. Pp viii, 327.
48. Richter, D.C. *Riotous Victorians.* Athens/London; Ohio UP; 1981. Pp xi, 185.
49. Shannon, R. *Gladstone; vol. 1: 1809–1865.* London; Hamilton; 1982.
50. Brooke, J.; Sorenson, M. (ed.). *W.E. Gladstone [Prime Ministers' papers series]: 4, autobiographical memoranda 1868–1894.* London; HMSO; 1981. Pp viii, 165.
51. Rice, C.D. *The Scots abolitionists 1833–1861.* Baton Rouge/ London; Louisiana State UP; 1981. Pp xii, 221.
52. O'Neill, C.F., 'The "contest for dominion": political conflict and decline of the Lowther "interest" in Whitehaven, 1820–1900,' *Northern History* 18 (1982), 133–52.
53. Purdue, A.W., 'Jarrow politics, 1885–1914: the challenge to Liberal hegemony,' ibid. 182–98.
54. Montgomery, F.A., 'Glasgow and the struggle for parliamentary reform,' *Scottish Historical R.* 61 (1982), 130–45.
55. Laqueur, T.W., 'The Queen Caroline affair: politics as art in the reign of George IV,' *J. of Modern History* 54 (1982), 417–66.
56. Claeys, G., 'A utopian tory revolutionary at Cambridge: the political ideas and schemes of James Bernard,' *Historical J.* 25 (1982), 583–603.
57. Skinner, J.T., 'The Liberal nomination controversy in Manchester, 1847,' *B. of the Institute of Historical Research* 55 (1982), 215–18.
58. Fletcher, R., 'British radicalism and German revisionism: the case of Eduard Bernstein,' *International History R.* 4 (1982), 339–70.
59. Pelling, H., 'The politics of the Osborne judgment,' *Historical J.* 25 (1982), 889–909.
60. Holmes, C., 'The Tredegar riots of 1911: anti-Jewish disturbances in south Wales,' *Welsh History R.* 11 (1982), 214–25.
61. Brock, M., ' "The eternal lack of motive": Raymond Asquith's buried talents,' Bc6, 479–88.
62. Hildebrand, K., 'Lord Clarendon, Bismarck und das Problem der

europäischen Abrüstung 1870. Möglichkeiten und Grenzen im britisch-preussischen Verhältnis am Vorabend des deutsch-französischen Krieges,' Bc19, 130–52.

63. Fladeland, B., ' "Our cause being one and the same": abolitionists and chartism,' Bc20, 69–99.
64. Dutton, H.I., ' "A fallacy, a delusion, and a snare": arbitration and conciliation in the Preston strike, 1853–4,' *T. of the Historic Soc. of Lancashire and Cheshire* 131 (1982 for 1981), 63–85.
65. Corp, E.T., 'A problem of promotion in the career of Sir Eyre Crow, 1905–20,' *Australian J. of Politics and History* 28 (1982), 236–49.
66. Bourne, K. *Palmerston: the early years 1784–1841.* London; Allen Lane; 1982. Pp xiv, 749.

(c) *Constitution, Administration and Law*

1. Cosgrove, R.A., 'The reception of analytic jurisprudence: the Victorian debate on the separation of law and morality, 1860–1900,' *Durham University J.* 74 (1982), 47–56.
2. Orth, J.V., 'English law and striking workmen: the Molestation of Workmen Act, 1859,' *J. of Legal History* 2 (1981), 238–57.
3. Parry, C.R., 'The General Post Office's Zanzibar shipping contracts, 1860–1914,' *Mariner's Mirror* 68 (1982), 57–67.
4. Tulloch, H., 'A.V. Dicey and the Irish question,' *Irish Jurist* 15/1 (1980), 137–65.
5. Dickson, R., 'Legal aspects of the Factory Act of 1856,' *J. of Legal History* 2 (1981), 276–84.
6. Smith, H., 'Judges and the lagging laws of compensation for personal injuries in the nineteenth century,' ibid. 258–75.
7. Weston, C.C., 'Salisbury and the Lords, 1868–1895,' *Historical J.* 25 (1982), 103–29.
8. Lilley, R.C., 'Attempts to implement the Bryce Commission's recommendations – and the consequences,' *History of Education* 11 (1982), 99–111.
9. Davies, E.R. *A history of the first Berkshire County Council.* Reading; County Secretariat; 1981. Pp 427.
10. Shanley, M.L., ' "One must ride behind": married women's rights and the divorce act of 1857,' *Victorian Studies* 25 (1982), 355–76.
11. Smith, P.J., 'The legislated control of river pollution in Victorian Scotland,' *Scottish Geographical Magazine* 98 (1982), 66–76.
12. Not used.
13. Pellew, J. *The Home Office 1848–1914: from clerks to bureaucrats.* London; Heinemann; 1982. Pp xi, 271.
14. Dickinson, F. (ed.). *Index to wills and administrations formerly*

preserved in the Probate Registry, Chester, 1834–1837. Record Soc. of Lancashire and Cheshire; 1980. Pp viii, 219.

15. Martin, G., 'Confederation rejected: the British debate on Canada, 1837–1840,' *J. of Imperial and Commonwealth History* 11 (1982), 33–57.
16. Strachan, H., 'Lord Grey and imperial defence,' Ic5, 1–23.
17. Bruce, A., 'Edward Cardwell and the abolition of purchase,' Ic5, 24–46.
18. Mayes, G.J., 'A poaching incident at Sudborough, 1837,' *Northamptonshire Past and Present* 6 (1982–3), 326–7.
19. Ford, T.H., 'Peterloo: the legal background,' *Durham University J.* (1982), 211–26.
20. Emsley, C., 'The Bedfordshire police 1840–1856: a case study in the working of the Rural Constabulary Act,' *Midland History* 7 (1982), 73–92.
21. Edwards, J.R.; Webb, K.M., 'The influence of company law on corporate reporting procedures, 1865–1929: an exemplification,' *Business History* 24 (1982), 259–79.
22. Hart, T., 'Urban growth and municipal government: Glasgow in a comparative context, 1846–1914,' Bc24, 193–219.

(d) *External Affairs*

1. Mahajan, S., 'The defence of India and the end of isolation: a study in the foreign policy of the Conservative government, 1900–1905,' *J. of Imperial and Commonwealth History* 10 (1982), 168–93.
2. Baumgart, W. *Imperialism: the idea and reality of British and French colonial expansion, 1880–1914.* Oxford UP; 1982. Pp 280.
3. Kohut, T.A., 'Kaiser Wilhelm II and his parents: an enquiry into the psychological roots of German policy towards England before the First World War,' *Kaiser Wilhelm II: new interpretations*, ed. J.C. Röhl and N. Sombart (Cambridge UP; 1982), 63–89.
4. Cecil, L., 'History as family chronicle: Kaiser Wilhelm II and the dynastic roots of the Anglo-German antagonism,' ibid. 91–119.
5. Steinberg, J., 'The Kaiser and the British: the state visit to Windsor, November 1907,' ibid. 121–41.
6. Danziger, C., 'The first Suez crisis,' *History Today* 32/9 (1982), 3–7.
7. Lightbown, R.W., 'Festival of India: British views of India,' ibid. 32/7 (1982), 23–7.
8. Curato, F., 'Lord Palmerston e il principe di Capua,' *Clio* 18 (1982), 78–107.
9. Morgan, G. *Anglo-Russian rivalry in central Asia: 1810–1895.* London; Cass; 1981. Pp xix, 264.

10. Hargreaves, J.D. *Aberdeenshire to Africa: northeast Scots and British overseas expansion.* Aberdeen UP; 1981. Pp viii, 95.
11. Desmond, R. *The India Museum 1801–1879.* London; HMSO; 1982. Pp xv, 215.
12. O'Mahoney, B.M.E. *Newhaven-Dieppe, 1825–1980: the history of an Anglo-French joint venture.* Wetherden; the author; 1980. Pp x, 160.
13. Corp, E.T., 'Sir William Tyrrell: the *eminence grise* of the British Foreign Office, 1912–1915,' *Historical J.* 25 (1982), 697–708.
14. Gaston, J.W.T., 'Trade and the late Victorian Foreign Office,' *International History R.* 4 (1982), 317–38.
15. *Anglo-Chinese relations, 1839–60.* Oxford UP for British Academy; 1982. Pp 398.
16. Rothschild, N.M.V. *'You have it, Madam': the purchase, in 1875, of Suez Canal shares by Disraeli and Baron Lionel de Rothschild.* London; the author; 1980. Pp 62.
17. Davis, J., 'Garibaldi and England,' *History Today* 32/12 (1982), 21–6.
18. Newbury, C., 'Cecil Rhodes and the South African connection: "A great imperial university"?,' Bc8, 75–96.
19. Lavin, D., 'Lionel Curtis and the idea of commonwealth,' Bc8, 97–121.
20. Gruner, W.D., 'Grossbritannien und die Julirevolution von 1830: Zwischen Legitimätsprinzip und nationalem Interesse,' *Francia* 9 (1982), 369–410.
21. Bucheim, C., 'Aspects of nineteenth-century Anglo-German trade rivalry reconsidered,' *J. of European Economic History* 10 (1981), 273–89.

(e) *Religion*

1. Hayes, A.J.; Gowland, D.A. (ed.). *Scottish Methodism in the early Victorian period: the Scottish correspondence of the Rev. Jabez Bunting 1800–57.* Edinburgh UP; 1981. Pp viii, 144.
2. Ker, I.T.; Gornall, T. (ed.). *The letters and diaries of John Henry Newman, vol. 4: The Oxford Movement, July 1833 to December 1834.* Oxford; Clarendon; 1980. Pp xv, 412.
3. Gilley, S., 'Vulgar piety and the Brompton Oratory, 1850–1860,' *Durham University J.* 74 (1981), 15–21.
4. Nussey, J.T.M., 'Hammond Robertson of Liversedge – bully or gentleman?,' *Yorkshire Arch. J.* 53 (1981), 97–109.
5. Dodd, V.A., 'Strauss's English propagandists and the politics of Unitarianism, 1841–1845,' *Church History* 50 (1981), 415–35.
6. MacLear, J.F., 'The idea of "American Protestantism" and British nonconformity, 1829–1840,' *J. of British Studies* 21 (1981), 68–89.
7. Matheney, M.P., 'Teaching prophet: the life and continuing

influence of Theodore Henry Robinson,' *Baptist Q.* 29 (1982), 199–216.

8. Jensen, G.E., 'A comparative study of Prussian and Anglican church-state reform in the nineteenth century,' *J. of Church and State* 23 (1981), 445–63.
9. Heeney, B., 'The beginning of Church feminism: women and the councils of the Church of England, 1897–1919,' *J. of Ecclesiastical History* 33 (1982), 89–109.
10. Frew, J., 'The "destroyer" vindicated? James Wyatt and the restoration of Henry VII's Chapel, Westminster Abbey,' *J. of the British Arch. Association* 134 (1981), 100–6.
11. Butler, P. *Gladstone: church, state and Tractarianism: a study of his religious ideas and attitudes.* Oxford; Clarendon; 1982.
12. Bellamy, V.N., 'Participation of women in the public life of the Church from Lambeth Conference 1867–1978,' *Historical Magazine of the Protestant Episcopal Church* 51 (1982), 81–98.
13. Leonard, E. *George Tyrrell and the Catholic tradition.* London; Darton, Longman & Todd; 1982. Pp 208.
14. Davies, E.T. *Religion and society in the nineteenth century.* Llandybie; Christopher Davies; 1981. Pp 100.
15. Arnstein, W. *Protestant versus catholic in mid-Victorian England: Mr Newdegate and the nuns.* Columbia/London; University of Missouri Press; 1982. Pp xii, 271.
16. Saumarez Smith, W.H., 'The growth of suffragan sees,' *Theology* 83 (1980), 424–30.
17. Holladay, J.D., '19th century evangelical activism: from private charity to state intervention, 1830–50,' *Historical Magazine of the Protestant Episcopal Church* 51 (1982), 53–79.
18. Dolbey, G.W., 'Northbrook Street church, Newbury,' *P. of the Wesley Historical Soc.* 43 (1981), 25–6.
19. Dean, W., 'The Methodist class meeting: the significance of its decline,' ibid. 41–8.
20. Machin, G.I.T., 'The last Victorian anti-ritualist campaign, 1895–1906,' *Victorian Studies* 25 (1982), 277–302.
21. Altholz, J.L., 'The mind of Victorian orthodoxy: Anglican responses to *Essays and Reviews*, 1860–1864,' *Church History* 51 (1982), 186–97.
22. Jones, I.G., 'Church reconstruction in Breconshire in the nineteenth century,' *Brycheiniog* 19 (1980–1), 7–26.
23. Johnson, D.A., 'Popular apologetics in late Victorian England: the work of the Christian Evidence Society,' *J. of Religious History* 11 (1981), 558–77.
24. Price, D.T.W., 'Kilvert and Breconshire,' *Brycheiniog* 19 (1980–1), 50–9.
25. Holladay, J.D., 'English Evangelicalism, 1820–1850: diversity and unity in "Vital Religion",' *Historical Magazine of the Protestant Episcopal Church* 51 (1982), 147–57.

26. Schultenover, D.G. *George Tyrell: in search of Catholicism.* Shepherdstown; Patmos Press; 1981. Pp xiii, 504.
27. Not used.
28. Scotland, N. *Methodism and the revolt of the field: a study of the Methodist contribution to agricultural trade unionism in East Anglia 1872–96.* Gloucester; Sutton; 1981. Pp 296.
29. Lough, A.G. *Dr. Pusey – restorer of the Church.* Newton Abbot; the author; 1981. Pp 166.
30. Stanley, B., 'C.H. Spurgeon and the Baptist Missionary Society, 1863–1866,' *Baptist Q.* 29 (1981), 319–28.
31. Not used.
32. Riden, P. *Building a parish: the history of St John the Evangelist, Newbold 1857–1982.* Newbold; the church; 1982. Pp 120.
33. Janet, R.J., 'Providence, prayer and cholera: the English general fast of 1832,' *Historical Magazine of the Protestant Episcopal Church* 51 (1982), 297–317.
34. Nimmo, D., 'Learning against religion, learning as religion; Mark Pattison and the Victorian crisis of faith,' Bc1, 311–24.
35. Walls, A.F., ' "The best thinking of the best heathen": learning and the missionary movement,' Bc1, 341–53.
36. Cockshut, A.O.J., 'Arnold, Hook, Ward: A Wiccamical sidelight on nineteenth-century religion,' Bc6, 375–402.
37. Gill, R., 'Priest and patron in a Northumberland parish,' Bc11, 146–59.
38. Pickering, W.S.F., 'The development of the diocese of Newcastle: I, An overall view; II, Battling with threatening forces,' Bc11, 104–45.
39. Milburn, G.E., 'Church-going in Northumberland in the period just prior to the foundation of the diocese [of Newcastle],' Bc11, 79–103.
40. Nicholson, M., 'A personal account of the diocese of Newcastle; I, The diocese and its bishops; II, The parishes, urban and rural,' Bc11, 53–78.
41. Jagger, P.J., 'The formation of the diocese of Newcastle,' Bc11, 24–52.
42. Hinchlift, P., 'Benjamin Jowett and the Church of England: on "why great men are never clergymen",' Bc14, 125–58.
43. Beardsley, C., 'Frederick William Robertson of Brighton: prince of preachers,' Bc17, 157–71.
44. Hennock, E.P., 'The Anglo-Catholics and church extension in Victorian Brighton,' Bc17, 173–88.
45. Briggs, A., 'The Salvation Army in Sussex 1883–1892,' Bc17, 189–208.
46. Rice, C.D., 'The missionary context of the British anti-slavery movement,' Bc20, 150–63.

47. Williams, C.P., 'Healing and evangelism: the place of medicine in later Victorian protestant missionary thinking,' Bc21, 271–85.
48. Martin, B.W. *John Henry Newman: his life and work.* London; Chatto & Windus; 1982. Pp 160.
49. Greenhalgh, D.M., 'The nineteenth century and after [at Wells cathedral],' Bc23, 179–203.

(f) *Economic Affairs*

1. Short, B., ' "The art and craft of chicken cramming": poultry in the Weald of Sussex 1850–1950,' *Agricultural History R.* 30 (1982), 17–30.
2. Nicholas, S., 'Total factor productivity growth and the revision of post-1870 British economic history,' *Economic History R.* 2nd ser. 35 (1982), 83–98.
3. Hartley, W.P., 'Springwood Colliery, Huddersfield: a portrait of a Yorkshire estate coal mine, 1862–1877,' *Yorkshire Arch. J.* 53 (1981), 93–6.
4. Redwood, C. *The Weston, Clevedon and Portishead Railway: the detailed study of an independent light railway.* Weston-super-Mare; Sequoia; 1981. Pp 183.
5. Michie, R.C. *Money, mania and markets: investment, company formation and the Stock Exchange in nineteenth-century Scotland.* Edinburgh; Donald; 1981. Pp ix, 287.
6. Kenny, S., 'Sub-regional specialization in the Lancashire cotton industry, 1884–1914: a study in organizational and locational change,' *J. of Historical Geography* 8 (1982), 41–63.
7. Gittins, L., 'Soapmaking in Britain, 1824–1851: a study in industrial location,' ibid. 29–40.
8. Buck, A. *Thomas Lester, his lace and East Midlands industry, 1820–1905.* Bedford; Ruth Bean; 1981. Pp x, 108.
9. Pollard, S., 'Sheffield and Sweet Auburn – amenities and living standards in the British industrial revolution: a comment,' *J. of Economic History* 41 (1981), 902–4. – Williamson, J.G., 'Some myths die hard – urban disamenities one more time: a reply,' ibid. 905–7.
10. Miller, C., 'The Gloucestershire Steam Plough Company, 1860–2,' *Bristol and Gloucestershire Arch. Soc. T.* 99 (1982 for 1981), 141–56.
11. Bartlett, J.N., 'Investment for survival: Culter Mills Paper Company Ltd. 1865–1914,' *Northern Scotland* 5 (1982), 31–56.
12. Springett, J., 'Landowners and urban development: the Ramsden estate and nineteenth-century Huddersfield,' *J. of Historical Geography* 8 (1982), 129–44.
13. Morris, J., 'State reform and the local economy,' *Economic*

History R. 2nd ser. 35 (1982), 292–300. – Schmiechen, J.A., 'State reform and the local economy: a reply,' ibid. 301–5.

14. Phillips, W.H., 'Induced innovation and economic performance in late Victorian British industry,' *J. of Economic History* 42 (1982), 97–103.
15. Eichengreen, B.J., 'The proximate determinants of domestic investment in Victorian Britain,' ibid. 87–95.
16. Kennedy, W.P., 'Economic growth and structural change in the United Kingdom, 1870–1914,' ibid. 105–14.
17. Moss, D.J., 'The private banks of Birmingham 1800–1827,' *Business History* 24 (1982), 79–94.
18. Timmins, J.G., 'Concentration and integration in the Sheffield crucible steel industry,' ibid. 61–78.
19. English, B., 'On the eve of the Great Depression: the economy of the Sledmere estate 1869–1878,' ibid. 24–47.
20. Harrison, A.E., 'F. Hopper & Co. – The problems of capital supply in the cycle manufacturing industry 1891–1914,' ibid. 3–23.
21. Not used.
22. Stang, G., 'Entrepreneurs and managers: the establishment and organization of British firms in Latin America in the nineteenth and early twentieth centuries,' *Historisk tidskrift* 1 (1982), 40–61.
23. Church, R., 'Markets and marketing in the British motor industry before 1914, with some French comparisons,' *J. of Transport History* 3rd ser. 3 (1982), 1–20.
24. Farnie, D.A. *The English cotton industry and the world market, 1815–1896.* Oxford; Clarendon; 1979. Pp xiii, 399.
25. Rennison, R.W. *Water to Tyneside: a history of the Newcastle and Gateshead Water Company.* The Company; 1979. Pp xx, 361.
26. Cain, P.J. *Economic foundations of English overseas expansion, 1815–1914.* London; Macmillan; 1980. Pp 85.
27. Robertson, C.H., 'John Gifford: a nineteenth-century cashier,' *Three Banks R.* 133 (1982), 50–8.
28. Moore, K.A. *The early history of freight conferences: background and main developments until around 1900.* London; National Maritime Museum; 1981. Pp ix, 73.
29. Hillier, R. *Clay that burns: a history of the Fletton brick industry.* London; London Brick Co.; 1981. Pp 100.
30. Hentschel, V., 'Produktion, Wachstum und Produktivität in England, Frankreich und Deutschland von der Mitte des 19. Jahrhunderts bis zum ersten Weltkrieg. Statistische Grenzen und Nöte beim internationalen wirtschafthistorischen Vergleich,' *Viertel jahrschrift für Sozial- und Wirtschaftsgeschichte* 68 (1981), 457–510.
31. Fernandez, M.A. *Technology and British nitrate enterprises in*

Chile, 1880–1914. Glasgow; Institute of Latin American Studies; 1981. Pp 18.

32. Anderson, R.C.; Gillham, J.C. *The tramways of East Anglia.* Broxbourne; Light Rail Transit Assoc.; 1981. Pp 65.
33. Fremdling, R., 'Britische Exporte und die Modernisierung der deutschen Eisenindustrie während der Frühindustrialisierung,' *Vierteljahrschrift für Sozial- und Wirtschaftsgeschichte* 68 (1981), 305–24.
34. Skingsley, T.A., 'Technical training and education in the English printing industry. Part I: The apprenticeship system. Part II: The pressures for change,' *J. of the Printing Historical Soc.* 13 (1978–9), 1–25; 14 (1979–80), 1–58.
35. More, C., 'Armaments and profits: the case of Fairfield,' *Business History* 2 (1982), 175–85.
36. Perks, R.B., 'Real profit-sharing: William Thomson & Sons of Huddersfield, 1886–1925,' ibid. 156–74.
37. Lloyd-Jones, R.; Le Roux, A.A., 'Marshall and the birth and death of firms: the growth and size distribution of firms in the early nineteenth-century cotton industry,' ibid. 141–55.
38. Morgan, D.H. *Harvesters and harvesting 1840–1900: a study of the rural proletariat.* London; Croom Helm; 1982. Pp viii, 224.
39. Crouzet, F. (A. Forster trs.). *The Victorian economy.* London; Methuen; 1982. Pp xiii, 430.
40. O'Brien, D.P.; Presley, J.R. (ed.). *Pioneers of modern economics.* London; Macmillan; 1981. Pp xix, 272.
41. Collison Black, R.D., 'W.S. Jevons, 1835–1882,' Hf40, 1–35.
42. O'Brien, D.P., 'A. Marshall, 1842–1924,' Hf40, 36–71.
43. Creedy, J., 'F.Y. Edgeworth, 1845–1926,' Hf40, 72–104.
44. Collard, D., 'A.C. Pigou, 1877–1959,' Hf40, 105–39.
45. Darnell, A., 'A.L. Bowley, 1869–1957,' Hf40, 140–74.
46. Presley, J.R., 'D.H. Robertson, 1890–1963,' Hf40, 175–202.
47. Davis, E.G., 'R.G. Hawtrey, 1879–1975,' Hf40, 203–33.
48. Shackle, G.L.S., 'F.A. Hayek, 1899– ,' Hf40, 234–61.
49. Not used.
50. Bonavia, M.R. *A history of the LNER, vol. 1: the early years, 1923–33.* London; Allen & Unwin; 1982. Pp xii, 90.
51. Turner, W.H.K., 'The localisation of early spinning mills in the historic linen region of Scotland,' *Scottish Geographical Magazine* 98 (1982), 77–86.
52. Roderick, G.; Stephens, M. (ed.). *Where did we go wrong? Industrial performance, education and the economy in Victorian Britain.* Lewes; Falmer Press; 1981. Pp 262.
53. Hart, P.; Clarke, R. *Concentration in British industry, 1935–75: a study of the growth, causes and effects of concentration in British manufacturing industries.* Cambridge UP; 1980. Pp xiv, 178.
54. Thomson, W.P.L. *The little general and the Rousay crofters: crisis*

and conflict on an Orkney crofting estate. Edinburgh; Donald; 1981. Pp x, 234.

55. Byles, A. *The history of the Monmouthshire Railway and Canal Company.* Cwmbran; Village Publishing; 1982.
56. Acton, R., 'The Market Rasen canal, 1801–1980,' *Lincolnshire History and Archaeology* 17 (1982), 59–64.
57. Bond, A.W. *The British tram: history's orphan.* Dunstable; Light Railway Soc.; 1980. Pp 75.
58. Capie, F.; Webber, A. *Total coin and coin in circulation in the U.K. 1868–1914.* London; City University; 1981. 33 leaves.
59. Bali, G.; Capie, F. *Concentration in British banking 1870–1920.* London; the same; 1982. Pp 20.
60. Wrigley, C. *The history of British industrial relations 1875–1914.* Brighton; Harvester; 1982. Pp xvi, 270.
61. Williams, L.J.; Jones, D., 'The wages of agricultural labourers in the nineteenth century: the evidence from Glamorgan,' *B. of the Board of Celtic Studies* 29 (1982), 749–61.
62. Weinberg, A. *The influence of Auguste Comte on the economics of John Stuart Mill.* London; E.G. Weinberg; 1982. Pp 406.
63. White, C.W., 'The Labour Exchange bill: Churchill as social reformer,' *Studies in History and Politics* 1 (1980), 11–27.
64. Fraser, W.H. *The coming of the mass market 1850–1914.* London; Macmillan; 1981. Pp x, 268.
65. Dodd, J.P., 'Wiltshire agriculture in 1854 – the value of the Board of Trade returns,' *Southern History* 4 (1982), 145–65.
66. Ferrier, R.W. *The history of the British Petroleum Company, vol. 1: The developing years 1901–1932.* Cambridge UP; 1982. Pp xxx, 801.
67. Sturgess, R.W., 'The Londonderry Trust, 1819–54,' *Archaeologia Aeliana* 5th ser. 10 (1982), 179–92.
68. Vamplew, W., 'The economics of a sports industry: Scottish gate-money football, 1890–1914,' *Economic History R.* 2nd ser. 35 (1982), 549–67.
69. Fussell, G.E., 'The Tariff Commission Report,' *Agricultural History R.* 30 (1982), 137–42.
70. Bailey, J.R., 'The struggle for survival in the Coventry ribbon and watch trades, 1865–1914,' *Midland History* 7 (1982), 132–52.
71. Rowan, A. *The creation of Shambellie: the story of a Victorian building contract.* Edinburgh; Royal Scottish Museum; 1982. Pp 64.
72. Vignoles, K.H. *Charles Blacker Vignoles, romantic engineer.* Cambridge UP; 1982. Pp xii, 187.
73. Anscomb, J.W., 'Woodford Halse: the village with a heart of steam,' *Northamptonshire Past and Present* 6 (1982–3), 341–50.
74. Jenkins, J.G. *Evan Thomas Radcliffe: a Cardiff shipowning company.* Cardiff; National Museum of Wales; 1982. Pp 92.

75. Moore, J.R., 'Halifax Corporation tramways – the story of a municipal tramway 1882–1939, part 4: "Along troubled lines" (1898–1908),' *T. of the Halifax Antiquarian Soc.* (1982 for 1981), 1–38.
76. Robinson, P.W., 'The emergence of the common brewer in the Halifax district,' ibid. 70–107.
77. Davis, S., 'Kells of Gloucester and Ross: agricultural implement makers,' *Bristol and Gloucestershire Arch. Soc. T.* 99 (1982 for 1981), 157–66.
78. Gulvin, C. (ed.)., 'Journal of Henry Brown, woollen manufacturer, Galashiels, 1828–1829,' Bc4, 53–135.
79. Vamplew, W. (ed.). 'The North British Railway Enquiry of 1866,' Bc4, 137–79.
80. Rae, T.I., 'The beginning and the end of the Lewis chemical works, 1857–1874,' Bc4, 181–212.
81. Bass, M., 'The financial foundations of the diocese of Newcastle,' Bc11, 160–9.
82. Oxborrow, J., 'Unemployment [c. 1850–1980],' Bc14, 15–33.
83. Capie, F.; Rodrik-Bali, G., 'Concentration in British banking 1870–1920,' *Business History* 24 (1982), 280–92.
84. Matthews, R.C.O.; Feinstein, C.H.; Odling-Smee, J. *British economic growth 1856–1973.* Oxford; Clarendon; 1982. Pp xxiv, 712.
85. McIvor, A. *Cotton employers' organisation and labour relations strategy 1890–1939.* London; Polytechnic of Central London; 1982. Pp 52.
86. Satre, L.J., 'After the match girls' strike: Bryant and May in the 1890s,' *Victorian Studies* 26 (1982), 7–31.
87. Slaven, A., 'Management and shipbuilding, 1890–1938: structure and strategy in the shipbuilding firm on the Clyde,' Bc24, 35–53.
88. Cameron, R., 'Banking and industrialisation in Britain in the nineteenth century,' Bc24, 102–11.
89. Munn, C.W., 'The development of joint-stock banking in Scotland, 1810–1845,' Bc24, 112–28.
90. Cottrell, P.L., 'London, Paris and silver, 1848–1867,' Bc24, 129–54.
91. Forsyth, W., 'Urban economic morphology in nineteenth-century Glasgow,' Bc24, 166–92.

(g) *Social Structure and Population*

1. Walkley, C. *The ghost in the looking glass: the Victorian seamstress.* London; Owen; 1981. Pp xi, 137.
2. *The London journal of Flora Tristan, 1842* [translated from *Promenades dans Londres*]. London; Virago; 1982. Pp 307.
3. Hall, A.A., 'Wages, earnings and real earnings in Teesside: a

reassessment of the ameliorist interpretation of living standards in Britain, 1870–1914,' *International R. of Social History* 26 (1981), 202–19.

4. Horn, P., 'Victorian villages from census returns,' *Local Historian* 15 (1982), 25–32.
5. Aronsfeld, C.C., 'German Jews in nineteenth-century Bradford,' *Yorkshire Arch. J.* 53 (1982), 111–17.
6. Agar, N.E. *The Bedfordshire farm worker in the nineteenth century*. Bedfordshire Historical Record Soc.; 1981. Pp ix, 213.
7. The WEA (Slough & Eton Branch) Local History Class. *A town in the making: Slough 1851*. Reading; Berkshire County Council [1981]. Pp 156.
8. Lockhart, D.G., 'Patterns of migration and movement of labour to the planned villages of north-east Scotland,' *Scottish Geographical Magazine* 98 (1982), 35–47.
9. Jennings, L.C., 'The French press and Great Britain's campaign against the slave trade, 1830–1848,' *Revue française d'histoire d'outre-mer* 67 (1982 for 1980), 5–24.
10. Colyer, R.J., 'Some aspects of occupation in nineteenth-century Cardiganshire,' *T. of the Honourable Soc. of Cymmrodorion* (1981), 79–97.
11. Hudson, K. *Where we used to work*. London; J. Baker; 1980. Pp viii, 162.
12. Jones, E. *Accountancy and the British economy 1840–1980: the evolution of Ernest & Whinney*. London; Batsford; 1981. Pp 288.
13. Not used.
14. Hodson, J.H.; Smith, J.H. (ed.). *Three Sundays in Wilmslow: 1851–1871*. Cheadle; Wilmslow Hist. Soc.; 1981. Pp viii, 66.
15. Bennet, E., 'Photographic treasures in the George Washington Wilson Collection,' *Aberdeen University R.* 49 (1982), 168–70.
16. Blair, A.G.J.W., 'Structural change in Aberdeen in the north east, 1851–1911,' *Northern Scotland* 5 (1982), 57–69.
17. Day, J.; Charlton, D.B., 'Excavation and field survey in Upper Redesdale: Part III,' *Archaeologia Aeliana* 5th ser. 9 (1981), 267–98; 'Part IV,' ibid. 10 (1982), 149–70.
18. Sandiford, K.A.P., 'The Victorians at play: problems of historiographical methodology,' *J. of Social History* 15 (1981–2), 271–88.
19. Richards, E., 'Highland emigrants to South Australia in the 1850s,' *Northern Scotland* 5 (1982), 1–29.
20. Johnson, R.L. *A Shetland country merchant: being an account of the life and times of James Williamson of Mid Yell 1800–1872*. Shetland Publishing; 1979. Pp 63.
21. Kent, R.A. *A history of British empirical sociology*. Aldershot; Gower; 1981. Pp viii, 228.
22. Lorimer, D.A. *Colour, class and the Victorians: English attitudes*

to the Negro in the mid-nineteenth century. Leicester UP; 1978. Pp 300.

23. Mayhew, H. *The Morning Chronicle survey of labour and the poor: the metropolitan districts.* Vols. 2–6. Horsham; Caliban; 1981/2. Pp 335; 277; 245; 248; 265.
24. Malchow, H.L. *Population pressures: emigration and government in late nineteenth-century Britain.* Palo Alto; Soc. for the Promotion of Science and Scholarship; 1979. Pp xi, 323.
25. Glynn, D., '"Exporting outcast London": assisted emigration to Canada, 1886–1914,' *Social History/Histoire sociale* 15 (1982), 209–38.
26. Walkowitz, J.R.; Caplan, J., 'Male vice and feminist virtue: feminism and the politics of prostitution in nineteenth-century Britain,' *History Workshop* 13 (1982), 77–93.
27. Boos, F. (ed.)., 'William Morris's socialist diary,' ibid. 1–75.
28. Durey, M., 'The survival of an Irish culture in Britain, 1800–1845,' *Historical Studies* 20 (1982), 14–35.
29. Bailey, V., 'Scouting for empire,' *History Today* 32/7 (1982), 5–9.
30. Thompson, F.M.L. (ed.). *The rise of suburbia.* Leicester UP; 1982. Pp xii, 274.
31. Not used.
32. Not used.
33. Crafts, N.F.R., 'Illegitimacy in England and Wales in 1911,' *Population Studies* 36 (1982), 327–31.
34. Barke, M.; Johnson, T., 'Emerging residential segregation in a nineteenth-century small town: the case of Falkirk,' *Scottish Geographical Magazine* 98 (1982), 87–102.
35. Roberts, E., 'Working-class standards of living in three Lancashire towns, 1890–1914,' *International R. of Social History* 27 (1982), 43–65.
36. Ashmore, O. *The industrial archaeology of north-west England.* Manchester UP; 1982. Pp 241.
37. Waters, M., 'The dockyard workforce: a picture of Chatham dockyard c. 1860,' *Archaeologia Cantiana* 97 (1982 for 1981), 79–94.
38. Jones, D. *Crime, protest, community and police in nineteenth-century Britain.* London; Routledge; 1982. Pp xi, 247.
39. Walvin, J. *A child's world: a social history of English childhood, 1800–1914.* Harmondsworth; Penguin; 1982. Pp 236.
40. Not used.
41. Thompson, F.M.L., 'The rise of suburbia,' Hg30, 2–25.
42. Rawcliffe, J.M., 'Bromley: Kentish market town to London suburb, 1841–81,' Hg30, 28–91.
43. Jahn, M., 'Suburban development in outer west London, 1850–1900,' Hg30, 94–156.
44. Treen, C., 'The process of urban development in north Leeds, 1870–1914,' Hg30, 158–209.

45. Carr, M.C., 'The development and character of a metropolitan suburb: Bexley, Kent,' Hg30, 212–67.
46. Reid, A., 'Labour and society in modern Britain,' *Historical J.* 25 (1982), 489–500.
47. Cannadine, D. (ed.). *Patricians, power and politics in nineteenth-century towns.* Leicester UP; 1982. Pp xi, 227.
48. Johnson, J.H.; Pooley, C.G. (ed.). *The structure of nineteenth century cities.* London; Croom Helm; 1982. Pp vi, 312.
49. Davidson, C. *A woman's work is never done.* London; Chatto & Windus; 1982. Pp 288.
50. Cohen, S.A. *English zionists and British Jews: the communal politics of Anglo-Jewry, 1895–1920.* Princeton UP; 1982. Pp xv, 349.
51. Cannadine, D.; Reeder, D. (ed.). *Exploring the urban past: essays in urban history by H.J. Dyos.* Cambridge UP; 1982. Pp xix, 258.
52. Service, A. *Edwardian interiors: inside the homes of the poor, the average and the wealthy.* London; Barrie & Jenkins; 1982. Pp 160.
53. Smith, D. *Conflict and compromise: class formation in English society. A comparative study of Birmingham and Sheffield.* London; Routledge; 1982. Pp xiii, 338.
54. Parsons, J.F. *J.E. Beale and the growth of Bournemouth, part 3: Business expansion 1905–1914.* Bournemouth Local Studies Publications; 1982. Pp 62.
55. Buchanan, R.A.; Williams, M. *Brunel's Bristol.* Bristol; Redcliffe; 1982. Pp 96.
56. [WEA Group], '1851 census returns for Halifax and Skircoat townships, part two,' *T. of the Halifax Antiquarian Soc.* (1982 for 1981), 39–69.
57. Wright, D.G., 'Mid-Victorian Bradford: 1850–1880,' *Bradford Antiquary* new ser. 47 (1982), 65–86.
58. Briggs, A. *Cities and countrysides: British and American experience (1860–1914).* Leicester; Victorian Studies Centre; 1982. Pp 20.
59. Spavold, J. (ed.). *Pits, pots and people: South Derbyshire in 1851.* Woodville; Local History Research Group; 1981. Pp 108.
60. Nash, R., 'Family and economic structure in nineteenth-century Wales: Llangernyw and Gwytherin in 1871,' *Welsh History R.* 11 (1982), 135–49.
61. Smith, S.R.B., 'The centenary of the London Chamber of Commerce: its origin and early policy,' *London J.* 8 (1982), 156–70.
62. Hoyle, S.R., 'The first battle for London: the Royal Commission on metropolitan termini, 1846,' ibid. 140–55.
63. Harrison, B., 'Women's health and the women's movement in Britain: 1840–1940,' Bc5, 15–71.

64. Dyhouse, C., 'Working-class mothers and infant mortality in England, 1895–1914,' Bc5, 73–98.
65. Delves, A., 'Popular recreation and social conflict in Derby, 1800–1850,' Bc7, 89–127.
66. Ashplant, T.G., 'London working men's clubs, 1875–1914,' Bc7, 241–70.
67. Rowe, D.J., 'The social and economic characteristics of Northumberland in the 1880s,' Bc11, 3–23.
68. Pounds, N.J.G., 'The social structure of Lostwithiel in the early nineteenth century,' Bc12, 30–48.
69. Holmes, C., 'The impact of immigration on British society 1870–1980,' Bc15, 172–202.
70. Roberts, E., 'Working wives and their families,' Bc15, 140–71.
71. Wall, R., 'Regional and temporal variations in the structure of the British household since 1851,' Bc15, 62–99.
72. Hair, P.E.H., 'Children in society, 1850–1980,' Bc15, 34–61.
73. Melling, J., 'Scottish industrialists and the changing character of class relations in the Clyde region c. 1880–1918,' Bc18, 61–142.
74. Eltis, D., 'Abolitionist perceptions of society after slavery,' Bc20, 195–213.
75. Bedale, C., 'Property relations and housing policy: Oldham in the late nineteenth and early twentieth century,' Ih12, 37–72.
76. Damer, S., 'State, class and housing: Glasgow, 1885–1919,' Ih12, 73–112.
77. Jackson, J.T., 'Long-distance migrant workers in nineteenth-century Britain: a case study of St Helen's glassmakers,' *T. of the Historic Soc. of Lancashire and Cheshire* 131 (1982 for 1981), 113–37.
78. Atkinson, B. *Trade unions in Bristol.* Bristol Branch of the Hist. Association; 1982. Pp 28.
79. Kellett, J.R., 'The social cost of mortality in the Victorian city,' Bc24, 147–65.
80. Caine, B., 'Beatrice Webb and the "woman question",' *History Workshop* 14 (1982), 23–44.

(h) *Social Policy*

1. Crowther, M.A. *The workhouse system 1834–1929: the history of an English social institution.* London; Batsford; 1981. Pp 305.
2. Weeks, J. *Sex, politics and society: the regulation of sexuality since 1800.* London; Longman; 1981. Pp xiii, 306.
3. Soloway, R., 'Counting the degenerates: the statistics of race deterioration in Edwardian England,' *J. of Contemporary History* 17 (1982), 137–64.
4. Crowther, M.A., 'Family responsibility and state responsibility

in Britain before the Welfare State,' *Historical J.* 25 (1982), 131–45.
5. Alexander, Z.; Dewjee, A., 'Mary Seacole,' *History Today* 31/9, (1981), 45.
6. Thorne, R., 'Hampstead Garden Suburb,' ibid. 32/5 (1982), 46–8.
7. Collins, H., 'The pattern of poor law removals in Nottinghamshire in the early nineteenth century,' *Local Population Studies* 27 (1981), 71–8.
8. Melling, J., 'Employers, industrial housing and the evolution of company welfare policies in Britain's heavy industry: West Scotland, 1870–1920,' *International R. of Social History* 26 (1981), 255–301.
9. Not used.
10. Thane, P. *The foundations of the welfare state.* London; Longman; 1982. Pp x, 383.
11. Royle, E., 'The Owenite legacy to social reform, 1845–1900,' *Studies in History and Politics* 1 (1980), 56–74.
12. Hebbert, M. *The inner city problem in historical context.* London; SSRC; 1980. Pp iii, 41.
13. Tregoning, D.; Cockerell, H. *Friends for life: Friends' Provident Life Office 1832–1982.* London; Melland; 1982. Pp 196.
14. Digby, A. *The poor law in nineteenth-century England.* London; Historical Association (pamphlet G.104); 1982. Pp 40.
15. Bartrip, P.W.J., 'British government inspection, 1832–1875: some observations,' *Historical J.* 25 (1982), 605–26.
16. Dingle, A.E., ' "The monster nuisance of all": landowners, alkali manufacturers, and air pollution, 1828–64,' *Economic History R.* 2nd ser. 35 (1982), 529–48.
17. Barker-Read, M., 'The public health question in the nineteenth century: public health and sanitation in a Kentish market town, Tonbridge 1850–1875,' *Southern History* 4 (1982), 167–89.
18. Boyd, N. *Josephine Butler, Octavia Hill, Florence Nightingale: three Victorian women who changed their world.* London; Macmillan; 1982. Pp xviii, 276.
19. Woods, D.C., 'The operation of the Masters and Servants' Act in the Black Country, 1858–1875,' *Midland History* 7 (1982), 93–115.
20. Leech, R. *Early industrial housing: the Trinity area of Frome.* London; HMSO; 1981. Pp viii, 44.
21. Lloyd, K., 'Social work in the diocese [of Newcastle],' Bc11, 228–46.
22. Holoham, A., 'The church, charity and charities,' Bc11, 216–27.
23. Gladstone, D.E., 'Secularisation and the care of the poor in Scotland,' Bc12, 49–61.
24. Craton, M., 'Slave culture, resistance and the achievement of emancipation in the British West Indies 1783–1838,' Bc20, 100–22.

25. Connolly, G.P., 'Little brother be at peace: the priest as holy man in the nineteenth-century ghetto,' Bc21, 191–206.
26. Aspinwall, B., 'Social catholicism and health: Dr and Mrs Thomas Low Nichols in Britain,' Bc21, 249–70.

(i) *Education*

1. Newton, J.S., 'The liberationists and the universities: Edward Miall and the struggle for university reform in the mid-nineteenth century,' *Durham University J.* 74 (1982), 31–46.
2. Binfield, C. *Belmont's Portias: Victorian nonconformists and middle-class education for girls.* London; Dr Williams's Trust; 1981. Pp 35.
3. Clark, E.A.G., 'The last of the voluntaryists: the Ragged School Union in the School Board era,' *History of Education* 11 (1982), 23–34.
4. Cowie, E.E., 'Stephen Hawtrey and a working-class Eton,' ibid. 71–86.
5. Fletcher, S., 'Co-education and the Victorian grammar school,' ibid. 87–98.
6. Evans, R.A., 'The university and the city: the educational work of Toynbee Hall, 1884–1914,' ibid. 113–25.
7. Marriott, S. *A backstairs to a degree: demands for an open university in late Victorian England.* University of Leeds; 1981. Pp iv, 107.
8. Black, R.D.C. (ed.). *Papers and correspondence of William Stanley Jevons, vol. 5: Papers on political economy.* London; Macmillan; 1981. Pp xiii, 357.
9. Hurt, J.S., 'Education and the working classes (a supplement),' *B. of the Soc. for the Study of Labour History* 43 (1981), 22–39.
10. Roderick, G.W.; Stephens, M.D., 'The influence of Welsh culture on scientific and technical education in Wales in the nineteenth century,' *T. of the Hon. Soc. of Cymmrodorion* (1981), 99–108.
11. Usher, H.J.K.; Black-Hawkins, C.D.; Carrick, G.J.; Smaggasgale, C.E.F.; Byrom, H.J.; Dean, M.E. *An angel without wings: the history of University College School 1830–1980.* London; The School; 1981. Pp 114.
12. Boylan, M.; Riley, G. *The University of Sheffield: an illustrated history.* Sheffield; The University; 1981. Pp 40.
13. Digby, A.; Searby, P. *Children, school and society in nineteenth-century England.* London; Macmillan; 1981. Pp 258.
14. Hare, P. *Victorian masters: a biographical essay on the nineteenth-century headmasters of Magdalen College School, Oxford.* Oxford; the school; 1979. Pp 18.
15. York, B., 'The role of the Victorian schoolmaster,' *Local Historian* 15 (1982), 137–43.

16. Not used.
17. Heesom, A. *The founding of the university of Durham*. Durham; Dean and Chapter; 1982. Pp 32.
18. York, B.A., 'Public opinion and the Kettering grammar school question 1883–88,' *Northamptonshire Past and Present* 6 (1982–3), 329–39.
19. Mason, D.M., 'Inspectors' reports and the select committee of 1864,' *History of Education* 11 (1982), 195–205.
20. Harte, N.B. *One hundred and fifty years of history teaching at University College London*. London; the College; 1982. Pp 32.
21. Tolley, B.H., 'The people's scientific university: science education in the East Midlands, 1860–1890,' *Midland History* 7 (1982), 116–31.
22. Marsden, W.E., 'Diffusion and regional variation in elementary education in England and Wales 1800–1870,' *History of Education* 11 (1982), 173–94.
23. Evans, W.G., 'The Aberdare Report and education in Wales 1881,' *Welsh History R.* 11 (1982), 150–72.
24. Gwyn, P., 'The "Tunding Row": George Ridding and the belief in "boy-government" [at Winchester],' Bc6, 431–77.
25. Tyson, J.C., 'The church and school education: I, Up to 1981 [sic: 1918],' Bc11, 270–90.
26. Hammerstein, N., 'Matthew Arnolds Vorschlag einer Reform der englischen Universitäten,' Bc19, 103–29.
27. Floud, R., 'Technical education and economic performance: Britain, 1850–1914,' *Albion* 14 (1982), 153–68.
28. Shafe, M. *University education in Dundee 1881–1981*. Dundee; the University; 1982. Pp vi, 214.
29. Broadway, C.M.; Buss, E.I. *The history of the [Dame Alice Harpur] school: 1882 B.G.M.S.–D.A.H.S. 1982*. Bedford; the school; 1982. Pp 190.
30. Jolley, M., 'Retrospective [in nursing and midwifery],' Ih21, 19–23.

(j) *Naval and Military*

1. Burroughs, P., 'The Ordnance Department and colonial defence, 1821–1855,' *J. of Imperial and Commonwealth History* 10 (1982), 125–49.
2. Dinwiddy, J.R., 'The early nineteenth-century campaign against flogging in the army,' *English Historical R.* 97 (1982), 308–31.
3. Van der Vat, D. *The grand scuttle: the sinking of the German fleet at Scapa Flow in 1919*. London; Hodder & Stoughton; 1982. Pp
4. Behenna, R.B. (ed.). *A Victorian sailor's diary: Richard Behenna of Veryan, 1833–1898*. Redruth; Institute of Cornish Studies; 1981. Pp 73.

5. Bruch, R. vom, ' "Deutschland und England. Heeres- oder Flottenverstärkung?" Politische Publizistik deutscher Hochschullehrer 1911/12,' *Militärgeschichtliche Mitteilungen* 21/1 (1981), 7–35.
6. Chamberlain, W.M., 'The characteristics of Australia's Boer War volunteers,' *Historical Studies* 20 (1982), 48–52.
7. Hamilton, C.I., 'The Victorian Navy,' *Historical J.* 25 (1982), 471–87.
8. French, D. *British economic and strategic planning 1905–1915.* London; Allen & Unwin; 1982. Pp x, 191.
9. Sinclair, K. (ed.). *A soldier's view of empire: the reminiscences of James Bodell, 1831–91.* London; Bodley Head; 1982. Pp 216.
10. Eglinton, E. *The last of the sailing coasters: reminiscences and observations of the days in the Severn trows, coasting ketches and schooners.* London; HMSO; 1982. Pp 131.
11. Beckett, I.F.W. *Rifleman firm: a study of the rifle volunteer movement 1859–1908.* Aldershot; Ogilby Trust; 1982. Pp xv, 368.
12. Perkins, R.; Douglas-Morris, K.J. *Gunfire in Barbary: Admiral Lord Exmouth's battle with the corsairs of Algiers in 1816 – the story of the suppression of white christian slavery.* Havant; Mason; 1982. Pp 200.
13. Ellis, F.E., 'Some early letters of Robert Fitzroy,' *Mariner's Mirror* 68 (1982), 391–409.
14. Downing, J.; Harris, E., 'Seven nineteenth-century buoys from H.M. Dockyard, Bermuda,' ibid. 411–20.
15. Mackichan, N.D., 'The William Fawcett of the P. & O.,' ibid. 421–8.
16. Osbon, G.A., 'Paddlewheel fighting ships of the Royal Navy,' ibid. 429–33.
17. Hirshfield, C., 'Liberal women's organizations and the war against the Boers, 1899–1902,' *Albion* 14 (1982), 27–49.
18. Beckett, I., 'H.O. Arnold-Forster and the volunteers,' Ic5, 47–68.
19. Gooch, N., 'Haldane and the "National Army",' Ic5, 69–86.
20. Westlake, R. *The rifle volunteers: the history of the rifle volunteers 1859–1908.* Chippenham; Picton; 1982. Pp xviii, 173.
21. Hughes, B.P., 'Siege artillery in the 19th century,' *J. of the Soc. for Army Historical Research* 60 (1982), 129–49.
22. Jackman, S.W., 'Crimean experiences, by William Love (ctd.),' ibid. 181–8.
23. Ereira, A., 'The hidden life of the British sailor,' *History Today* 32/12 (1982), 27–32.
24. Cox, B.W.; Prevezer, M., 'The Brodrick cap,' *J. of the Soc. for Army Historical Research* 60 (1982), 213–25.
25. Hankinson, A. *Man of Wars [William Howard Russell].* London; Heinemann; 1982.

(k) *Science and Medicine*

1. Smith, F.B. *Florence Nightingale: reputation and power.* London; Croom Helm; 1982. Pp xii, 216.
2. Bowers, B. *A history of electric light and power.* Stevenage; Peregrinus; 1982.
3. Bratchell, D.F. *The impact of Darwinism: texts and commentary illustrating nineteenth-century religious, scientific and literary attitudes.* Amersham; Avebury; 1981. Pp 140.
4. Ospovat, D. *The development of Darwin's theory: natural history, natural theology, and natural selection, 1838–1859.* Cambridge UP; 1981. Pp xii, 301.
5. Cowell, B.; Wainwright, D. *Behind the blue door: the history of the Royal College of Midwives, 1881–1981.* London; Bailliere Tindall; 1981. Pp 111.
6. Brent, P. *Charles Darwin: a man of enlarged curiosity.* London; Heinemann; 1981. Pp 536.
7. Woodhouse, J., 'Eugenics and the feeble-minded: the parliamentary debates of 1912–14,' *History of Education* 11 (1982), 127–37.
8. Tolstoy, I. *James Clerk Maxwell: a biography.* Edinburgh; Canongate; 1981. Pp viii, 184.
9. Berridge, V.; Edwards, G. *Opium and the people: opiate use in nineteenth-century England.* London; Allen Lane; 1981. Pp xxx, 369.
10. Spencer, E.M., 'Notes on the history of dental dispensaries,' *Medical History* 26 (1982), 47–66.
11. Carter, K.C., 'Nineteenth-century treatments for rabies as reported in the *Lancet*,' ibid. 67–78.
12. Manlitz, R.C., 'Metropolitan medicine and the man-midwife: the early life and letters of Charles Locock,' ibid. 25–46.
13. Porter, R., 'The descent of genius: Charles Darwin's brilliant career,' *History Today* 32/7 (1982), 16–22.
14. Cooke, A.M., 'Queen Victoria's medical household,' *Medical History* 26 (1982), 307–20.
15. Checkland, O.; Lamb, M. (ed.). *Health care as social history: the Glasgow case.* Aberdeen UP; 1982. Pp xx, 285.
16. Jacyna, L.S., 'Somatic theories of mind and the interests of medicine in Britain, 1850–1879,' *Medical History* 26 (1982), 233–58.
17. Smith, T., 'The Balliol-Trinity laboratories,' Bc14, 185–224.
18. Secord, J.A., 'King of Siluria: Roderick Murchison and the imperial theme in nineteenth century British geology,' *Victorian Studies* 25 (1982), 413–42.
19. Gilley, S., 'The Huxley-Wilberforce debate: a reconsideration,' Bc1, 325–40.

20. Kevles, D.J., 'Genetics in the United States and Great Britain 1890–1930: a review and speculations,' Bc5, 193–215.
21. Searle, G.R., 'Eugenics and class,' Bc5, 217–42.
22. Mackenzie, D., 'Sociobiologies in competition: the Biometrician-Mendelian debate,' Bc5, 243–88.
23. Oddy, D.J., 'The health of the people,' Bc15, 121–39.
24. Winter, J.M., 'The decline of mortality in Britain 1870–1950,' Bc15, 101–20.
25. Ritter, G.A., 'Motive und Organisationsformen der internationalen Wissenschaftsbeziehungen und die Anfänge einer auswärtigen Kulturpolitik im deutschen Kaiserreich vor dem Ersten Weltkrieg,' Bc19, 153–200.
26. Alter, P., 'Internationale Wissenschaft und nationale Politik. Zur Zusammenarbeit der wissenschaftlichen Akademien im frühen 20. Jahrhundert,' Bc19, 201–21.
27. Pickstone, J.V., 'Establishment and dissent in nineteenth-century medicine: an exploration of some correspondence and connections between religious and medical belief-systems in early industrial England,' Bc21, 165–89.
28. Barrow, L., 'Anti-establishment healing: spiritualism in Britain,' Bc21, 225–47.
29. Walls, A.F., ' "The heavy artillery of the missionary army": the domestic importance of the nineteenth-century medical missionary,' Bc21, 287–97.
30. Anning, S.T.; Walls, W.K.J. *A history of the Leeds School of Medicine.* Leeds UP; 1982. Pp xiv, 170.
31. Speakman, C. *Adam Sedgwick: geologist and dalesman, 1785–1873. A biography in twelve themes.* Broad Oak; Broad Oak Press; 1982. Pp 145.

(l) *Intellectual and Cultural*

1. Hobson, A. *The art and life of J.W. Waterhouse RA, 1849–1917.* London; Studio Vista; 1980. Pp x, 208.
2. Wood, C. *The Pre-Raphaelites.* London; Weidenfeld & Nicolson; 1981. Pp 160.
3. Shattock, J.; Wolff, M. (ed.). *The Victorian periodical press: samplings and soundings.* Leicester UP; 1982. Pp xx, 400.
4. Bayley, S. *The Albert Memorial: the monument in its social and architectural context.* London; Scolar; 1981. Pp 160.
5. McCrimmon, B. *Power, politics and print: the publication of the British Museum Catalogue 1881–1900.* Hamden, Conn.; Linnet; 1981. Pp 186.
6. Ormond, R.; Rishel, J.; Hamlyn, R. *Sir Edwin Landseer.* London; Thames & Hudson; 1981. Pp 223.
7. Shanley, M.L., 'Marital slavery and friendship: John Stuart Mill's *The Subjection of Women,' Political Theory* 9 (1981), 229–47.

8. Langham, I. *The building of British social anthropology: W.H.R. Rivers and his Cambridge disciples in the development of kinship studies, 1898–1931.* Dordrecht/London; Reidel; 1981. Pp xxxii, 392.
9. Hunt, J.D. *The wider sea: a life of John Ruskin.* London; Dent; 1982. Pp xv, 512.
10. McFadzean, R. *The life and work of Alexander Thomson.* London; Routledge; 1979. Pp xvi, 304.
11. Rose, A. *Pre-Raphaelite portraits.* Yeovil; Oxford Illustrated Press; 1981. Pp 144.
12. Arneson, R.J., 'Prospects for community in a market economy [on J.S. Mill],' *Political Theory* 9 (1982), 207–27.
13. Harding, F.W.J., 'The Welsh excursions of Thomas Stringer contributed to the European Magazine and London Review, 1819–21; part II, North Wales,' *T. of the Honourable Soc. of Cymmrodorion* (1981), 51–78.
14. Sakula, A., 'Baroness Burdett-Coutts' garden party: the International Medical Congress, London, 1881,' *Medical History* 26 (1982), 183–90.
15. Sullivan, E.P., 'A note on the importance of class in the political theory of John Stuart Mill,' *Political Theory* 9 (1982), 248–56.
16. Nadel, I.B.; Schwarzbach, T.S. (ed.). *Victorian artists and the city: a collection of critical essays.* New York/Oxford; Pergamon; 1980. Pp xvi, 170.
17. Henderson, H., 'Carlyle and the book clubs: a new approach to publishing?,' *Publishing History* 6 (1982 for 1979), 37–62.
18. Shelden, M., 'Dickens, "The Chimes", and the anti-corn law league,' *Victorian Studies* 25 (1982), 328–53.
19. Herendeen, W.H., 'The Doré controversy: Doré, Ruskin, and Victorian taste,' ibid. 305–27.
20. Mackenzie, D.A. *Statistics in Britain 1865–1930: the social construction of scientific knowledge.* Edinburgh UP; 1981. Pp viii, 306.
21. Witt, J. *William Henry Hunt (1790–1864): life and work with a catalogue.* London; Barrie & Jenkins; 1982. Pp 264.
22. Howard, J. *Darwin.* Oxford UP; 1982. Pp viii, 101.
23. Martin, D.E. *John Stuart Mill and the land question.* Hull; the University; 1981. Pp 61.
24. Heron, R. *Cecil Aldin: the story of a sporting artist.* Exeter; Webb & Bower; 1981. Pp 208.
25. Allan, M. *William Robson 1838–1935: father of the English flower garden.* London; Faber & Faber; 1982. Pp 255.
26. Booth, M.R. (ed.). *Victorian theatrical trades: articles from the Stage 1883–1884.* London; Soc. for Theatre Research; 1981. Pp ix, 56.
27. MacCarthy, F. *British design since 1880: a visual history.* London; Lund Humphries; 1982. Pp 229.

28. Rooke, T.; Lago, M. (ed.). *Burne-Jones talking.* London; Murray; 1982.
29. Goodman, J. *The Mond legacy: a family saga.* London; Weidenfeld & Nicolson; 1982. Pp xv, 272.
30. George, W. *Darwin.* London; Fontana; 1982. Pp 160.
31. Taylor, R. *George Washington Wilson: artist and photographer 1823–93.* Aberdeen UP; 1982. Pp x, 204.
32. Finley, G. *Turner and George the Fourth in Edinburgh 1822.* London; Tate Gallery & Edinburgh UP; 1981. Pp viii, 86.
33. Britain, I. *Fabianism and culture.* Cambridge UP; 1982.
34. Ramm, A. *Gladstone as man of letters.* Oxford; Somerville College; 1982. Pp 16.
35. Brocklebank, J. *Victorian stone carvers in Dorset churches, 1856–1880.* Wimborne; Dovecote; 1979. Pp 72.
36. Le Quesne, A.L. *Carlyle.* Oxford UP; 1982. Pp x, 99.
37. Colloms, B. *Victorian visionaries.* London; Constable; 1982. Pp 284.
38. Nettleship, L.E., 'William Fremantle, Samuel Barnett and the broad church origins of Toynbee Hall,' *J. of Ecclesiastical History* 33 (1982), 564–79.
39. Howell, R., 'Cromwell and the imagery of nineteenth century radicalism: the example of Joseph Cowen,' *Archaeologia Aeliana* 5th ser. 10 (1982), 193–7.
40. Soffer, R.N., 'Why do disciplines fail? The strange case of British sociology,' *English Historical R.* 97 (1982), 767–802.
41. Goldstein, D.S., 'The organizational development of the British historical profession, 1884–1921,' *B. of the Institute of Historical Research* 55 (1982), 180–93.
42. Barker, N. *A sequel to an enquiry: the forgeries of H. Buxton Forman and T.H. Wise re-examined.* London; Scolar; 1982. Pp 422.
43. Metcalf, A., 'Organized sport in the mining communities of south Northumberland, 1800–1889,' *Victorian Studies* 27 (1982), 469–95.
44. Hunt, B.D. *Sailor-scholar: Admiral Sir Herbert Richmond 1871–1946.* Waterloo, Ont.; Wilfred Laurier UP; 1982. Pp xii, 259.
45. Smith, H., 'Philip Webb's restoration of Forthampton court,' *Architectural History* 24 (1981), 92–102.
46. Powers, A., ' "Architects I have known": the architectural career of S.D. Adshead,' ibid. 103–23.
47. Harris, J. *William Talman, maverick architect.* London; Allen & Unwin; 1982. Pp 54.
48. Allthorpe-Guyton, M.; Stevens, J. *A happy eye: a school of art in Norwich 1845–1982.* Norwich; Jarrold; 1982. Pp 144.
49. Read, B. *Victorian sculpture.* New Haven; Yale UP for Paul Mellon Center; 1982. Pp x, 414.
50. Bell, Q. *A new and noble school: the Pre-Raphaelites.* London; Macdonald; 1982. Pp 192.

51. Block, E., 'James Sully, evolutionist psychology, and late Victorian Gothic fiction,' *Victorian Studies* 25 (1982), 443–67.
52. Brendon, P. *The life and death of the press barons.* London; Secker & Warburg; 1982. Pp 279.
53. Blau, E. *Ruskinian gothic: the architecture of Deane and Woodland 1845–1861.* Princeton UP; 1982. Pp xix, 219.
54. Ganzel, D. *Fortune and men's eyes: the career of John Payne Collier.* Oxford UP; 1982. Pp x, 454.
55. Heyck, T.W. *The transformation of intellectual life in Victorian England.* London; Croom Helm; 1982. Pp 262.
56. Blakiston, J.M.G., 'The fellows' Library [at Winchester] : Sir Thomas Phillipps and after,' Bc6, 403–29.
57. Yeo, E., 'Culture and constraint in working-class movements, 1830–1855,' Bc7, 155–86.
58. Howkins, A., 'The taming of Whitsun: the changing face of a nineteenth-century rural holiday,' Bc7, 187–208.
59. Summerfield, P., 'The Effingham Arms and the Empire: deliberate selection in the evolution of music hall in London,' Bc7, 209–40.
60. Pickering, W.S.F., 'The upsurge of building in the early days of the diocese [of Newcastle] and the position today,' Bc11, 170–8.
61. Schmidt, C., 'Classical studies at Balliol in the 1860s: the undergraduate essays of Gerald Manley Hopkins,' Bc14, 159–84.
62. Mommsen, W.J., 'Zur Entwicklung des Englandbildes der Deutschen seit dem Ende des 18. Jahrhunderts,' Bc19, 375–97.
63. Joseph, T. *George Grossmith: biography of a Savoyard.* Bristol; the author; 1982. Pp x, 212.
64. Stevens, L.R., 'Darwin's humane reading: the anaesthetic man reconsidered,' *Victorian Studies* 26 (1982), 51–63.

I. BRITAIN SINCE 1914

See also Ha2, 3, 8, c9, e12, f1, 29, 34, 75, 85, 87, g12, 21, h2, i20, 29, 18, 44, 52, 62. Items Hf50, 53 are misplaced and belong to this Section.

(a) *General*

1. Johnson, H. *Wings over Brooklands: the story of the birthplace of British aviation.* Weybridge; Whittet Books; 1981. Pp 157.
2. Cottesloe, G. (baroness). *The story of the Battersea Dogs' Home.* Newton Abbot; David & Charles; 1979. Pp 175.
3. Judd, D. *Lord Reading: Rufus Isaacs, first marquess of Reading, lord chief justice and viceroy of India, 1860–1935.* London; Weidenfeld & Nicolson; 1982. Pp x, 316.

4. Baudis, D., 'Deutschland und Grossbritannien in der Zeit des ersten Weltkrieges: Versuch einer vergleichenden Betrachtung einiger Aspekte der wirtschaftlichen und sozialen Entwicklung,' *Jahrbuch für Wirtschaftsgeschichte* (1981/III), 49–78.
5. Marwick, A. *British society since 1945.* London; Allen Lane; 1982. Pp 303.
6. Gibson, M.L. *Aviation in Northamptonshire: an illustrated history.* Northamptonshire Libraries; 1982. Pp vii, 360.
7. Brown, R.D. *East Anglia.* Lavenham; Dalton; 1981. Pp x, 166.
8. Barty-King, H. *The AA: a history of the first 75 years of the Automobile Association 1905–1980.* Basingstoke; AA; 1980. Pp 319.
9. Seabrook, J. *Working-class childhood.* London; Gollancz; 1982. Pp 224.
10. Chew, D.N. *The life and writings of Ada Nield Chew.* London; Virago; 1982. Pp xxiv, 255.
11. Madgwick, P.J.; Steeds, D.; Williams, L.J. *Britain since 1945.* London; Hutchinson; 1982. Pp vii, 379.
12. Block, M. *The Duke of Windsor's war.* London; Weidenfeld & Nicolson; 1982. Pp xvii, 397.
13. Fisher, N. *Harold Macmillan: a biography.* Idem; 1982. Pp xi, 404.
14. Eccles, D. *By safe hands: the wartime letters of David and Sybil Eccles.* London; Bodley Head; 1982. Pp 384.
15. Vernon, B. (ed.). *Margaret Cole 1893–1980.* London; Fabian Soc.; 1982. Pp 19.

(b) *Politics*

1. Gilbert, M. *Churchill's political philosophy* [lecture]. Oxford UP for British Academy; 1981. Pp 119.
2. Vernon, B.D. *Ellen Wilkinson.* London; Croom Helm; 1982. Pp 272.
3. Adelman, P. *The decline of the Liberal party, 1910–1931.* London; Longman; 1981. Pp vii, 940.
4. Campbell, J., 'F.E. Smith: tory democrat or social democrat?,' *History Today* 32/5 (1982), 5–10.
5. Ball, S.R., 'Asquith's decline and the general election of 1918,' *Scottish Historical R.* 61 (1982), 44–61.
6. Fraser, P., 'British war policy and the crisis of Liberalism in May 1915,' *J. of Modern History* 54 (1982), 1–26.
7. Fraser, P., 'Lord Beaverbrook's fabrications in *Politicians and the War 1914–1916*,' *Historical J.* 25 (1982), 147–66.
8. Martin, R.M. *TUC: the growth of a pressure group, 1868–1976.* Oxford; Clarendon; 1980. Pp xiii, 394.
9. Williamson, P., ' "Safety First": Baldwin, the Conservative party and the 1929 general election,' *Historical J.* 25 (1982), 385–409.

10. Not used.
11. Crosland, S. *Tony Crosland.* London; Cape; 1982.
12. Fair, J.D., 'The second Labour government and the politics of electoral reform, 1929–1931,' *Albion* 13 (1981), 276–301.
13. Carsten, F.L. *War against war: British and German radical movements in the first world war.* London; Batsford; 1982. Pp 285.
14. Brett, T.; Gilliatt, S.; Pople, A., 'Planned trade, Labour party policy and US intervention: successes and failures of postwar reconstruction,' *History Workshop* 13 (1982), 130–42.
15. Kennedy, T.C. *The hound of conscience: a history of the No-Conscription Fellowship, 1914–1919.* Fayettesville; University of Arkansas Press; 1981. Pp ix, 322.
16. Hart, M., 'The Liberals, the war and the franchise,' *English Historical R.* 97 (1982), 820–32.
17. Woodhouse, T., 'The general strike in Leeds,' *Northern History* 18 (1982), 252–62.
18. Jupp, J. *The radical left in Britain, 1931–1941.* London; Cass; 1982. Pp viii, 261.
19. Brock, M. & E. (ed.). *H.W. Asquith: letters to Venetia Stanley.* Oxford UP; 1982.
20. Close, D.H., 'The realignment of the British electorate in 1931,' *History* 67 (1982), 393–404.
21. Beck, P.J., 'Labour's way to peace,' *B. of the Soc. for the Study of Labour History* 43 (1982), 11–13.
22. Vowles, J., 'A Guild Socialist programme in action,' ibid. 16–21.
23. Lowe, R., 'Hours of labour: negotiating industrial legislation in Britain, 1919–39,' *Economic History R.* 2nd ser. 35 (1982), 254–71.
24. Warde, A. *Consensus and beyond: development of Labour party strategy since the second world war.* Manchester UP; 1982. Pp 243.
25. Dunleavy, P. *The politics of mass housing in Britain, 1945–1975: a study of corporate and professional influence in the welfare state.* Oxford; Clarendon; 1981. Pp xvi, 447.
26. Allen, V.L. *The militancy of British miners.* Shipley; Moor; 1981. Pp xix, 337.
27. Frow, E. & R. *Engineering struggles: episodes in the story of the shop stewards' movement.* Manchester; Working Class Movement Library; 1982. Pp 496.
28. James, A.J.; Thomas, J.E. *Wales at Westminster: a history of the parliamentary representation of Wales 1800–1979.* Llandysul; Gomer; 1982. Pp xv, 284.
29. Bell, G. *Troublesome business: the Labour party and the Irish question.* London; Pluto; 1982. Pp 168.
30. Barker, R. *Conscience, government and war: conscientious objec-*

tion in Great Britain 1939–45.* London; Routledge; 1982. Pp x, 174.

31. Kingsford, P. *The hunger marchers in Britain, 1920–1939.* London; Lawrence & Wishart; 1982. Pp 244.
32. Harris, K. *Attlee.* Weidenfeld & Nicolson; 1982. Pp ix, 630.
33. Pronay, N.; Spring, D.W. *Propaganda, politics and film.* London; Macmillan; 1982. Pp ix, 302.
34. Pronay, N., 'The political censorship of films in Britain between the wars,' Ib33, 98–125.
35. Ramsden, J.A., 'Baldwin and film,' Ib33, 126–43.
36. Hogenkamp, B., 'The workers' film movement in Britain, 1929–39,' Ib33, 144–70.
37. Harrison, T., 'Films and the home front: the evaluation of their effectiveness by Mass Observation,' Ib33, 234–45.
38. Edwards, O.D., 'Divided treason and divided loyalties: Roger Casement and others,' *T. of the Royal Historical Soc.* 5th ser. 32 (1982), 153–74.
39. Mortimer, J.E. *History of the Boilermakers' Society, vol. 2: 1906–1939.* London; Allen & Unwin; 1982. Pp x, 355.
40. Negrine, R., 'The press and the Suez crisis: a myth re-examined,' *Historical J.* 25 (1982), 975–83.
41. Hennessy, P.; Brownfeld, G., 'Britain's cold war security purge: the origins of positive vetting,' ibid. 965–73.
42. Roskill, S., 'Lord Cecil and the historians,' ibid. 953–4; Thompson, J.A., 'Lord Cecil and Stephen Roskill,' ibid. 955–6.
43. Rose, N., 'The resignation of Anthony Eden,' ibid. 911–31.
44. Jones, J.G., 'Wales and the "new socialism", 1926–1929,' *Welsh History R.* 11 (1982), 173–99.
45. Husbands, C.T., 'The London borough council elections of 6 May 1982: results and analysis,' *London J.* 8 (1982), 177–90.
46. Greenville, J.A.S., 'British propaganda, the newsreels and Germany 1933 to 1939,' Bc19, 281–93.
47. Balfour, M., 'A war-time exercise in empathy,' Bc19, 294–311.
48. Thompson, A.F., 'Winchester and the Labour party: three "gentlemanly rebels",' Bc6, 489–503.
49. Grieves, K.R., 'The Liverpool dock batallion: military intervention in the Mersey docks, 1915–1918,' *T. of the Historic Soc. of Lancashire and Cheshire* 131 (1982 for 1981), 139–58.
50. Pimlott, B.; Cook, C. *Trade unions in British politics.* London; Longman; 1982. Pp 320.

(c) *Constitution, Administration and Law*

1. Pearce, R.D., 'The Colonial Office in 1947 and the transfer of power in Africa: an addendum to John Cell,' *J. of Imperial and Commonwealth History* 10 (1982), 211–15.

2. Lee, J.M.; Petter, M. *The Colonial Office, war and redevelopment policy.* London; Temple Smith; 1982. Pp 320.
3. Moon, P.; Blake, D.M.; Carter, L. (ed.). *The transfer of power 1942–47, vol. 10: the Mountbatten viceroyalty – formulation of a plan 22 March–30 May 1947.* London; HMSO; 1981. Pp cxxvi, 1077.
4. Eder, N.R., 'Malingering and the administration of health insurance in Britain, 1913–1936,' *Studies in History and Politics* 1 (1980), 115–36.
5. Beckett, I.; Gooch, J. (ed.). *Politicians and defence: studies in the formulation of British defence policy 1845–1970.* Manchester UP; 1981. Pp xxii, 202.
6. Simkins, P., 'Kitchener and the expansion of the Army,' Ic5, 87–109.
7. Bond, B., 'Leslie Hore-Belisha at the War Office,' Ic5, 110–31.
8. Gordon, C., 'Duncan Sandys and the independent nuclear deterrent,' Ic5, 132–53.
9. Nailor, P., 'Denis Healey and rational decision-making in defence,' Ic5, 154–77.
10. Burk, K. (ed.). *War and the state: the transformation of British government, 1914–1919.* London; Allen & Unwin; 1982. Pp 189.
11. French, D., 'The rise and fall of "business as usual",' Ic10, 7–31.
12. Wrigley, C., 'The Ministry of Munitions: an innovatory department,' Ic10, 32–56.
13. Turner, J., 'Cabinets, committees, and secretariats: the higher direction of the war,' Ic10, 57–83.
14. Burk, K., 'The Treasury: from impotence to power,' Ic10, 84–107.
15. Lowe, R., 'The Ministry of Labour, 1916–19: a still, small voice,' Ic10, 108–34.
16. Harris, J., 'Bureaucrats and businessmen in British food controls, 1916–19,' Ic10, 135–56.
17. Cline, P., 'Winding down the war economy: British plans for peacetime recovery, 1916–19,' Ic10, 157–81.
18. Thomas, I.A. *The creation of the Welsh Office: conflicting purposes in institutional change.* Glasgow; Univ. of Strathclyde; 1981. Pp iv, 80.
19. McKenzie, A.W. *The treatment of enemy property in the United Kingdom during and after the second world war.* Chislehurst; the author; 1981. Pp 62.
20. Fraser, D. *Municipal reform and the industrial city.* Leicester UP; 1982. Pp x, 165.
21. Kirk-Green, A., 'Margery Perham and colonial administration: a direct influence on indirect rule,' Bc8, 122–43.

(d) *External Affairs*

1. Rothwell, V. *Britain and the Cold War, 1941–1947.* London; Cape; 1982. Pp 551.
2. Gates, E.M. *End of the affair: the collapse of the Anglo-French alliance, 1939–40.* London; Allen & Unwin; 1981. Pp xviii, 630.
3. Medlicott, W.N.; Dakin, D.; Bennett, G. (ed.). *Documents on British foreign policy 1919–1939, first series: Papers from the Foreign Office archives, vol. 22 (Central Europe and the Balkans 1921, Albania 1921–2).* London; HMSO; 1980. Pp cxii, 885.
4. Stivers, W., 'International politics and Iraqi oil, 1918–1928: a study of Anglo-American diplomacy,' *Business History R.* 55 (1981), 517–40.
5. Hanak, H., 'Sir Stafford Cripps as ambassador in Moscow, June 1941–January 1942,' *English Historical R.* 97 (1982), 332–44.
6. Young, J.W., 'The Foreign Office and the departure of General de Gaulle, June 1945–January 1946,' *Historical J.* 25 (1982), 209–16.
7. Davis, L.E.; Huttenback, R., 'The political economy of British imperialism: measures of benefits and support,' *J. of Economic History* 42 (1982), 119–30.
8. Tomlinson, B.R., 'The political economy of the Raj: the decline of colonialism,' ibid. 133–7.
9. Bonjour, E., 'England und der schweizerische Widerstandswille 1939/40,' *Schweizerische Zeitschrift für Geschichte* 31 (1981), 332–5.
10. Winkel, H., 'Boykott und Gegenboykott: zu den deutsch-englischen Handelsbeziehungen im Jahre 1933,' *Preussen, Deutschland und der Westen*, ed. H. Bodensieck (Göttingen; Musterschmidt; 1980), 179–202.
11. Aigner, D., ' "For the defence of freedom and peace": eine politische Neugruppierung in England 1936 im Licht bisher unveröffentlichter deutscher Botschaftsberichte,' ibid. 203–21.
12. Parker, R.A.C., 'Dr. Schacht und die Briten: Auswirkungen von Schachts Paris-Reise im August 1936,' ibid. 222–8.
13. Ashton, S.R. *British policy towards the Indian states, 1905–1939.* London; Curzon Press; 1982. Pp 244.
14. Steininger, R., 'Die Rhein-Ruhr Frage im Kontext britischer Deutschlandspolitik 1945/46,' *Politische Weichenstellungen im Nachkriegsdeutschland 1945–1953*, ed. H.A. Winkler (Geschichte und Gesellschaft, Sonderheft 5; Göttingen; Vandenhoeck & Ruprecht; 1979), 111–66.
15. Ovendale, R., 'Britain, the U.S.A. and the European cold war, 1945–8,' *History* 67 (1982), 217–36.
16. Schmidt, G., 'Politische Tradition und wirtschaftliche Faktoren in der britischen Friedensstrategie 1918/19,' *Vierteljahrshefte für Zeitgeschichte* 29 (1981), 131–88.

17. Kluke, P., 'Winston Churchill und die alliierte Intervention im revolutionären Russland,' *Innen- und Aussenpolitik: Primat oder Interdependenz?*, ed. U. Altermatt et al. (Bern/Stuttgart; Paul Haupt; 1980), 127–47.
18. Uhlig, R., 'Königswinter – Symbol deutsch-britischer Verständigung nach dem Zweiten Weltkrieg,' *Geschichte und Gegenwart*, ed. H. Boockmann et al. (Neumünster; Wachholtz; 1980), 491–529.
19. Hauser, O., 'England und Hitler 1936–1939,' ibid. 365–80.
20. Haworth, B., 'The British Broadcasting Corporation, Nazi Germany and the Foreign Office, 1933–1936,' *Historical J. of Film, Radio and Television* 1 (1981), 47–55.
21. Short, K.R.M., ' "The White Cliffs of Dover": promoting Anglo-American alliance in World War II,' ibid. 2 (1982), 3–25.
22. Schmidt, H.-I., 'Wirtschaftliche Kriegsziele Englands und interalliierte Kooperation: Die Pariser Wirtschaftskonferenz 1916,' *Militärgeschichtliche Mitteilungen* 29/1 (1981), 37–54.
23. Glees, A. *Exile politics during the second world war: the German Social Democrats in Britain*. Oxford; Clarendon; 1982.
24. Gallagher, J. (ed. A. Seal). *The decline, revival and fall of the British Empire*. Cambridge UP; 1982. Pp xxvii, 211.
25. Hathaway, R.M. *Ambiguous partnership: Britain and America, 1944–1947*. New York/Guildford; Columbia UP; 1981. Pp x, 410.
26. Pearce, R.D. *The turning point in Africa: British colonial policy, 1938–48*. London; Cass; 1982. Pp 223.
27. Nish, I.H. (ed.). *Anglo-Japanese alienation 1919–1952*. Cambridge UP; 1982. Pp x, 305.
28. Hosoya, C., 'Britain and the United States in Japan's view of the international system, 1919–37,' Id27, 3–26.
29. Nish, I.A., 'Japan in Britain's view of the international system, 1919–37,' Id27, 27–55.
30. Hosoya, C., 'Britain and the United States in Japan's view of the international system [after 1937],' Id27, 57–75.
31. Usui, K., 'A consideration of Anglo-Japanese relations: Japanese views on Britain, 1937–41,' Id27, 77–96.
32. Hagihara, N., 'Anglo-Japanese attitudes, 1940–1,' Id27, 97–102.
33. Lowe, P., 'Britain and the opening of the war in Asia, 1937–41,' Id27, 103–22.
34. Probert, H., 'British strategy and the far eastern war, 1941–5,' Id27, 157–75.
35. Thorne, C., 'Wartime British planning for the post-war Far East,' Id27, 199–225.
36. Watanabe, A., 'From bitter enmity to cold partnership: Japanese views of the United Kingdom, 1945–52,' Id27, 229–55.
37. Daniels, G., 'Britain's view of post-war Japan, 1945–9,' Id27, 257–77.

38. Reynolds, D. *The creation of the Anglo-American alliance: a study in competitive cooperation.* London; Europa; 1981. Pp xiii, 397.
39. Northedge, F.S.; Wells, A. *Britain and Soviet communism: the impact of a revolution.* London; Macmillan; 1982. Pp viii, 280.
40. Buckley, R. *Occupation diplomacy: Britain, the United States and Japan, 1945–1952.* Cambridge UP; 1982. Pp x, 294.
41. Ellwood, D.W., 'Showing the world what it owed to Britain: foreign policy and "cultural propaganda",' Ib33, 50–73.
42. Taylor, P.M., 'British official attitudes towards propaganda abroad, 1918–29,' Ib33, 23–49.
43. Reynolds, D., 'Roosevelt, the British Left, and the appointment of John G. Winant as United States ambassador to Britain in 1941,' *International History R.* 4 (1982), 393–413.
44. Cole, C.R., 'The conflict within: Sir Stephen Tallents and planning propaganda overseas before the second world war,' *Albion* 14/1 (1982), 50–71.
45. Marks, S., 'Ménage à trois: the negotiations for an Anglo-French-Belgian alliance in 1922,' *International History R.* 4 (1982), 524–52.
46. Stoff, M.B., 'The Anglo-American oil agreement and the war-time search for foreign policy,' *Business History R.* 55 (1981), 59–74.
47. Canning, P., 'Yet another failure for appeasement? The case of the Irish ports,' *International History R.* 4 (1982), 371–92.
48. Charmley, J., 'Harold Macmillan and the making of the French Committee of Liberation,' ibid. 553–67.
49. Tomlinson, B.R., 'The contraction of England: national decline and the loss of empire,' *J. of Imperial and Commonwealth History* 11 (1982), 58–72.
50. Singh, A.I., 'Imperial defence and the transfer of power in India, 1946–1947,' *International History R.* 4 (1982), 568–88.
51. Andrew, C.M., 'British intelligence and the breach with Russia in 1927,' *Historical J.* 25 (1982), 957–64.
52. Lawlor, S., 'Greece, March 1941: the politics of British military intervention,' ibid. 933–46.
53. Hauner, M., 'Anspruch und Wirklichkeit: Deutschland als dritte Macht in Afghanistan, 1915–1939,' Bc19, 222–44.
54. Fromm, H., 'Das Dritte Reich im Urteil eines Engländers: Harold Nicolson und die Deutschen 1933–1945,' Bc19, 245–62.
55. Bussmann, W., 'Masstäbe diplomatischer Urteilsbildung im Foreign Office während der Rheinlandskrise 1936,' Bc19, 263–80.
56. Rudzio, W., 'Grossbritannien als sozialistische Besatzungsmacht in Deutschland: Aspekte des deutsch-britischen Verhältnisses 1945–1948,' Bc19, 341–52.
57. Schwabe, K., 'Adenauer und England,' Bc19, 353–74.

58. Alexander, G.M. *The prelude to the Truman doctrine: British policy in Greece 1944–1947.* Oxford; Clarendon; 1982.

(e) *Religion*

1. Studdert-Kenedy, G. *Dog-collar democracy: the Industrial Christian Fellowship 1919–1929.* London; Macmillan; 1982. Pp xv, 228.
2. Williams, B. *The Franciscan revival in the Anglican communion.* London; Darton, Longman & Todd; 1982. Pp 208.
3. Morris, P. *The chapel on the hill: a history of Surbiton Hill Methodist church: 1882–1982.* Surbiton; the author; 1981. Pp ix, 91.
4. Lowndes, W. *The Quakers of Fritchley, 1863–1980.* Fritchley; Friends' Meeting House; 1981. Pp vii, 272.
5. Mews, S., 'The revival of spiritual healing in the Church of England 1920–26,' Bc21, 299–31.
6. Homan, R., 'Age of miracles: the pentecostal revival in Sussex,' Bc17, 223–42.
7. Dodd, P., 'The Church in its industrial setting,' Bc11, 247–69.
8. Ward Davis, C., 'One man's answer [parish priest in Byker, 1927–44],' Bc11, 204–15.
9. Robbins, K., 'Religion and identity in modern British history,' Bc10, 465–87.
10. Sefton, H.R., 'The Church of Scotland and Scottish nationhood,' Bc10, 549–55.
11. White, G., ' "No-one is free from parliament": the Worship and Doctrine measure in parliament, 1974,' Bc10, 557–65.

(f) *Economic Affairs*

1. Foldes, L.; Watson, P., 'Quarterly return to investment in ordinary shares, 1919–1970,' *Economica* 49 (1982), 201–5.
2. Bagwell, P.S. *The railwaymen: history of the National Union of Railwaymen, vol. 2: The Beeching era and after.* London; Allen & Unwin; 1982. Pp 456.
3. Harvey, C.E. *The Rio Tinto Company: an economic history of a leading international mining concern, 1873–1954.* Penzance; Alison Hodge; 1981. Pp xiv, 390.
4. Nock, O.S. *A history of the LMS (Steam Past), vol. 1: the first years 1923–1930; vol. 2: the record breaking 'thirties', 1931–9.* London; Allen & Unwin; 1982. Pp 94, 96.
5. Jones, G., 'Lombard Street on the Riviera: the British clearing banks and Europe 1900–1960,' *Business History* 2 (1982), 186–210.
6. Pearce, D. *United Kingdom energy policy: an historical overview 1945–1982.* University of Aberdeen; 1982. Pp 64.

7. Winton, J.R. *Lloyds Bank 1918–1969.* Oxford UP; 1982. Pp viii, 210.
8. Gilbert, J.C. *Keynes's impact on monetary economics.* London; Butterworths; 1982. Pp viii, 280.
9. Reader, W.J. *Bowater: a history.* Cambridge UP; 1981. Pp xv, 426.
10. Clarke, R. (ed. A. Cairncross). *Anglo-American collaboration in war and peace 1942–1949.* Oxford; Clarendon; 1982. Pp xxiii, 215.
11. Macleod, I.; Wilson, G. *Structural engineering in Scotland: a review of developments 1931–1981.* London; Pentech Press; 1981. Pp 143.
12. Wurm, C.A., 'Der Exporthandel und die britische Wirtschaft 1919–1939,' *Vierteljahrschrift für Sozial- und Wirtschaftsgeschichte* 68 (1981), 191–224.
13. Buxton, N.K.; Aldcroft, D.H. (ed.). *British industry between the wars.* London; Scolar Press; 1979. Pp 308.
14. Porter, J.H., 'Cotton and wool textiles,' If13, 25–47.
15. Buxton, N.K., 'Coalmining,' If13, 48–78.
16. Parkinson, J.R., 'Shipbuilding,' If13, 79–102.
17. Warren, K., 'Iron and steel,' If13, 103–28.
18. Gourvish, T.R., 'Mechanical engineering,' If13, 129–55.
19. Reader, W.J., 'The chemical industry,' If13, 156–78.
20. Miller, M.; Church, R.A., 'Motor manufacturing,' If13, 179–215.
21. Fearon, P., 'Aircraft manufacturing,' If13, 216–40.
22. Catterell, R.E., 'Electrical engineering,' If13, 241–75.
23. Harrop, J., 'Rayon,' If13, 276–302.
24. Gamble, A. *Britain in decline: economic policy, political strategy and the British state.* London; Macmillan; 1981. Pp xxi, 279.
25. Campbell, R.H., 'Costs and contracts: lessons from Clyde shipbuilding between the wars,' Bc24, 54–79.
26. Richards, A.B. *Touche Ross & Co. 1899–1981: the origins and growth of the United Kingdom firm.* London; the firm; 1981. Pp xiii, 145.
27. Dummett, G.A. *From little acorns: a history of the A.P.V. Company Limited.* London; Hutchinson Benham; 1981. Pp xiv, 247.
28. Masefield, P.G. *To ride the storm: the story of the airship R. 101.* London; Kimber; 1982. Pp 560.
29. Gordon, B. *One hundred years of electricity supply 1881–1981.* Hove; Southeastern Electricity Board; 1981. Pp 83.
30. Gould, W.T.S.; Hodgkiss, A.G. *The resources of Merseyside.* Liverpool UP; 1982. Pp xiv, 198.
31. Aspinall, P.J.; Hudson, D.M.; Lawton, R. *Ellesmere Port: the making of an industrial borough.* Neston: Borough Council; 1982. Pp 328.
32. Eatwell, J. *Whatever happened to Britain? The economics of decline.* London; Duckworth; 1982. Pp 168.

33. Moggeridge, D.E. (ed.). *The collected writings of John Maynard Keynes, vol. 20: Activities 1929–1931 – rethinking employment and unemployment policies.* London; Macmillan; 1981. Pp xii, 668.
34. Moggeridge, D.E. *Ditto, vol. 21: Activities 1931–1939, world crises and policies in Britain and America.* The same; 1982. Pp xiii, 632.
35. Coad, R. *Laing: the biography of Sir John W. Laing, C.B.E. (1879–1978).* London; Hodder & Stoughton; 1979. Pp 238.
36. Channon, G., 'The Great Western Railway under the British Railways Act of 1921,' *Business History R.* 5 (1981), 188–216.
37. Griffin, A.R. *The Nottinghamshire coalfield 1881–1981: a century of progress.* Ashbourne; Moorland Publications; 1981. Pp 145.
38. Duncan, S., 'Chemical industry in its historical context,' *The Chemical Industry*, ed. D.H. Sharp & T.F. West (Chichester; Ellis Horwood; 1982), 40–61.
39. Pollard, S. *The wasting of the British economy.* London; Croom Helm; 1982. Pp 192.
40. Whetham, E.H. *Agricultural economists in Britain 1900–1940.* Oxford; Institute of Agricultural Economics; 1981. Pp vi, 97.
41. McGoldrick, J., 'Crisis and the division of labour: Clydeside shipbuilding in the inter-war period,' Bc18, 143–85.
42. Wybrow, P., 'The Scottish labour movement and the offshore oil industry,' Bc18, 251–77.
43. Hannah, L. *Engineers, managers and politicians: the first fifteen years of nationalised electricity supply in Britain.* London; Macmillan; 1982. Pp xiii, 336.

(g) *Social Structure and Population*

1. Lee, E.A.M.; Vaisey, M.H., 'The army agent 1661–1918, part II: 1918 onwards,' *Three Banks R.* 132 (1981), 63–9.
2. *Fifty years of adult study: University of London Goldsmiths' College School of Adult and Social Studies Golden Jubilee, 1931–1981.* London; the University; 1981. Pp 112.
3. Pissarides, C.A., 'Staying on at school in England and Wales,' *Economica* 48 (1981), 345–63.
4. Joshi, H.E., 'Secondary workers in the employment cycle: Great Britain, 1961–1974,' ibid. 29–44.
5. Webster, C., 'Healthy or hungry thirties?,' *History Workshop* 13 (1982), 110–29.
6. Brandon, P.F., 'A twentieth-century squire in his landscape,' *Southern History* 4 (1982), 191–220.
7. Williamson, B. *Class, culture and community: a biographical study of social change in mining.* London; Routledge; 1982. Pp xiv, 245.

8. Sherrington, G. *English education, social change and war, 1911–20.* Manchester UP; 1981. Pp xiii, 194.
9. Stead, P., 'The people and the pictures: the British working class and film in the 1930s,' Ib33, 77–97.
10. Gallagher, R., 'The Vale of Leven 1914–1925: changes in working class organisation and action,' Bc18, 186–211.
11. Watt, I., 'Occupational stratification and the sexual division of labour: Scotland since 1945,' Bc18, 212–50.
12. Stead, P., 'The voluntary response to mass unemployment in South Wales,' Bc12, 97–117.
13. Norton, B., 'Psychologists and class,' Bc5, 289–314.
14. Miliband, R. *Capitalist democracy in Britain.* Oxford UP; 1982.

(h) *Social Policy*

1. Ravetz, A. *Remaking cities: contradictions of the recent urban environment.* London; Croom Helm; 1980. Pp 375.
2. Dunleavy, P. *The politics of mass housing in Britain, 1945–1975: a study of corporate power and professional influence in the welfare state.* Oxford; Clarendon; 1981. Pp xvi, 447.
3. Marsh, J., 'The unemployed and the land,' *History Today* 32/4 (1982), 16–20.
4. Garside, W.R., 'Unemployment and the school-leaving age in inter-war Britain,' *International R. of Social History* 26 (1981), 159–70.
5. Smith, H., 'The problem of "equal pay for equal work" in Great Britain during World War II,' *J. of Modern History* 53 (1981), 652–72.
6. Summerfield, P., 'Education and politics in the British armed forces in the second world war,' *International R. of Social History* 26 (1981), 133–58.
7. Cullingworth, J.B. *Environmental planning, 1939–1969, vol. 4: Land values, compensation and betterment.* London; HMSO; 1980. Pp xv, 582.
8. Evans, B.J., 'Further education pressure groups: the campaign for continued and technical education in 1944,' *History of Education* 11 (1982), 45–55.
9. Pater, J.E. *The making of the National Health Service.* London; King Edward's Hospital Fund; 1981. Pp xii, 210.
10. Kogan, M. *The politics of educational change.* Manchester UP; 1978. Pp 172.
11. Macnicol, J. *The movement for family allowances, 1918–45: a study on social policy development.* London; Heinemann; 1980. Pp xiii, 243.
12. Melling, J. (ed.). *Housing, social policy and the state.* London; Croom Helm; 1980. Pp 233.

13. Finnigan, R., 'Housing policy in Leeds between the wars,' Ig12, 113–38.
14. Melling, J., 'Clydeside housing and the evolution of state rent control, 1900–1929,' Ig12, 139–67.
15. Byrne, D., 'The standard of council housing in inter-war North Shields – a case study on the politics of reproduction,' Ig12, 168–93.
16. Dale, J., 'Class struggle, social policy and state structure: central-local relations and housing policy, 1919–1939,' Ig12, 194–223.
17. Lowe, R., 'Welfare legislation and the unions during and after the first world war,' *Historical J.* 25 (1982), 437–41. – Whiteside, N., 'Industrial labour and welfare legislation after the first world war: a reply,' ibid. 443–6.
18. Jones, G., 'Eugenics and social policy between the wars,' *Historical J.* 25 (1982), 717–28.
19. Younghusband, E. *The newest profession: a short history of social work.* Sutton; Community Care; 1981. Pp 46.
20. Starkie, D. *The motorway age: road and traffic policies in post-war Britain.* Oxford; Pergamon; 1982. Pp xiii, 176.
21. Allan, P.; Jolley, M. (ed.). *Nursing, midwifery and health visiting since 1900.* London; Faber; 1982. Pp 316.
22. Pyne, R.H., 'The General Nursing Councils,' Ih21, 33–49.
23. Jolley, M., 'General nursing,' Ih21, 64–79.
24. Watkin, B., 'Before and after the National Health Service,' Ih21, 50–63.
25. Kratz, C.R., 'District nursing,' Ih21, 80–91.
26. Owens, G.M., 'Health visiting,' Ih21, 92–105.
27. Everest, R., 'Mental illness nursing,' Ih21, 106–24.
28. Birchenall, P.D., 'Mental handicap nursing,' Ih21, 125–40.
29. Saunders, D.M., 'Sick children's nursing,' Ih21, 141–50.
30. Slaney, B.M., 'Occupational health nursing,' Ih21, 150–7.
31. Blenkinsop, D., 'The preparation of nurse managers,' Ih21, 158–73.
32. Green, M.D., 'The preparation of "teachers",' Ih21, 174–9.
33. Bent, E.A., 'The growth and development of midwifery,' Ih21, 180–95.
34. Hayward, J.C.; Lelean, S.R., 'Nursing research,' Ih21, 196–214.
35. Cowie, A.V., 'Organised labour,' Ih21, 215–32.
36. Rye, D.H., 'Prospective [on nursing and midwifery], post-1980,' Ih21, 285–98.
37. Searby, P. *The training of teachers in Cambridge University: the first sixty years, 1879–1939.* Cambridge University Dept of Education; 1982. Pp 45.
38. Smart, R. *Bedford Training College, 1882–1982: a history of a Froebel college and its schools.* Bedford; the College; 1982. Pp xv, 178.

39. Vinson, A.J., 'Unemployment relief works in Southampton between the wars: a case study,' Bc12, 63–95.
40. Hogg, G.W., 'The Church and school education: 2. From 1981 [i.e. 1918] to the present,' Bc11, 291–312.

(i) *Naval and Military*

1. Conduit, B.D.P., 'Britain's arctic gamble: the Russo-Finnish war, 1939–40,' *History Today* 32/3 (1982), 26–32.
2. Terraine, J., 'The spectre of the bomber,' *History Today* 32/4 (1982), 4–9.
3. Vaughan, E.C. *Some desperate glory: the diary of a young officer, 1917.* London; Warne; 1981. Pp xi, 232.
4. Hinsley, F.H.; Thomas, E.E.; Ransom, C.F.G.; Knight, R.C. *British intelligence in the Second World War: its influence on strategy and operations* (vol. 2). London; HMSO; 1981. Pp xv, 850.
5. Strawson, J. *El Alamein – desert victory.* London; Dent; 1981. Pp 191.
6. Love, R.W., 'Anglo-American naval diplomacy and the British Pacific Fleet, 1942–1945,' *American Neptune* 42 (1982), 203–16.
7. Whetton, J.T.; Ogden, R.H. *Z location, or, Survey in war: the story of the 4th Durham Survey Regiment.* Bolton; Ogden; 1982. Pp 195.
8. Sweetman, J. *Operation Chastise: the dams raid, epic or myth?* London; Jane's; 1982. Pp xiv, 218.
9. Sturtivant, R. *Fleet air arm at war.* London; Ian Allan; 1982. Pp 144.
10. Compton-Hall, R. *The underwater war 1939–1945.* Poole; Blandford Press; 1982. Pp 160.
11. Keegan, J. *Six armies in Normandy.* London; Cape; 1982. Pp 320.
12. Brook-Shepherd, G. *November 1918: the last act of the Great War.* London; Collins; 1982. Pp 461.
13. Wark, W.K., 'British Intelligence on the German Air Force and aircraft industry, 1933–1939,' *Historical J.* 25 (1982), 627–48.
14. Connell, G.G. *Arctic destroyers: the 17th flotilla.* London; Kimber; 1982.
15. Cocker, M. *Destroyers of the Royal Navy 1893–1981.* London; Ian Allan; 1981. Pp 136.
16. Eriksen, K.E., 'Great Britain and the problem of bases in the Nordic area, 1945–1947,' *Scandinavian J. of History* 7 (1982), 135–63.
17. Bidwell, S.; Graham, D. *Fire-power: British army weapons and theories of war 1904–1945.* London; Allen & Unwin; 1982. Pp xvi, 327.

18. Baden-Powell, D. *Operation Jupiter: SOE's secret war in Norway.* London; Hale; 1982. Pp 208.
19. Beesley, P. *Room 40: British naval intelligence 1914–18.* London; Hamilton; 1982. Pp 352.
20. Beevor, J.G. *SOE: recollections and reflections 1940–1945.* London; Bodley Head; 1981. Pp 269.
21. Doughty, M. *Merchant shipping and war: a study of defence planning in twentieth-century Britain.* London; Royal Historical Soc. (Studies in History 31); 1982. Pp ix, 218.
22. Messenger, C. *Terriers in the trenches: the Post Office Rifles at war 1914–1918.* Chippenham; Picton; 1982. Pp xii, 170.
23. Winstone, H.V.F. *Leachman, 'OC Desert': the life of Lieutenant-Colonel Gerard Leachman, D.S.O.* London; Quartet; 1982. Pp x, 246.
24. Messenger, C. *Cologne: the first 1000-bomber raid.* London; Ian Allan; 1982. Pp 64.
25. Denham, H.M. *Dardanelles.* London; Murray; 1981. Pp 224.
26. Fraser, D. *Alanbrooke.* London; Collins; 1982. Pp 591.
27. Ride, E. *BAAG: Hong Kong resistance 1942–1945.* Oxford UP; 1981. Pp xiv, 347.
28. Price, A. *The Spitfire story.* London; Jane's; 1982. Pp 256.
29. Smith, P.C.; Dominy, J.R. *Cruisers in action 1939–1945.* London; Kimber; 1982. Pp 320.
30. Stewart, A. *Hurricane: the war exploits of the fighter aircraft.* London; Kimber; 1982. Pp 336.
31. Golley, J. *The big drop: the guns of Merville, June 1944.* London; Jane's; 1982. Pp 174.
32. Levin, R. *The other Ultra.* London; Hutchinson; 1982.
33. Kinsey, G.; Wilkins, A.F. *Orfordness – secret site: a history of the establishment 1915–1980.* Lavenham; Dalton; 1981. Pp xi, 180.
34. Chichester, M.; Wilkinson, J. *The uncertain ally: British defence policy 1960–1990.* Aldershot; Gower; 1982. Pp xvii, 246.
35. Wiggan, R. *Hunt the Altmark.* London; Hale; 1982. Pp 176.
36. Wettern, D. *The decline of British seapower.* London; Jane's; 1982. Pp 452.
37. Mosley, L. *The druid [Nazi spy].* London; Eyre Methuen; 1982. Pp 256.
38. Pronay, N., 'The news media at war,' Ib33, 173–208.
39. Collier, B. *Hidden weapons: allied secret or undercover services in World War II.* London; Hamilton; 1982. Pp xviii, 386.
40. Holmes, R.; Kemp, A. *The bitter end: the fall of Singapore 1941–1942.* Chichester; Anthony Bird; 1982.
41. Anderson, R.W., 'Naming a generation of Cunarders,' *American Neptune* 42 (1982), 295–300.
42. Kettenacker, L., 'Preussen in der alliierten Kriegszielplanung, 1939–1947,' Bc19, 312–40.

43. Hughes, C. *Mametz: Lloyd George's 'Welsh army' at the Battle of the Somme.* Gerrards Cross; Orion Press; 1982. Pp 160.
44. Robertson, A.J., 'Lord Beaverbrook and the supply of aircraft, 1940–1941,' Bc24, 80–100.
45. Fernbach, D., 'Tom Wintringham and socialist defence strategy,' *History Workshop* 14 (1982), 63–91.

(j) *Intellectual and Cultural*

1. Moggridge, D.E. (ed.). *The collected writings of John Maynard Keynes, vol. 25: Activities 1940–1944.* London; Macmillan for Royal Economic Soc.; 1980. Pp xiv, 522.
2. Not used.
3. MacKenna, R.O. *Glasgow University Athletic Club: the story of the first hundred years.* Glasgow; the Club; 1981. Pp 128.
4. Hawkes, J. *Mortimer Wheeler: adventurer in archaeology.* London; Weidenfeld & Nicolson; 1982. Pp xii, 387.
5. Husemann, H., 'Zu den deutsch-englischen Universitätsbeziehungen während der letzten hundert Jahre,' *Geschichte und Gegenwart*, ed. H. Boockmann et al. (Neumünster; Wachholtz; 1980), 459–90.
6. Topping, J. *The beginnings of Brunel University: from technical college to university.* Oxford UP; 1982. Pp xii, 449.
7. Hyman, A. *Charles Babbage: pioneer of the computer.* Oxford UP; 1982. Pp xi, 287.
8. Richards, J., 'The British Board of Film Censors and content control in the 1930s: images of Britain & foreign affairs,' *Historical J. of Film, Radio and Television* 1 (1981), 95–116; 2 (1982), 39–48.
9. Robertson, J.C., 'British film censorship goes to war,' ibid. 2 (1982), 49–64.
10. Haynes, R. *The Society for Psychical Research, 1882–1982.* London; MacDonald; 1982. Pp xv, 240.
11. Fisher, P. *External examinations in secondary schools in England and Wales 1944–1964.* Leeds; Museum of the History of Education; 1982. Pp iv, 83.
12. Burnet, C. *Three centuries to Concorde.* London; Mechanical Engineering Publications; 1979. Pp xii, 276.
13. Brown, J. *Gardens of a golden afternoon: the story of a partnership: Edwin Lutyens and Gertrude Jekyll.* London; Allen Lane; 1982. Pp 208.
14. Beauman, S. *The Royal Shakespeare Company: a history of ten decades.* Oxford UP; 1982.
15. Bass, H. *Glorious Wembley: the official history of Britain's foremost entertainment centre.* Enfield; Guinness Superlatives; 1982. Pp 176.

16. Reisman, D. *State and welfare: Tawney, Galbraith and Adam Smith.* London; Macmillan; 1982. Pp viii, 254.
17. Young, M. *The Elmhirsts of Dartington: the creation of an Utopian community.* London; Routledge; 1982. Pp x, 381.
18. James, T.J.H. (ed.). *Excavating in Egypt: the Egypt Exploration Society, 1882–1982.* London; British Museum Publications; 1982. Pp 192.
19. Devereux, W.A. *Adult education in Inner London 1870–1980.* London; Shepheard-Walwyn; 1982.
20. Clapp, B.W. *The University of Exeter: a history.* Exeter; the University; 1982. Pp xiv, 208.
21. Reckitt, B.N. *A history of the Sir James Reckitt Charity 1921–1979.* Withernsea; the Trustee; 1981. Pp 53.
22. *The landscape of Oxford's green belt.* Oxford University Dept for External Studies; 1981. Pp v, 88.
23. Perry, G. *Forever Ealing [films].* London; Pavilion Books; 1981.
24. Moore, G.H. *The University of Bath: the formative years 1949–1969: a short history of the circumstances which led to the foundation of the University of Bath.* Bath UP; 1982. Pp 110.
25. Lucas, R. *The voice of a nation? A concise account of the BBC in Wales, 1923–1973.* Llandysul; Gomer; 1981. Pp 233.
26. Yorke, M. *Eric Gill: a man of flesh and spirit.* London; Constable; 1981. Pp 304.
27. Forman, H., 'The non-theatrical distribution of film by the Ministry of Information,' Ib33, 221–33.
28. Dalrymple, I., 'The Crown Film Unit, 1940–43,' Ib33, 209–20.
29. Buchan, W. *John Buchan: a memoir.* London; Buchan & Enright; 1982. Pp 272.
30. Durant, J.R., 'Innate character in animals and man: a perspective on the origins of ethology,' Bc5, 157–92.
31. Sutherland, G., 'Measuring intelligence: English Local Education Authorities and mental testing, 1919–1939,' Bc5, 315–35.

J. MEDIEVAL WALES

(a) *General*

1. Davies, W. *Wales in the early middle ages.* Leicester UP; 1982. Pp 280.
2. Smith, L.B., 'The death of Llywelyn ap Gruffyd: the narratives reconsidered,' *Welsh History R.* 11 (1982), 200–13.

(b) *Politics*

1. Owen, D.H., 'Welsh and English princes of Wales,' *History Today* 32/12 (1982), 11–15.

2. Rowland, I.W., 'William de Braose and the lordship of Brecon,' *B. of the Board of Celtic Studies* 30 (1982), 123–33.

(c) *Constitution, Administration and Law*

1. Sheringham, J.G.T., 'Bullocks with horns as long as their ears,' *B. of the Board of Celtic Studies* 29 (1982), 691–708.
2. Williams, D.H. *Welsh history through seals.* Cardiff; Amgueddfa Genedlaethol Cymru; 1982. Pp 48.
3. Jones, G.R.J., 'Early customary tenures in Wales and open-field agriculture,' Bc3, 202–25.
4. Davies, W., 'The latin-charter tradition in western Britain, Brittany and Ireland in the early medieval period,' Bc13, 258–80.
5. Taylor, A.J., 'The Conwy particular accounts for Nov. 1285–Sept. 1286,' *B. of the Board of Celtic Studies* 30 (1982), 134–47.

(d) *External Affairs*

(e) *Religion*

1. Evans, D.H., 'Excavations at Llanthony priory, 1978,' *Monmouthshire Antiquary* 4 (1980), 5–43.
2. Williams, D.H., 'Usk nunnery,' ibid. 44–5.

(f) *Economic Affairs*

1. Boon, G.C. *Cardigan silver and the Aberystwyth mint in peace and war.* Cardiff; National Museum of Wales; 1981. Pp xiii, 287.
2. Williams-Davies, J. *Welsh sheep and their wool.* Llandysul; Gomer; 1981. Pp 74.
3. Jenkins, J.G. *From fleece to fabric: the technological history of the Welsh woollen industry.* Ibid.; 1981. Pp 37.
4. Faull, M.L., 'Celtic numerals for counting sheep,' *Local Historian* 15 (1982), 21–3.
5. Jones, J.E.T., 'Old fairs in Wales,' *J. of the Merioneth Historical and Record Soc.* 9/1 (1981), 3–16.

(g) *Social Structure and Population*

1. Powell, R.F.P., 'Notes on a place-names element peculiar to Breconshire,' *Brycheiniog* 19 (1980–1), 83–95.

(h) *Naval and Military*

(i) *Intellectual and Cultural*

1. Peden, A., 'Science and philosophy in Wales at the time of the Norman Conquest: a Macrobius manuscript from Llabadarn,' *Cambridge Medieval Celtic Studies* 2 (1981), 21–45.
2. Huws, D., 'Llawysgrif Hendregadredd,' *National Library of Wales J.* 22 (1981), 1–26.
3. Moore, D., 'Early views of towns in Wales and the borders,' *T. of the Honourable Soc. of Cymmrodorion* (1981), 35–50.
4. Bartlett, R. *Gerald of Wales, 1146–1223.* Oxford; Clarendon; 1982. Pp 350.
5. Roberts, B.F. *Gerald of Wales.* Cardiff; University of Wales Press; 1982. Pp 124.
6. Jackson, K., 'Gildas and the names of the British princes,' *Cambridge Medieval Celtic Studies* 3 (1982), 30–40.
7. Thomson, D., 'Cistercians and schools in late medieval Wales,' ibid. 76–80.
8. Oates, J.C.T., 'Notes on the later history of the oldest manuscript of Welsh poetry: the Cambridge Juvencus,' ibid. 81–7.
9. Hamp, E.P., '*Lloegr*: the Welsh name for England,' ibid. 4 (1982), 83–5.
10. Lewis, J.M., 'A medieval gold finger-ring from Llanrithyd, South Glamorgan,' *Antiquaries J.* 62 (1982), 129–31.

K. SCOTLAND BEFORE THE UNION

(a) *General*

1. Good, G.L.; Tabraham, C.J., 'Excavations at Threave Castle, Galloway,' *Medieval Archaeology* 25 (1981), 90–140.
2. Dodgshon, R.A. *Land and society in early Scotland.* Oxford; Clarendon; 1982.
3. McIvor, I.; Thomas, M.C.; Breeze, D.J., 'Excavations on the Antonine Wall fort of Rough Castle, Stirlingshire, 1957–61,' *P. of the Soc. of Antiquaries of Scotland* 110 (1981 for 1978–80), 230–85.
4. Richmond, I.A. (ed. Hanson, W.S.), 'A Roman fort at Inveresk, Midlothian,' ibid. 286–304.
5. Rowntree Bodie, W.G., 'Introduction to the Rothes papers,' ibid. 404–31.
6. Miller, M., 'Hiberni reversuri,' ibid. 305–27.
7. Slade, H.G., 'Arbuthnot House, Kincardineshire,' ibid. 432–74.
8. Johnston, D.B., 'Letters and papers of the Setons of Mounie, including the papers of Dr. James Anderson,' *Northern Scotland* 5 (1982), 71–9.

9. Lenman, B., 'Reinterpreting Scotland's last two centuries of independence [review article],' *Historical J.* 25 (1982), 217–28.
10. Caldwell, D.H. (ed.). *Scottish weapons and fortifications 1100–1800.* Edinburgh; John Donald; 1981. Pp xvii, 452.
11. Mitchison, R. *A history of Scotland* (2nd ed.). London; Methuen; 1982. Pp 468.
12. Kenworthy, J. (ed.). *Agricola's campaigns in Scotland: Scottish Archaeological Forum 12.* Edinburgh UP; 1981. Pp 114.
13. Jackson, K., '*Varia*: I. Bede's *Urbs Giudi*: Stirling or Cramond?,' *Cambridge Medieval Celtic Studies* 2 (1981), 1–7.
14. Booth, C.G. *A list of Islay people.* Isle of Islay Museums Trust; 1982. 30 leaves.
15. James, I.E. *The goldsmiths of Aberdeen.* Aberdeen; Bieldside Books; 1981. Pp 156.
16. Urquhart, J. *Dumfries: the remarkable story of its common seal and coat of arms with a wealth of local history.* Dumfries; the author; 1981. Pp xiii, 168.
17. Murray, J.C. *Excavations in the medieval burgh of Aberdeen, 1973–82.* Edinburgh; Soc. of Antiquaries of Scotland; 1982.
18. MacDonald, M. (ed.). *A Lorn miscellany of history and tradition.* Oban; Lorn Arch. and Historical Soc.; 1982. Pp 76.
19. Royal Commission of the Ancient and Historical Monuments of Scotland. *Argyll: an inventory of the monuments; vol. 4: Iona.* Edinburgh; HMSO; 1982. Pp xvi, 296.
20. Smith, A.M., 'A Scottish aristocrat's diet, 1671,' *Scottish Historical R.* 61 (1982), 146–57.
21. Linnard, W., 'Timber floating: an early record on the Tay and the use of coracles or currachs,' *Scottish Studies* 25 (1982), 77–9.
22. Oftedal, M., 'Names of lakes on the Isle of Lewis in the Outer Hebrides,' *P. of the Eighth Viking Congress*, ed. H. Bekker-Nielsen et al. (Odense UP; 1981), 183–7.
23. Hunter, J.; Morris, C.D., 'Recent excavations at the Brough of Birsay, Orkney,' ibid. 245–58.
24. Houston, R.A. (ed.). *Records of a Scottish village: Lasswade 1650–1750.* Cambridge; Chadwick-Healey; 1982. Pp 32 + microfiche.
25. McLean, A. *The place names of Cowal: their meaning and history.* Dunoon Observer; 1982. Pp 137.
26. Webster, B. (ed.). *Regesta regum Scotorum, vol. 6: The acts of David II, king of Scots 1329–1371.* Edinburgh UP; 1982. Pp xiii, 571.

(b) *Politics*

1. Head, D.M., 'Henry VIII's Scottish policy: a reassessment,' *Scottish Historical R.* 61 (1982), 1–24.
2. Murray, J.E.L. & J.K.R., 'Notes on the vicit leo testoons of Mary

Queen of Scots,' *British Numismatic J.* 50 (1981 for 1980), 81–90.

3. Anderson, P.D. *Robert Stewart: earl of Orkney, lord of Shetland 1533–1593.* Edinburgh; Donald; 1982. Pp viii, 245.
4. Macdougall, N. *James III: a political study.* Edinburgh; Donald; 1982. Pp 338.
5. Reid, N., 'The kingless kingdom: the Scottish guardianship of 1286–1306,' *Scottish Historical R.* 61 (1982), 105–29.
6. Anderson, M.O., 'Dalriada and the creation of the kingdom of the Scots,' Bc13, 106–32.
7. Barrow, G.W.S., 'Popular courts in early medieval Scotland: some suggested place-name evidence,' *Scottish Studies* 25 (1982), 1–24.
8. Cowan, E.J., 'The Angus Campbells and the origin of the Campbell-Ogilvie feud,' ibid. 25–38.
9. Scott, R.M. *Robert the Bruce, king of Scots.* London; Hutchinson; 1982. Pp xviii, 254.
10. Hewitt, G.R. *Scotland under Morton 1572–80.* Edinburgh; Donald; 1982. Pp vii, 232.
11. Furgol, E.M., 'The military and ministers as agents of presbyterian imperialism in England and Ireland, 1640–1648,' Bc45, 95–115.

(c) *Constitution, Administration and Law*

1. Stevenson, D., 'The "Letter on sovereign power" and the influence of Jean Bodin on political thought in Scotland,' *Scottish Historical R.* 61 (1982), 25–43.
2. Macqueen, H.L., 'The brieve of right in Scots law,' *J. of Legal History* 3 (1982), 52–70.
3. Walkes, D.M. (ed.). *Stair tercentenary studies.* Edinburgh; Stair Soc.; 1981. Pp viii, 267.
4. Walker, D.M., 'Stair's contributions to Scots law,' Kc3, 250–2.
5. Luiz, K., 'Stair from a foreign standpoint,' Kc3, 239–50.
6. Lawson, F.H., 'Stair from an English standpoint,' Kc3, 227–39.
7. Blackie, J.W.G., 'Stair's later reputation as a jurist,' Kc3, 207–27.
8. Paton, G.C.H., 'Comparison between the Institutions and other institutional writings,' Kc3, 201–27.
9. MacCormick, D.N., 'Stair as an analytical jurist,' Kc3, 187–99.
10. Stein, P.G., 'The theory of law,' Kc3, 181–7.
11. Walker, D.M., 'The content of the Institutions,' Kc3, 151–79.
12. Halliday, J.M., 'Feudal law as a source,' Kc3, 136–50.
13. Cary, A.J., 'The law of nature and nations as a source,' Kc3, 127–36.
14. Robertson, J.J., 'Canon law as a source,' Kc3, 112–27.
15. Gordon, W.M., 'Roman law as a source,' Kc3, 107–12.

16. Walker, D.M., 'The structure and arrangement of the Institutions,' Kc3, 100–5.
17. Hutton, G.M., 'Stair's philosophic precursors,' Kc3, 87–99.
18. Hutton, G.M., 'Stair's aim in writing the Institutions,' Mc3, 79–87.
19. Walker, D.M., 'The background of the Institutions,' Kc3, 69–78.
20. Hutton, G.M., 'Stair's public career,' Kc3, 1–68.
21. Smith, L.M., 'Sackcloth for the sinner or punishment for the crime? Church and secular courts in Cromwellian Scotland,' Bc25, 116–32.

(d) *External Affairs*

1. Cooney, J. *Scotland and the papacy.* Edinburgh; Harris; 1982. Pp 126.

(e) *Religion*

1. Drexler, M., 'The extant abridgements of Walter Bower's Scotichronicon,' *Scottish Historical R.* 61 (1982), 62–7.
2. Morrill, J., 'Seventeenth-century Scotland [review article],' *J. of Ecclesiastical History* 33 (1982), 266–71.
3. Lynch, M. *Edinburgh and the Reformation.* Edinburgh; Donald; 1981. Pp xv, 416.
4. Larner, C. *Enemies of God: the witch-hunt in Scotland.* London; Chatto & Windus; 1981. Pp x, 244.
5. *The 17th century witch craze in West Fife: a guide to the printed sources.* Dunfermline District Libraries; 1980. 30 leaves.
6. Somerville, R. (ed.). *Scotia pontificia: papal letters to Scotland before the pontificate of Innocent III.* Oxford; Clarendon; 1982. Pp xiii, 177.
7. Miner, J.N., 'Church and community in later medieval Glasgow: an introductory essay,' *Histoire sociale/Social History* 15 (1982), 5–33.
8. Cowan, I.B. *The Scottish Reformation: church and society in sixteenth-century Scotland.* London; Weidenfeld; 1982. Pp x, 244.
9. Lenman, B., 'The Scottish episcopal clergy and the ideology of Jacobitism,' Bc22, 36–48.
10. Williamson, A.H., 'Scotland, antichrist and the invention of Great Britain,' Bc25, 34–58.

(f) *Economic Affairs*

1. Gauldie, E. *The quarries and the feus: a history of Invergowrie.* Dundee; Waterside Press; 1981. Pp 106.

(g) *Social Structure and Population*

1. Sanderson, M.H.B. *Scottish rural society in the sixteenth century*. Edinburgh; Donald; 1982. Pp ix, 286.
2. Booth, C.G. *Index of pre 1855 gravestone inscriptions in Islay.* Isle of Islay Museums Trust; 1981. 32 leaves.
3. Love, J.A., 'Shielings of the Isle of Rum,' *Scottish Studies* 25 (1982), 39–63.
4. Lamont, W.D., ' "House" and "pennyland" in the Highlands and Isles,' ibid. 65–76.
5. Hunter, J.R., 'Medieval Berwick-upon-Tweed,' *Archaeologia Aeliana* 5th ser. 10 (1982), 67–124.

(h) *Naval and Military*

1. Graham, E.F., 'The Scottish marine during the Dutch wars,' *Scottish Historical R.* 61 (1982), 67–74.
2. Crawford, I.A., 'War or peace – Viking colonisation in the northern and western Isles of Scotland reviewed,' *P. of the Eighth Viking Congress*, ed. H. Bekker-Nielsen et al. (Odense UP; 1981), 259–69.
3. Reid, S. *Scots armies of the civil war, 1639–1651.* Leigh-on-Sea; Partizan Press; 1982. Pp 50.

(i) *Intellectual and Cultural*

1. Withers, C.W.J., 'The geographical extent of Gaelic in Scotland 1698–1806,' *Scottish Geographical Magazine* 97 (1981), 130–9.
2. Gillies, W., 'Arthur in Gaelic tradition, part I: folktales and ballads,' *Cambridge Medieval Celtic Studies* 2 (1981), 47–72.
3. Stevenson, D., 'Scotland's first newspaper, 1648,' *The Bibliothek* 10 (1981), 123–6.
4. Dunbar, J.T. *The costume of Scotland.* London; Batsford; 1981. Pp 212.
5. Houston, R., 'The literacy myth? Illiteracy in Scotland 1630–1760,' *Past and Present* 96 (1982), 81–102.
6. Twiss, G.P.; Chennell, P. *Famous rectors of St. Andrews.* St Andrews; Alvie; 1982. Pp 143.
7. Not used.
8. Durkan, J., 'Giovanni Ferrerio and religious humanism in sixteenth-century Scotland,' Bc1, 181–94.
9. Miller, M., 'Matriliny by treaty: the Pictish foundation-legend,' Bc13, 133–61.
10. Henderson, I., 'Pictish art and the Book of Kells,' Bc13, 79–105.
11. Reid, D. (ed.). *The party-coloured mind: prose relating to the*

conflict of church and state in seventeenth century Scotland. Edinburgh; Scottish Academic Press; 1982. Pp x, 221.

12. Evans, D.W., 'James Watson of Edinburgh: a bibliography of works from his press, 1695–1722,' *Edinburgh Bibliographical Soc. T.* 5/2 (1982), 5–158.
13. Mason, R.A., '*Rex stoicus*: George Buchanan, James VI and the Scottish polity,' Bc25, 9–33.
14. Macinnes, A.T., 'Scottish Gaeldom, 1638–1651: the vernacular response to the covenanting dynamic,' Bc25, 59–94.
15. Ouston, M., 'York in Edinburgh: James VII and the patronage of learning in Scotland, 1679–1688,' Bc25, 133–55.
16. Alcock, L., 'Forteriot: a Pictish and Scottish royal church and palace,' Bc27, 211–40.

L. IRELAND TO ca. 1640

(a) *General*

1. Frame, R. *English lordship in Ireland, 1318–1361.* Oxford; Clarendon; 1982. Pp 360.
2. Löwe, H. (ed.). *Die Iren und Europa im früheren Mittelalter.* Stuttgart; Lett-Cotta; 1982. Pp xviii, 1083.
3. Ó Corráin, D. (ed.). *Irish antiquity: essays and studies presented to Professor M.J. O'Kelly.* Cork; Tower Books; 1982. Pp xxviii, 350.
4. Ó Cuív, B., 'A fragment of Irish annals,' *Celtica* 14 (1982 for 1981), 83–103.
5. Sheane, M. *Ulster and the middle ages.* Stockport; Highfield; 1982. Pp 195.

(b) *Politics*

1. Ó Corráin, D., 'Foreign connections and domestic politics: Killaloe and the Uí Briain in twelfth-century hagiography,' Bc13, 213–31.
2. O'Brien, A.F., 'The territorial ambitions of Maurice FitzThomas, first earl of Desmond, with particular reference to the barony and manor of Inchiquin, co. Cork,' *P. of the Royal Irish Academy* 82:C:3 (1982), 59–88.
3. Dunne, T.J., 'The Gaelic response to conquest and colonisation: the evidence of the poetry,' *Studia Hibernica* 20 (1982 for 1980), 7–30.
4. Flanagan, M.T., 'Mac Dalbaig, a Leinster chieftain,' *J. of the Royal Soc. of Antiquaries of Ireland* 111 (1982 for 1981), 5–13.

5. Hunter, R.J. et al. *The plantation in Ulster in Strabane barony, co. Tyrone, c. 1600–41.* Londonderry; New University of Ulster; 1982. Pp vii, 61.

(c) *Constitution, Administration and Law*

1. Harris, F.W., 'The rebellion of Sir Cahir O'Doherty and its legal aftermath,' *Irish Jurist* new ser. 15 (1980), 298–325.
2. Ellis, S.G., 'Historical revision XIX: The Irish customs administration under the early Tudors,' *Irish Historical Studies* 22 (1981), 271–7.
3. Bradshaw, B., 'A treatise for the reformation of Ireland 1554–5,' *Irish Jurist* new ser. 16 (1981), 299–315.
4. Brand, P., 'Ireland and the literature of the early common law,' ibid. 95–113.
5. Turner, R.V., 'Roger Huscarl: professional lawyer in England and royal justice in Ireland, c. 1199–1230,' ibid. 290–8.
6. Harris, F.W., 'The commission of 1609: legal aspects,' *Studia Hibernica* 20 (1982 for 1980), 31–55.
7. Melia, D.F., 'The Irish church in the Irish laws,' Bc27, 363–78.

(d) *External Affairs*

1. Contreni, J.J., 'The Irish in the western Carolingian empire,' La2, 758–98.
2. Löwe, H., 'Die Iren und Europa im früheren Mittelalter,' La2, 1013–40.
3. James, E., 'Ireland and western Gaul in the Merovingian period,' Bc13, 362–86.

(e) *Religion*

1. O'Dwyer, P. *Céli Dé: spiritual reform in Ireland, 750–900.* Dublin; Editions Tailliura; 1981. Pp xvi, 213.
2. Angenendt, A., 'Die irische Peregrinatio und ihre Auswirkungen auf dem Kontinent vor dem Jahre 800,' La2, 52–97.
3. Berschin, W., 'Ich Patricius: Die Autobiographie des Apostels der Iren,' La2, 9–25.
4. Bullough, D.A., 'The missions to the English and Picts and their heritage (to c. 800),' La2, 80–98.
5. Bulst, N., 'Irizches Mönchtum und cluniazensizche Klosterreform,' La2, 958–69.
6. Eberl, I., 'Das Irenkloster Honau und seine Regel,' La2, 219–38.
7. Fanning, T., 'Early Christian sites in the barony of Corkaguiney,' La3, 241–6.
8. Gamber, K., 'Irische Liturgiebücher und ihre Verbreitung auf dem Kontinent,' La2, 536–48.

9. Kahl, H.-D., 'Zur Rolle der Iren im östlichen Vorfeld des agilolingischen und frühkarolingischen Baiern,' La2, 375–98.
10. Koller, H., 'Die Iren und die Christianisierung der Baiern,' La2, 342–74.
11. Kottje, R., 'Überlieferung und Rezeption der irischen Bussbücher auf dem Kontinent,' La2, 511–24.
12. Müller, W., 'Der Anteil der Iren an der Christianisierung der Alemannen,' La2, 330–41.
13. Ó Corráin, D., 'The early Irish churches: some aspects of organization,' La3, 327–42.
14. Richter, M., 'Der irische Hintergrund der angelsächsischen Mission,' La2, 120–37.
15. Schäferdiek, K., 'Columbans Wirken im Frankenreich (591–612),' La2, 171–201.
16. Sheehy, M.P., 'The Collectio Canonum Hibernensis – a Celtic phenomenon,' La2, 525–35.
17. Vogt, H.J., 'Zur Spiritualität des frühen irischen Mönchtums,' La2, 26–51.
18. Wendehorst, A., 'Die Iren und die Christianisierung Mainfrankens,' La2, 319–29.
19. Werner, M., 'Iren und Angelsachsen in Mitteldeutschland: Zur vorbonifatianischen Mission in Hessen und Thüringen,' La2, 239–318.
20. Binchy, D.A., 'A pre-Christian survival in medieval Irish hagiography,' Bc13, 165–78.
21. Not used.
22. Stancliffe, C., 'Red, white and blue martyrdom,' Bc13, 21–46.
23. Bethell, D.L.T., 'The originality of the early Irish Church,' *J. of the Royal Soc. of Antiquaries of Ireland* 111 (1982 for 1981), 36–49.
24. McCone, K., 'Brigit in the seventh century: a saint with three lives?,' *Peritia* 1 (1982), 107–45.
25. Ní Dhonnchadha, M., 'The guarantor list of Cáin Adomnáin, 697,' ibid. 178–215.
26. Ó Muraíle, N., 'Doire na bhFlann alias Doire Eidhneach: an historical and onomastic study,' *Studia Hibernica* (1982 for 1980), 111–39.
27. Ó Riain, P., 'Towards a methodology in early Irish hagiography,' *Peritia* 1 (1982), 146–99.
28. Ó Riain-Raedel, D., 'Aspects of the promotion of Irish saints' cults in medieval Germany,' *Zeitschrift für keltische Philologie* 39 (1982), 220–34.
29. Picard, J.M., 'The purpose of Adomnán's *Vita Columbae*,' *Peritia* 1 (1982), 160–77.
30. Sharpe, R., '*Vitae S Brigitae*: the oldest texts,' ibid. 81–106.
31. Sharpe, R., 'Palaeographical considerations in the study of the

Patrician documents in the Book of Armagh (Dublin, Trinity College, MS 52),' *Scriptorium* 36 (1982), 3–28.

32. Sharpe, R., 'St Patrick and the see of Armagh,' *Cambridge Medieval Celtic Studies* 4 (1982), 33–59.
33. Davies, W., 'Clerics as rulers: some implications of the terminology of ecclesiastical authority in early medieval Ireland,' Da2, 81–97.
34. Hurley, V., 'The early church in the south-west of Ireland: settlement and organisation,' Bc27, 297–332.
35. Mytum, H., 'The location of early churches in northern county Clare,' Bc27, 351–62.

(f) *Economic Affairs*

1. Binchy, D.A., 'Brewing in eighth-century Ireland,' Bc2, 3–6.
2. Mac Eoin, G., 'The early Irish vocabulary of mills and milling,' Bc2, 13–19.
3. Mac Niocaill, G., 'Investment in early Irish agriculture,' Bc2, 7–9.
4. Wallace, P.F., 'Anglo-Norman Dublin: continuity and change,' La3, 247–68.
5. Broderick, G., 'The baronial possessions of Bangor and Saul in Man,' *B. of the Ulster Place-Name Soc.* 2nd ser. 4 (1981–2), 24–6.
6. Childs, W., 'Ireland's trade with England in the later middle ages,' *Irish Economic and Social History* 9 (1982), 5–33.
7. Doherty, C., 'Some aspects of hagiography as a source for Irish economic history,' *Peritia* 1 (1982), 300–28.
8. Lydon, J., 'A fifteenth-century building account from Dublin,' *Irish Economic and Social History* 9 (1982), 73–5.

(g) *Social Structure and Population*

1. Barry, T.B., 'Archaeological excavations at Dunbeg promontory fort, county Kerry, 1977,' *P. of the Royal Irish Academy* 81 C (1981), 295–329.
2. Duffy, P.J., 'The territorial organization of Gaelic landownership and its transformation in County Monaghan, 1591–1640,' *Irish Geography* 14 (1981), 1–26.
3. Simpson, M.L.; Dickson, A., 'Excavations in Carrickfergus, co. Antrim, 1972–79,' *Medieval Archaeology* 25 (1981), 78–159.
4. Wallace, P., 'The origins of Dublin,' Bc2, 129–43.
5. Canny, N. *The upstart earl: a study of the social and mental world of Richard Boyle, first earl of Cork, 1566–1643.* Cambridge UP; 1982. Pp xii, 211.
6. Mac Niocaill, G. *Irish population before Petty: problems and possibilities.* Dublin; National University of Ireland; 1981. Pp 11.

7. O'Brien, A.F., 'The settlement of Imokilly and the formation and descent of the manor of Inchiquin, co. Cork,' *J. of the Cork Historical and Arch. Soc.* 87 (1982), 21–6.
8. Sawyer, P., 'The Vikings and Ireland,' Bc13, 345–61.
9. Wailes, B., 'The Irish "royal sites" in history and archaeology,' *Cambridge Medieval Celtic Studies* 3 (1982), 1–29.
10. Warner, R.B., 'A case study: Clochar Macc nDaimíni,' *B. of the Ulster Place-Name Soc.* 2nd ser. 4 (1981–2), 27–31.
11. Smyth, A.P. *Celtic Leinster: towards an historical geography of early Irish civilization 500–1600.* Blackrock; Irish Academic Press; 1982. Pp 212.

(h) *Naval and Military*

(i) *Intellectual and Cultural*

1. Bradley, J.; Manning, C., 'Excavations at Duiske Abbey, Graiguenamanagh, co. Kilkenny,' *P. of the Royal Irish Academy* 81 C (1981), 397–426.
2. Brannon, N.E.; Blades, B.S., 'Dungiven Bawn re-edified,' *Ulster J. of Archaeology* 3rd ser. 43 (1981 for 1980), 91–6.
3. Garton, T., 'A Romanesque doorway at Lillaloe,' *J. of the British Arch. Association* 134 (1981), 31–57.
4. Johnston, J.D., 'Settlement and architecture in county Fermanagh, 1610–41,' *Ulster J. of Archaeology* 3rd ser. 43 (1981 for 1980), 79–89.
5. Loeber, R., 'Sculptured memorials to the dead in early 17th-century Ireland: a survey from *Monumenta Eblanae* and other sources,' *P. of the Royal Irish Academy* 81 C (1981), 267–93.
6. Loeber, R. *A biographical dictionary of architects in Ireland 1600–1720.* London; Murray; 1981. Pp 127.
7. Ó Cuív, B., 'Medieval Irish scholars and classical Latin literature,' *P. of the Royal Irish Academy* 81 C (1981), 239–48.
8. Nic Ghiollamhaith, A., 'Dynastic warfare and historical writing in North Munster, 1276–1350,' *Cambridge Medieval Celtic Studies* 2 (1981), 73–89.
9. Anton, H.H., 'Pseudo-Cyprian: De duodecim abusivis saeculi und sein Einfluss auf den Kontinent, insbesondere auf die karolingischen Fürstenspiegel,' La2, 568–617.
10. Autenrieth, J., 'Irische Handschriftenüberlieferung auf der Reichenau,' La2, 903–15.
11. Beierwaltes, W., 'Eriugena: Aspekte seiner Philosophie,' La2, 799–818.
12. Berschin, W., 'Griechisches bei den Iren,' La2, 501–10.
13. Brincken, A.-D. von den, 'Marianus Scottus als Universalhistoriker iuxta veritatem evangelii,' La2, 970–1012.

14. Brown, T.J., 'The Irish element in the insular system of scripts to circa A.D. 850,' La2, 101–19.
15. Canny, N., 'The formation of the Irish mind: religion, politics and Gaelic Irish literature 1580–1750,' *Past and Present* 95 (1982), 91–116.
16. Düchting, R., 'Sedulius Scottus – ein "Heilger Drei König mehr" aus dem Abendland,' La2, 866–75.
17. Duft, J., 'Irische Handschriftenüberlieferung in St. Gallen,' La2, 916–40.
18. Harbison, P., 'Early Irish churches,' La2, 618–29.
19. Hennig, J., 'Irlandkunde in der festländischen Tradition irischer Heiliger,' La2, 686–96.
20. Herren, M., 'Sprachliche Eigentümlichkeiten in den hiberno-lateinischen Texten des 7. und 8. Jahrhunderts,' La2, 425–33.
21. Jacobsen, P., 'Carmina Columbani,' La2, 434–67.
22. Kelly, J.F., 'Hiberno-Latin theology,' La2, 549–67.
23. Leonardi, C., 'Gli Irlandesi in Italia: Dungal e la controversia iconoclastica,' La2, 746–57.
24. Macdonald, A., 'Notes on monastic archaeology and the Annals of Ulster, 650–1050,' La3, 304–19.
25. Münxelhaus, B., 'Der Beitrag Irlands zur Musik des frühen Mittelalters,' La2, 630–8.
26. Ó Riain, P., 'The Irish element in Welsh hagiographical tradition,' La3, 291–303.
27. Prinz, F., 'Die Rolle der Iren beim Aufbau der merowingischen Klosterkultur,' La2, 202–18.
28. Rädle, F., 'Die Kenntnis der antiken lateinischen Literatur bei den Iren in der Heimat und auf dem Kontinent,' La2, 484–500.
29. Reichl, L., 'Zur Frage des irischen Einflusses auf die altenglische weltliche Dichtung,' La2, 138–70.
30. Riché, P., 'Les Irlandais et les princes carolingiens aux VIIIe et IXe siècle,' La2, 735–45.
31. Schaller, D., 'Die Siebensilberstrophen "de mundi transitu" – eine Dichtung Columbans?,' La2, 468–83.
32. Schrimpf, G., 'Der Beitrag des Johannes Scottus Eriugena zum Prädestinationsstreit,' La2, 819–65.
33. Semmler, J., 'Iren in der lothringischen Klosterreform,' La2, 941–57.
34. Spilling, H., 'Irische Handschriftenüberlieferung in Fulda, Mainz und Würzburg,' La2, 876–902.
35. Strasser, I., 'Irisches im Althochdeutschen?,' La2, 399–424.
36. Tristram, H.L.C., 'Das Europabild in der mittelirischen Literatur,' La2, 697–734.
37. Wais, K., 'Volkssprachliche Erzähler Alt-Irlands im Rahmen der Euopäischen Literaturgeschichte,' La2, 639–85.
38. Wright, D.H., 'The Irish element in the formation of Hiberno-Saxon art: calligraphy and metalwork,' La2, 99–100.

39. Dumville, D.N., 'Latin and Irish in the *Annals of Ulster*,' Bc13, 320–41.
40. Hamlin, A., '*Dignatio diei dominici*: an element in the iconography of Irish crosses?', Bc13, 69–75.
41. Harrison, K., 'Episodes in the history of Easter cycles in Ireland,' Bc13, 307–19.
42. Mac Cana, P. *The learned tales of Medieval Ireland.* Dublin Institute for Advanced Studies; 1980. Pp ix, 159.
43. Sims-Williams, P., 'The evidence of vernacular Irish literary influence on early medieval Welsh literature,' Bc13, 235–57.
44. Bishop, T.A.M., '*Periphyseon*: the descent of the uncompleted copy,' Bc13, 281–304.
45. Wright, N., 'The *Hisperica Famina* and Caelus Sedulius,' *Cambridge Medieval Celtic Studies* 4 (1982), 61–76.
46. Harrington, J.P., 'A Tudor writer's tracts on Ireland: his rhetoric,' *Eire-Ireland* 17/2 (1982), 92–103.
47. Law, V. *The insular Latin grammarians.* Woodbridge; Boydell; 1982. Pp xiv, 131.
48. Law, V., 'Notes on the dating and attribution of anonymous Latin grammars of the early middle ages,' *Peritia* 1 (1982), 250–67.
49. Ó Cróinín, D., 'Mo-Sinnu moccu Min and the computus of Bangor,' ibid. 281–95.
50. Waddell, J., 'An unpublished High Cross on Aran, county Galway,' *J. of the Royal Soc. of Antiquaries of Ireland* 111 (1982 for 1981), 29–35.
51. O'Driscoll, R. (ed.). *The Celtic consciousness.* Portlaoise; Dolmen Press; 1982. Pp xxxi, 642.
52. Jacobs, N., 'The Green Knight: an unexplored Irish parallel,' *Cambridge Medieval Celtic Studies* 4 (1982), 1–4.
53. Hamlin, A., 'Early Irish stone carving: content and context,' Bc27, 283–96.

M. IRELAND SINCE ca. 1640

(a) *General*

1. Longford, Frank Pakenham earl of; McHardy, A. *Ulster.* London; Weidenfeld & Nicolson; 1981. Pp viii, 260.
2. Harrison, G. *The Irish civil war.* Dublin; Gill & Macmillan; 1981. Pp 142.
3. O'Farrell, P., 'Whose reality? The Irish famine in history and literature,' *Historical Studies* 20 (1982), 1–13.
4. Moody, T.W.; Martin, F.X.; Byrne, F.J. (ed.). *A new history of*

Ireland, vol. VIII: A chronology of Irish history to 1876. Oxford; Clarendon; 1982. Pp 591.

5. Boyce, D.G. *Nationalism in Ireland.* London; Croom Helm; 1982. Pp 441.
6. Doyle, D.N. *Ireland, Irishmen and revolutionary America, 1760–1820.* Dublin; Mercier; 1982. Pp xix, 257.
7. Drudy, P.J. (ed.). *Ireland: land, politics and people* (Irish Studies 2). Cambridge UP; 1982. Pp viii, 331.
8. Drudy, P.J., 'Land people and the regional problem in Ireland,' Ma7, 191–216.
9. McAleese, D., 'Political independence, economic growth and the role of economic policy,' Ma7, 271–95.

(b) *Politics*

1. Hayton, D., 'The crisis in Ireland and the disintegration of Queen Anne's last ministry,' *Irish Historical Studies* 22 (1981), 193–215.
2. Kerr, D., 'Peel and the political involvement of the priests,' *Archivum Hibernicum* 36 (1981), 16–25.
3. Comerford, R.V., 'Patriotism as pastime: the appeal of fenianism in the mid-1860s,' *Irish Historical Studies* 22 (1981), 239–50.
4. Hawkins, F.M.A., 'Defence and the role of Erskine Childers in the treaty negotiations of 1921,' ibid. 251–70.
5. Dwyer, T.R. *Michael Collins and the Treaty: his differences with de Valera.* Dublin; Mercier; 1981. Pp 172.
6. Garvin, T. *The evolution of Irish nationalist politics.* Dublin; Gill & Macmillan; 1981. Pp xii, 244.
7. Newsinger, J., 'Old Chartists, Fenians and new socialists,' *Eire-Ireland* 17/2 (1982), 19–45.
8. Garvin, T., 'Defenders, Ribbonmen and others: underground political networks in pre-famine Ireland,' *Past and Present* 96 (1982), 133–55.
9. Hayton, D.W., 'Divisions in the whig junto in 1709: some Irish evidence,' *B. of the Institute of Historical Research* 55 (1982), 206–14.
10. Bowman, J. *De Valera and the Ulster Question, 1917–1973.* Oxford; Clarendon; 1982. Pp 384.
11. Moody, T.W. *Davitt and the Irish revolution, 1846–1882.* Oxford UP; 1982. Pp xxiv, 674.
12. D'Arcy, F.A., 'The National Trades' Political Union and Daniel O'Connell, 1830–1848,' *Eire-Ireland* 17/3 (1982), 7–16.
13. Van Voris, J., 'Daniel O'Connell and women's rights – one letter,' ibid. 35–9.
14. McKillen, B., 'Irish feminism and nationalist separatism, 1914–23,' ibid. 52–67.
15. Rodner, W.S., 'Leaguers, covenanters, moderates: British support for Ulster, 1913–1914,' ibid. 68–85.

16. McMinn, R., 'The myth of "Route" Liberalism in county Antrim 1869–1900,' ibid. 17/1 (1982), 137–49.
17. Ford, T.H., 'The re-making of a Unionist: A.V. Dicey and the second home rule bill,' ibid. 107–36.
18. Beames, M. *Peasant rebellion and social transformation in pre-Famine Ireland.* Brighton; Harvester; 1982. Pp 224.
19. Beames, M.R., 'The Ribbon Societies: lower-class nationalism in pre-Famine Ireland,' *Past and Present* 97 (1982), 128–43.
20. Bew, P.; Patterson, H. *Sean Lemass and the making of modern Ireland.* Dublin; Gill & Macmillan; 1982.
21. Elliott, M. *Partners in revolution: the United Irishmen and France.* New Haven/London; Yale UP; 1982.
22. McCartney, D. (ed.). *The world of Daniel O'Connell.* Dublin; Mercier; 1980. Pp viii, 185.
23. Bew, P., 'The Land League ideal: achievements and contradictions,' Ma7, 77–92.
24. Higgins, M.D.; Gibbons, J.P., 'Shopkeeper-graziers and land agitation in Ireland, 1895–1900,' Ma7, 93–118.
25. Bax, M., 'The small community in the Irish political process,' Ma7, 119–40.
26. Ó Tuathaigh, M.A.G., 'The land question, politics and Irish society, 1922–1960,' Ma7, 167–89.

(c) *Constitution, Administration and Law*

1. Fanning, R., 'The response of the London and Belfast governments to the declaration of the Republic of Ireland, 1948–49,' *International Affairs* 58 (1981–2), 95–114.
2. Smith, B.A., 'The Irish General Prisons Board, 1877–1885: efficient deterrence or bureaucratic ineptitude?,' *Irish Jurist* 15/1 (1980), 122–36.
3. Buckland, P., 'Who governed Northern Ireland; The royal assent and the Local Government Bill 1922,' *Irish Jurist* 15/2 (1980), 326–40.
4. O'Hara, B.J. *The evolution of Irish industrial relations law and practice.* Tallaght; Folens; 1981. Pp 146.
5. Reamonn, S. *History of the Revenue Commissioners.* Dublin; Institute of Public Administration; 1981. Pp xii, 385.
6. Golding, G.M. *George Gavan Duffy 1882–1951: a legal biography.* Blackrock; Irish Academic Press; 1982. Pp xvi, 224.

(d) *External Affairs*

(e) *Religion*

1. Carroll, K.L., 'Quakerism in Connaught, 1656–1978,' *J. of the Friends' Historical Soc.* 54 (1979), 185–206.

2. Gallagher, T., 'Religion, reaction, and revolt in Northern Ireland: the impact of Paisleyism in Ulster,' *J. of Church and State* 23 (1981), 423–44.
3. Corish, P.J. *The catholic community in the seventeenth and eighteenth centuries.* Dublin; Helicon; 1981. Pp vii, 156.
4. Walsh, K., 'The opening of the Vatican archives (1880–1881) and Irish historical research,' *Archivum Hibernicum* 36 (1981), 34–43.
5. Purcell, M., 'Dublin diocesan archives: Murray papers,' ibid. 51–140.
6. Purcell, M., 'Sidelights on the Dublin diocesan archives,' ibid. 44–50.
7. Rushe, D. *Edmund Rice: the man and his times.* Dublin; Gill & Macmillan; 1981. Pp xi, 156.
8. Connolly, S.J. *Priests and people in pre-famine Ireland, 1780–1845.* Dublin; Gill & Macmillan; 1982. Pp 338.
9. James, F.G., 'The Church of Ireland and the patriot movement in the late eighteenth century,' *Eire-Ireland* 17/2 (1982), 46–55.
10. Hamell, P.J. *Maynooth: students and ordinations index 1795–1895.* Birr; the compiler; 1982. Pp 199.
11. Bailie, W.D. (ed.). *A history of congregations in the Presbyterian Church in Ireland 1610–1982.* Presbyterian Historical Soc. of Ireland; 1982. Pp 808.
12. Kerr, D.A. *Peel, priests and politics: Sir Robert Peel's administration and the Roman Catholic Church in Ireland 1841–46.* Oxford UP; 1982. Pp 399.
13. Holmes, R.F.G., 'Ulster presbyterianism and Irish nationalism,' Bc10, 535–55.

(f) *Economic Affairs*

1. O'Hare, F. *The divine gospel of discontent: story of the Belfast dockers and carters strike 1907.* Belfast; Connolly Bookshop; 1981. Pp 32.
2. Collins, B., 'Proto-industrialization and pre-famine emigration,' *Social History* 7 (1982), 127–46.
3. Fairley, J. *Irish whales and whaling.* Belfast; Blackstaff Press; 1981. Pp 218.
4. Forde, F. *The long watch: the history of the Irish mercantile marine in World War II.* Dublin; Gill & Macmillan; 1981. Pp xi, 147.
5. Hughes, N.J. *Irish engineering 1760–1960.* Dublin; Institute of Engineers of Ireland; 1982. Pp viii, 159.
6. Went, A.E.J., 'Historical notes on the fisheries of the estuary of the river Shannon,' *J. of the Royal Soc. of Antiquaries of Ireland* 111 (1982 for 1981), 107–18.
7. Longfield, A.K., 'Blarney and Cork: printing on linen, cotton and

paper in the eighteenth and early nineteenth centuries,' ibid. 81–101.

8. Ryder, M., 'The Bank of Ireland, 1721: land, credit and dependency,' *Historical J.* 25 (1982), 557–82.
9. Greaves, C.D. *The Irish Transport and General Workers' Union: the formative years 1909–1923.* Dublin; Gill & Macmillan; 1982. Pp ix, 363.
10. Vaughan, W.E., 'Farmer, grazier and gentleman: Edward Delany of Woodtown, 1851–99,' *Irish Economic and Social History* 9 (1982), 53–72.
11. Clune, M.J., 'Horace Plunkett's resignation from the Irish Department of Agriculture and Technical Instruction 1906–1907,' *Eire-Ireland* 17/1 (1982), 57–73.
12. O'Neill, J.W., 'A look at Captain Rock: agrarian rebellion in Ireland, 1815–1845,' ibid. 17/3 (1982), 17–34.
13. Commins, P., 'Land politics and agricultural development,' Ma7, 217–40.
14. Matthews, A., 'The state and Irish agriculture, 1950–1980,' Ma7, 241–69.

(g) *Social Structure and Population*

1. Rutherford, G. *Gravestone inscriptions, county Antrim, vol. 2: parishes of Glynn, Kilroot, Raloo and Templecorran.* Ulster Historical Foundation; 1981. Pp xv, 174.
2. Mullaly, F. *The silver salver: the story of the Guinness family.* London; Granada; 1981. Pp xii, 255.
3. Walker, B.M. *Sentry Hill: an Ulster farm and family.* Dundonald; Blackstaff Press; 1981. Pp xii, 167.
4. O'Dowd, A. *Meitheal: a study of co-operative labour in rural Ireland.* Dublin; Comhairle Bhealoideas Eireann; 1981. Pp 181.
5. Bartlett, T., 'The O'Haras of Annaghmore *c.* 1600–*c.* 1800: survival and revival,' *Irish Economic and Social History* 9 (1982), 34–52.
6. Malcolmson, A.P.W. *The pursuit of the heiress: marriage in Ireland 1750–1820.* Ulster Historical Foundation; 1982. Pp x, 70.
7. Ó Danachair, C., 'An Rí (the king): an example of traditional social organisation,' *J. of the Royal Soc. of Antiquaries of Ireland* 111 (1982 for 1981), 14–28.
8. Clark, S., 'The importance of agrarian classes: agrarian class structure and collective action in nineteenth-century Ireland,' Ma7, 11–36.
9. Fitzpatrick, D., 'Class, family and rural unrest in nineteenth-century Ireland,' Ma7, 37–75.
10. Hannan, D.F., 'Peasant models and the understanding of social and cultural change in rural Ireland,' Ma7, 141–65.

11. Bannon, M.J., 'Urban growth and urban land policy,' Ma7, 297–323.

(h) *Naval and Military*

(i) *Intellectual and Cultural*

1. Sligo, Denis Browne marquess of. *Westport House and the Brownes.* Ashbourne; Moorland Publishing; 1982. Pp 112.
2. McElligott, T.J. *Secondary education in Ireland 1870–1921.* Blackrock; Irish Academic Press; n.d. [1981]. Pp x, 200.
3. Curl, J.S. *The history, architecture and planning of the estates of the Fishmongers' Company in Ulster.* Ulster Architectural Heritage Soc.; 1981. Pp 76.
4. Vance, N., 'Celts, Carthaginians and constitutions: Anglo-Irish literary relations 1780–1820,' *Irish Historical Studies* 22 (1981), 216–38.
5. Towey, J., 'Summerhill 1880,' *Archivum Hibernicum* 36 (1981), 26–33.
6. McDowell, R.B.; Webb, D.A. *Trinity College Dublin, 1592–1952: an academic history.* Cambridge UP; 1982. Pp xxiii, 580.
7. Freyer, G. *W.B. Yeats and the anti-democratic tradition.* Dublin; Gill & Macmillan; 1981. Pp x, 143.
8. Turpin, J., 'Ireland's progress: the Dublin exhibition of 1907,' *Eire-Ireland* 17/1 (1982), 31–8.
9. Bowman, J.; O'Donoghue, R. (ed.). *Portraits: Belvedere College 1832–1982.* Dublin; Gill & Macmillan; 1982.
10. O'Farrell, P., 'Whose reality? The Irish Famine in history and literature,' *Historical Studies* 20 (1982), 1–13.

(j) *Local History*

1. Maybin, J.M. *Belfast Corporation tramways: 1905–1954.* Broxbourne; Light Rail Transport Association; 1981. Pp 83.
2. Mac Coil, L. *The book of Blackrock* (2nd ed.). Blackrock; Carraig; 1981. Pp 155.
3. Carson, W.H. *The dam builders: the story of the men who built the Silent Valley reservoir.* Newcastle, Co. Down; Mourne Observer Press; 1981. Pp xv, 102.
4. Rankin, J.F. *The heritage of Drumbo.* The Parish; 1982. Pp iv, 125.
5. Gribbon, S. *Edwardian Belfast.* Belfast; Appletree Press; 1982. Pp 64.
6. Bardon, J. *Belfast.* Belfast; Blackstaff; 1982. Pp 304.
7. Beckett, J.C. *Belfast: the making of a city 1800–1914.* Belfast; Appletree Press; 1982.
8. O'Brien, J.V. *'Dear dirty Dublin': a city in distress, 1899–1916.* Berkeley/London; University of California Press; 1982. Pp xiv, 338.

AUTHOR INDEX

Author Index

Author Index

SUBJECT INDEX